LEARNING AND MEMORY

LEARNING AND MEMORY

Major Ideas, Principles, Issues and Applications

ROBERT W. HOWARD

PRAEGER   Westport, Connecticut
                           London

AL HARRIS LIBRARY
SOUTHWESTERN OKLA. STATE UNIV.
WEATHERFORD, OK 73096

Library of Congress Cataloging-in-Publication Data

Howard, Robert W.
    Learning and memory : major ideas, principles, issues and
applications / Robert W. Howard.
      p.   cm.
    Includes bibliographical references and index.
    ISBN 0–275–94641–X (alk. paper)
    1. Learning, Psychology of. 2. Memory.
BF318.H69 1995
153.1—dc20   94–180177

British Library Cataloguing in Publication Data is available.

Copyright © 1995 by Robert W. Howard

All rights reserved. No portion of this book may be
reproduced, by any process or technique, without the
express written consent of the publisher.

Library of Congress Catalog Card Number: 94–180177
ISBN: 0–275–94641–X

First published in 1995

Praeger Publishers, 88 Post Road West, Westport, CT 06881
An imprint of Greenwood Publishing Group, Inc.

Printed in the United States of America

The paper used in this book complies with the
Permanent Paper Standard issued by the National
Information Standards Organization (Z39.48–1984).

10 9 8 7 6 5 4 3 2 1

Copyright Acknowledgments

The author and publisher gratefully acknowledge permission to reprint previously
copyrighted material:

An excerpt from W. G. Chase, ed. *Visual information processing*. Orlando, FL: Academic Press. Copyright © 1973 by Academic Press.
Figure 3.5. From H. P. Bahrick. Semantic memory content in permastore: Fifty years
of memory for Spanish learned in school. *Journal of Experimental Psychology: General*
113: 1–24. Copyright © 1984 by the American Psychological Association.
Figure 7.2. From D. E. Rumelhart and J. L. McClelland. *Parallel Distributed Processing*. Cambridge, MA: MIT Press. Copyright © 1986 by MIT Press.

Contents

Preface   vii

1   The Ability to Learn and Remember   1

2   Learning and Memory in Evolution and in Animals   29

3   Structures and Processes of the Memory System   55

4   Knowledge   83

5   Skills and Expertise   111

6   Effects of Age, Intelligence, and Styles on Learning and
     Memory   135

7   Machine Learning: Symbolic and Connectionist   163

8   Applications   183

References   213

Index   243

298438

Preface

Learning and memory is a topic of great importance that has long been at center stage in psychology and is also studied in such disciplines as philosophy, biology, education, artificial intelligence (AI), and linguistics. The topic is a major concern in many applied areas as well. In the last few decades, much progress has been made in understanding this complex, crucial ability. Nevertheless, its study is still somewhat fragmented. Psychologists still use several different approaches based on different assumptions and methodologies, and there are several subfields that sometimes communicate little with each other and with the mainstream. The organization of most learning and memory textbooks still reflects this fragmentation. Typically the first half deals with learning, mostly in animals and from a behavioral perspective, and the second deals with memory, mostly in humans and from a cognitive perspective. The two halves are rarely linked. Some books mainly present material from just a cognitive or behavioral perspective. Introductory psychology textbooks often still take "learning" to refer to topics studied by behaviorists and cover it in a different section from work on memory. By and large, behavioral researchers still mostly study learning, and cognitive researchers (aside from those using connectionist techniques) mostly study memory. There are, however, increasing links between them, and cognitively oriented researchers have been looking more at learning processes in the last decade.

The first aim of this book is to try to bring some additional order to a vast and sprawling field by overviewing the entire area aside from its physiology. This book describes the major approaches and their basic assumptions, the key issues about learning and memory, and various subfields and topics usually not included in mainstream books, such as nonconnectionist machine learning, constraints on knowledge, skill learning, prenatal learning, and application areas such as industrial design and the law. I have tried to bring these together as much as possible and sketch out links between them. The book also presents some new theoretical work on topics such as the classification of learning processes and concept learning. The book therefore can be read to see what the field is all about, what its parts are and how they interrelate, and what its major principles and applications are.

The second (and related) aim is to survey the key ideas in the field, starting with major philosophical issues, and examining their cultural manifestations and various derivational issues. The reader can see what the key ideas are, where they come from, and how various research areas derive from them. To keep the book readable and its length manageable, I have not gone into great detail at points. The book could easily be expanded into a 1,200-page tome, but that would defeat its purpose.

The book can be used by several audiences. One is professionals working in the area, in related basic research or applied areas of psychology, and in related disciplines. The book can update knowledge of what is going on in the field and in outlying subfields. Graduate students and advanced undergraduates in psychology, education, and related disciplines also can use it to get a broad perspective on what the field is all about and what major principles have been derived. Learning is vastly improved if learners have a broad framework to hang details on, which this book will provide. To make the book accessible to a wide audience, I have kept the style as simple as possible and started each topic right at the beginning. And, I have stressed throughout the importance of the ability to learn and remember in everyday life.

1

The Ability to Learn and Remember

It is easy to see how important something is when it is impaired or gone. So it is with the crucial human ability to learn and remember, its importance revealed by various brain-damaged persons. A very striking case is "HM" (Milner, 1966). In 1953 surgeons lesioned his hippocampus and temporal lobes to try to relieve symptoms of severe epilepsy. The symptoms were reduced, but he gained a new problem—a much impaired ability to acquire factual information. He seemed quite normal on initial contact. His general intelligence and immediate memory were intact; he could learn simple skills and readily recall events that occurred before his operation. But his deficits would soon become apparent. He could not recall events occurring after the operation, hold the thread of a conversation for long, or learn to recognize new faces. He would repeat stories, reread magazines without them seeming familiar, and after some years could no longer recognize his own face in the mirror. He got very upset when told about a friend's death, but could not retain the information for long and would get just as upset on being told again. He seemed stuck in a single moment, believing the date to be 1953. In later years a little new factual information somehow seemed to get through. He was dimly aware of a few major historical events.

Another illustrative case is Clive Wearing, a talented British broadcaster and musician who contracted the viral brain disease encephalitis in his forties (Baddeley, 1990). After many weeks in a coma he awoke, but with brain damage that greatly affected his memory. He could recall few details of his past life (mostly just general features) and had lost much world knowledge (such as the author of *Romeo and Juliet*). He had great difficulty learning new factual information. He thought he had recovered conscious- ness just a few moments before. He would greet his wife joyously in the morning, as though he had not seen her for a long time, then would forget the incident and repeat the greeting later. He could not venture out without getting lost, or say who he was, where he lived, or why he had gone out. Like HM, he was stuck in a single moment, with a poor sense of past and future.

The ability to learn and remember is indeed crucial. Almost every aspect of our thinking and behavior depends heavily on learning, and learning is central to our daily functioning. Humans continually need to gather and store information about the world to behave adaptively, to bring past experience to bear. So, the study of this capability is at center stage in psychology and is very important in such disciplines as artificial intelligence (AI), philosophy, biology, education, and linguistics.

THE CONCEPT OF LEARNING AND THE CONCEPT OF MEMORY

Everyone knows what learning is, but most would be hard-pressed to define it. There are several definitions, but none is universally accepted. Here are some oft-used ones.

1. "A relatively permanent change in behavior that occurs as a result of practice." The change must be relatively permanent (e.g., not due to transient reactions to stimuli, such as a startle response) and must be due to practice rather than fatigue, drugs, injury, and so on. This definition is favored by behaviorists (described later) and is still commonly cited in introductory psychology text-books.
2. "Organized knowledge which grows and becomes better organized" (Charniak and McDermott, 1985, 610).
3. "Any process whereby people or machines increase their knowledge or their skill" (Stillings et al., 1987, 189).
4. "An experience-dependent generation of enduring internal representations, and/or experience-dependent lasting modification in such representations" (Dudai, 1989, 6). (A representation is information in the nervous system that stands for something in the world.) This definition is favored in neuroscience.
5. "The acquisition of knowledge and/or skills." Knowledge in this sense is factual information—e.g., that Paris is the capital of France and that 1+1=2—and skills are co-ordinations of perception and action, such as the skills of typing and car driving.

The definitions have some commonalities. Learning is seen as a lasting change of some sort, and in four definitions involves acquiring information. Dudai (1989) looks at a variety of definitions of learning and notes some other commonalities: learning occurs after individual experience (rather than being the kind of information acquisition of a species over many generations that is coded in the genes) and is a process rather than an instantaneous change. Some definitions hold that learning improves the organism, but it is easy to think of cases of learning that do not. For instance, patients receiving chemotherapy sometimes develop an aversion to a food eaten just before treatment. This does not improve them at all.

One can argue about which definition is best. This book will use the fifth one because it is broad enough to encompass a very wide variety of phenomena in humans, other animals, and machines. Some everyday human examples are a child learning to tie a shoelace, to speak a native language, to recite a poem verbatim, and to fear dogs after a painful bite. Further examples are the perceptual sharpening that allows a wine taster to discriminate various wine vintages and an expert tennis player to learn the likely actions that follow various postures of an opponent, attitude change after hearing a persuasive speech, slowly ceasing to notice background noise after moving to a new house, and adaptation to sensory disturbance after wearing a distorting pair of prisms (Bedford, 1993). One can include astronauts learning to function in microgravity and the acquisition of very general problem-solving skills after a training course (e.g., Feuerstein et al., 1980). Some examples in animals are a rat learning to press a bar for food or to avoid a novel food after becoming nauseous after eating some, a newly hatched duckling approaching and thereafter following the first moving object it encounters, and tadpoles injected with a chemical before hatching preferring that chemical after hatching. A computer example is Samuel's (1959) checker-playing program, which learned to improve its skill by playing itself and humans. An instance of learning can occur very rapidly or involve a long, slow process that can take years. So many phenomena are labeled instances of learning that some ask whether the category is too broad to be useful, if "learning" is a natural kind (Churchland, 1986). The category is broad, but the concept is very useful.

Although the category seems very broad, neurophysiologists see learning as a special case of neural plasticity (e.g., Squire, 1987; Churchland and Sejnowski, 1992). Many neurons show plasticity, the ability to change their structure or function to make the organism more adaptable. The brain continually modifies and updates itself, and most brain functions, such as perception and thermoregulation, are modifiable if the need arises. As Squire put it, "Plasticity is evident in such diverse phenomena as drug tolerance, enzyme production, sprouting of axon terminals after a brain lesion, and strictly synaptic events such as facilitation" (4).

Learning is the acquisition of information, and memory is that information's persistence in the nervous system over time; for a few seconds, days, or a lifetime. Memory preserves information for immediate or later use, and without it, of course, learning would have no purpose. Learning and memory are very closely linked, however, because the contents of memory largely determine what is likely to be learned and how rapidly and well it is. What is already known is a major determinant of (and limit on) what else can be acquired. Here are two illustrations of this important principle.

Figure 1.1
A Random Arrangement of Chess Pieces (Left) and a Chess Position that Could Actually Occur in a Game (Right). The Blocks in the Lower Diagram Enclose the Unitary Patterns that the Expert Sees.

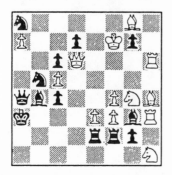 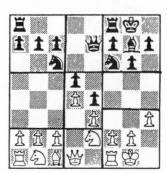

Figure 1.1 presents two chess positions. One could occur in an actual game and one is a random piece arrangement that would not. Chase and Simon (1973) had chess experts and novices view such positions for five seconds each and then reproduce them from memory. With the random positions, the experts and novices alike correctly placed about six pieces. The experts did much better than the novices with the real positions, typically placing almost all pieces correctly. The experts' knowledge allowed them to group pieces into larger units and acquire much more information at a glance.

A second example is this passage:

The procedure is actually quite simple. First you arrange things into different groups. Of course, one pile may be sufficient depending on how much there is to do. If you have to go somewhere else due to lack of facilities that is the next step, otherwise you are pretty well set. It is important not to overdo things. That is, it is better to do too few things at once than too many. In the short run, this may not seem important but complications can easily arise. A mistake can be expensive as well. At first the whole procedure will seem complicated. Soon, however, it will become just another facet of life. It is difficult to foresee any end to the necessity for this task in the immediate future, but then one can never tell. After the procedure is completed one arranges the materials into different groups again. Then they can be put in their appropriate places. Eventually they will be used once more and the whole cycle will then have to be repeated. However, that is part of life. (Bransford and Johnson, 1973)

Most readers find the passage hard to understand and recall few details when tested. However, if it is titled "Washing Clothes," readers find it more comprehensible and recall more details. Knowledge of washing clothes can help them acquire information in the passage.

Another link is that much learning occurs through manipulation of one's existing knowledge base. A good example of the power of such manipulation is Lenat's (1976) computer program AM. It had a knowledge base of mathematical concepts and some heuristics and in a long run derived many more concepts from it, many quite well known to mathematics. Researchers in such disciplines as mathematics and philosophy largely acquire new knowledge by manipulating existing knowledge.

Finally, the ability to learn and remember is an important contributor (along with other processes) to various broad processes. One such is human development. From birth to age twenty or so, a person alters from a nearly helpless infant who knows and can do relatively little to a very capable individual with much knowledge and many cognitive and physical capabilities. When psychologists speak of developmental change, they typically see it as involving some sort of growth, resulting in increased capacity to think and learn, and as being tied to underlying maturational change (Canfield and Ceci, 1992). The idea of maturation is of physiological changes that proceed relatively independently of learning according to a genetic timetable and that allow more things to be learned. For example, a child's ability to walk, climb, run, and jump depends on growing muscle tissue and maturing motor areas in the brain. The child can only do these things when the nervous system has matured sufficiently. The nervous system is still maturing into adolescence, and capacity changes can be tied to physiological changes (see Chapter 6). Once the maturational readiness is there, learning may be very rapid. Jensen (1989) gives the sad example of "Isabelle," kept from birth to age six in a semi-dark room by a deaf-mute mother. She was nonverbal and acted like an infant but when placed in a normal environment quickly learned to speak. However, maturational readiness is a somewhat problematical concept. Sometimes the postulated age limits for some learning turn out to be wrong. For instance, Jean Piaget's theory of cognitive development posited various minimum ages at which children could learn various things, but training studies have pushed these limits well back (Halford, 1993). The important point here is that learning and maturation are different processes that both contribute to development.

Another broad process to which the ability to learn contributes is animal domestication, defined by Price (1984) as "that process by which a population of animals becomes adapted to man and the captive environment." Domestication is a very complex process, and only some species are readily liable to domestication. Price lists some key traits: social animals that live in large hierarchical groups which include both sexes, males dominant over females, having a critical period after birth or hatching for the development of a species bond, omnivorous, adaptable to many conditions, and with low reactivity to humans and to sudden changes in environment. Learning is one key process involved. For instance, some animals may become imprinted onto humans (see Chapter 2), and get used to (habituate to) humans, the captive environment, foods provided, and so on. Several processes of genetic change also contribute. Price cites artificial selection, such as for tameness or small size, and natural selection in captivity. Animals selected by humans to be parents do not always reproduce due to stress, space deprivation, and the like, but those tolerant of such stressors may do so. A third key process is relaxation of some aspects of natural selection. Behaviors important in nature are less important in captivity (such as food and shelter seeking and predator avoidance), so genetic and phenotypic variation in such characters may increase. In addition, an individual's development may speed up in captivity. Price cites a study in which domesticated and wild Norway rats were reared under identical conditions with a rich diet. The domestic strain reached sexual maturity and bred earlier. Again, learning is just a contributor to domestication.

SOME THINGS THAT HUMANS NEED TO LEARN AND DO LEARN

As mentioned, virtually all aspects of human thought and behavior depend heavily on learning. Our sense of identity, how we perceive the world, react to various stimuli, eat, work, and organize our daily activities are affected by acquired information. Children must acquire an immense amount of knowledge and many skills to become functional in the natural and social environments. They need a huge knowledge base to understand natural language and perform everyday activities. And learning must continue throughout the lifetime to support daily functioning. This section briefly outlines some important things that people need to learn and some functions of memory in daily life to give some idea of its importance. Some things need only be learned briefly, such as the day's weather report, a spouse's mood, and the morning's schedule. Some things need to be acquired and retained for life, examples being speaking a native language and how to drive a car.

Some Things People Need to Learn and Retain for Long Periods

Children in a hunter-gatherer or agricultural society must learn many things: a native language, how various objects are manipulated, perhaps how to hunt, how to deal well with others, their culture's mores, how to identify many objects (such as local plants, animals, and lakes and streams), places and routes, many general rules, and countless discriminations (for instance, between ripe and unripe fruit and ambitious and unambitious persons). In a complex technological society, children may need to learn much more: skills such as reading and writing, driving and typing, how to use many machines, repair various artifacts, and so on. They must learn much factual knowledge: historical events, games, foods, other cultures, world geography, and so on. Children need to refine their Newtonian knowledge of how the world works: that things fall to earth, weak tree branches break easily, objects move further the harder they are hit, and so on. (Some such knowledge is innate; for instance, infants avoid precipices without having to experience a fall, as in Gibson, 1991.) Children need to acquire many basic concepts and continually learn new ones, such as *virtual reality, the information superhighway,* and *cocooning.*

Children also need to learn many contingencies, relations between their actions and consequences and between various environmental events. In the vernacular, they need to learn the "causal structure of the world." Some contingencies are quite simple and are easily learned; for example, that pitching a baseball harder makes it harder to hit, that hot water washes dishes better than cold, and that punching someone may induce him to punch back. But many contingencies are quite complex, do not always hold, and need much knowledge to understand and use. Some examples are the complex contingencies needed to succeed in business, rise in a profession, and conduct scientific research. Knowledge to contingencies is essential to adaptive behavior, so they are of much interest to everyone. News media often feature reports of newly discovered contingencies or convincing new evidence for known ones. Some examples are:

Long-term jogging may damage the knees.

Ingesting aluminium may lead to Alzheimer's disease.

Buying stock X now may double your investment in a year.

Of course, many "contingencies" that people "know" and use are spurious, and millions use whole systems of spurious contingencies as guides to action, such as astrology and numerology. It is a paradox that humans are so prone to acquire contingencies that do not hold. Even pigeons may learn what Skinner (1948) called "superstitions." He placed pigeons in a box and delivered food at regular intervals independent of what the pigeons did. Later, the birds repeated various behaviors before food arrival, evidently believing that these actions brought food. (A British newspaper later came up with the amusing but misleading statement, "Psychologist B.F. Skinner believes that pigeons are superstitious.")

Another kind of knowledge is what events are likely to follow other events; for example, thunder after lightning and a rise in unemployment after a stock market crash. These do not involve an action by the individual.

Contingencies can be learned from instruction, observation of others, or direct experience. Acquiring knowledge of causal contingencies from experience can be difficult because so many contingencies are probabilistic (a consequence does not always follow) and variable. Furthermore, contingencies may hold for a time and then change, an example being those for successful courtship in the United States. Much research is being done on how people learn about contingencies and distinguish between accidental correlations between events and causal relations (e.g., Allan, 1993). Some causal knowledge is probably innate and people get progressively better at separating accidental and causal sequences as they get older (Cheng, 1993). Increasing knowledge also can help a person better learn them.

Cohen (1989) describes many more things that humans need to learn: identity, location, and function of many objects, recipes for actions (such as cooking a meal or changing a flat tire), and life experiences. Humans also need to learn much information about various people: kin, friends, workmates, acquaintances, and so on. People need to learn and remember their names, faces, quirks, habits, relation to oneself, and so on. Cohen cites studies that show that we recognize people from many cues about them: clothes, gait, context in which we encounter them, build, and so on. People also need to keep track of changing relations with others and events in their lives.

There must be a practical limit to how many other persons the average individual can reasonably keep track of and "groom" relationships with. Much information must be acquired and kept current, and the load climbs with each person added on. Indeed, politicians who must keep track of many persons often use written files. Dunbar (1993) extrapolated from the relation in primates between neocortex size and group size to estimate about 150 persons reasonably can be kept up with. Interestingly, 150 is a common group size in hunter-gatherer societies and in technological ones.

Updating Existing Knowledge

Much learning in daily life can be labeled "updating." With time, one's existing knowledge may become only partially accurate or even obsolete and must be altered to be kept current. Professional knowledge is a clear example: knowledge in engineering or medicine rapidly becomes obsolete and practitioners must read much and/or attend refresher courses to stay current. It is also common in daily life. People need to update their knowledge of others; that they recently married or retired, or got a new hairstyle, that one has a new secretary or new workplace building, that the physical environment recently changed, that a new freeway has gone through or an oft-used bridge has collapsed. An aircraft traffic controller needs to continually update knowledge of various aircraft headings, altitudes, and speeds, and a newspaper editor needs to update knowledge of developments in news stories, reporter deployments, and the current state of the newspaper's production cycle. Bjork (1978) distinguishes between two types of updating. Destructive updating is getting rid of no longer current information, and structural updating is encoding new information with old as part of a series (e.g., the latest development in a news story).

Updating may sometimes break down under stress or inattention. Old habits may reinstate themselves and cause disaster. Bjork cites this as a problem in the military. When personnel are trained on new equipment, actions suitable for old equipment may intrude into performance.

If a person does not update, he or she can become confused, error prone, and increasingly inefficient (Bjork, 1978). Kausler (1990) gives some idea of what life might be like without it. A person's attitudes would be frozen, he or she could not learn new skills, a foreign language, new concepts (such as *timeshare real estate* and *grunge*), that the front door has a new lock, that a step on the staircase recently became a hazard, or remember ways that various problems had been solved. A non-updater could not keep up with world and local affairs and societal changes in customs and fashions. The case of HM shows how important updating is.

Learning about Sources of Knowledge

Another kind of knowledge that people often need to retain (or be able to infer) is knowledge of where certain information was acquired. Information is learned from many sources, and some are more reliable than others. Source knowledge is an important guide to action in daily life. For instance, it is helpful to know whether "Product Y is excellent for cleaning" was acquired from an ad or a consumer organization. Being unclear about sources may even produce delusions and hallucinations and lead to maladaptive behavior (Johnson et al., 1993).

Marcia Johnson and her colleagues have extensively investigated human memory for sources. Johnson dubbed this function "source monitoring," an extension of her earlier notion of "reality monitoring." The latter is being able to discriminate between things actually experienced and things imagined or dreamed of; for instance, whether one really did turn off the iron before leaving the house or just imagined doing so. Source monitoring is retaining information that allows one to distinguish between fact and fantasy, reliable and unreliable sources, actions performed or just intended, and so on. People may only retain degrees of source knowledge. Consider the 1980 Mt. St. Helens' eruption. One may recall who told one of the event, or where, or when, and why one was told. One may also have varying degrees of confidence about the accuracy of one's source knowledge.

Johnson et al. present much evidence that humans are quite good at keeping track of sources. They also argue that source knowledge is not directly stored but is inferred if and when it is needed. People may use various strategies and facts to identify sources; for instance, the knowledge that events perceived are remembered more vividly than events imagined or that only a certain person could have told one about the upcoming company restructure. But surely such knowledge is sometimes stored directly. Consider the vivid memory that many persons have of when they heard about the assassination of John F. Kennedy. The trace typically includes knowledge of exactly where they were and how they learned about the event.

Acquiring Information Needed to Support Daily Activities

Cohen (1989) points out that memory is essential to support many everyday activities and thinking. Of course, thinking would not be possible without memory. Memory is needed to hold information about ongoing actions, for instance. A simple example is running an errand. One needs to construct the sequence of elements, hold it in memory, compute the best route, set priorities, and so on. Goschke and Kuhl (1993) carried out an interesting study that suggested that knowledge of such intentions is held in a more active state than knowledge for other things. Subjects memorized two texts that described simple activities and were told that they would have to execute one of the scripts. In a later recognition test, words from the script to be executed were recognized faster. Perhaps they have a heightened level of activation until actually executed.

The Human Ability to Learn and Remember Is Severely Overtaxed

As Cohen (1989) points out, the ability to learn and remember is sorely overloaded in a technological society. The memory system evolved to cope with the lesser demands of a hunter-gatherer society in which few major events occur and people interact with relatively few others, need learn many fewer skills, and rarely venture far from a restricted home locale. However, people cope with overload in various ways. For instance, we forget information that is not needed, actively select and learn what is important, recall useful gist rather than unimportant details, organize bits of information into larger units, and automate complex action sequences to free up attention for other things. We place things into categories and treat them as category members rather than individual things. We collapse memories of many events into generalizations and may forget the individual events. For instance, rather than remember all instances of being bitten by a dog, we can remember, "Dogs bite." People also leave much information computable rather than directly stored (Cohen, 1989). And people rely on numerous external aids, such as notebooks, diaries, computers, and secretaries. These aids have allowed a massive store of knowledge to accumulate over the generations, and better ways to process it have amplified human capabilities. Even researchers in memory favor such aids rather than strategies to improve recall (Park et al., 1990). As Cohen points out, despite its limits, the human memory apparatus does a fine job under the circumstances.

THE HISTORY OF THE STUDY OF LEARNING AND MEMORY

The study of learning and memory has a long and complex history. There have been a variety of different approaches to its study, various subfields which at times have had little or no contact with each other, and other disciplines at times have influenced the mainstream. Examples of the latter are AI, ethology, neurophysiology, and linguistics. Much of the field's history is an effort to find a useful approach to studying a very complex and variable subject matter. This section will examine some key strands and milestones needed to understand the present situation in the field.

Learning and memory are so central to human life that early humans must have worked out some basic principles. People inevitably would notice that they readily forgot some sorts of material but not others, that more was forgotten as time passes, and that memory for events might have become quite distorted with time. Indeed, Kreutzer et al. (1975) found that American ten-year-olds knew such generalizations as "meaningful material is easier to recall," "more study time increases the amount learned," and "savings in time to learn may occur when once-familiar material is relearned."

Philosophical Beginnings

The formal study of learning and memory began with speculations by the Ancient Greek philosophers. Plato proposed a wax tablet model of memory in which information is stored like impressions in wax and forgetting is the erosion of the impressions with time. Plato also held that fundamental concepts are innate and experience only brings them forward. Aristotle analyzed knowledge into types and laid down some principles by which ideas are linked together (Boring, 1950). Examples are that ideas are likely to be associated if they are similar, if they contrast, or if they occur simultaneously.

Plato and Aristotle also set the stage for a debate of enormous weight: Where does an individual's knowledge come from? There are three general possibilities (Anderson, 1989): knowledge is inbuilt, it comes from experience, or it is derived from manipulating existing knowledge. There are major philosophical positions that all or much knowledge originates in a certain way. Empiricism holds that all knowledge is acquired from experience, and nativism that at least some is inbuilt. Bolles (1988) points out that some philosophers have held that all knowledge is learned but none has held that all is innate.

The English philosopher John Locke (1632–1704) wrote at length on empiricism. Locke held that the mind at birth is a "tabula rasa," a blank slate on which experience would write. Everything a human knows and becomes capable of derives from experience. Bower and Hilgard (1981) list some specific tenets of the view. First, the mind is like a machine, operating according to laws. Second, humans see things as they actually are; they see reality directly, a view called naive realism. Third, new knowledge is acquired by directly copying sense impressions or by linking known ideas together. So, complex notions as that of an orange are built up in the mind by associating simpler ideas, such as roundness, the color orange, and so on.

The German philosopher Immanuel Kant (1724–1804) wrote at length on nativism. Kant conceded that much knowledge is acquired from experience but argued that some must be inbuilt. Fundamental concepts such as time, space, and causality are too complex to be learned. Such knowledge is present at birth, or it emerges later through maturation. Piattelli-Palmarini (1989) suggests some mechanisms that may be at work here. He notes that experience alters the strength of connections between neurons and/or prunes away little-used pathways and neurons. Nature produces many neurons and pathways and only some are selected for survival. He argues that experience does not instruct, it selects from what is already there. In a sense, therefore, all that a person can learn is present in the brain already. He offered an analogy to the immune system, which does not tailor-make new antibodies for previously unencountered invaders. It has the capacity to make one for every invader it might encounter. The environment selects from what is already there. There is strong evidence for such inbuilt programming for language acquisition. Humans evidently have inbuilt principles for which the parameters are set by a given native language. Gazzaniga (1992) expands on the extreme view that all learning is selection from existing innate knowledge.

The issue of pure empiricism versus nativism has had a big impact in many realms (e.g., Bolles, 1988), because the view adopted affects many things. Consider education. Many "progressive" schools lean toward nativism and give children much freedom to explore and construct knowledge for themselves, believing that experience brings forward knowledge already there. Some very traditional schools lean toward empiricism and see children as empty vessels to be filled with rote-learned knowledge. A second example is about the philosophical principles underlying a given society. Empiricism is a major pillar of American society. Indeed, John Locke's political philosophy was a major inspiration for the Founding Fathers: the Declaration of Independence says, "All men are created equal." An important assumption is that later social class and wealth differences are partly due to unequal effort and use of opportunities, and many see the role of government as only to provide equal opportunities. Violating this principle can lead to great controversy. Consider the derivational issue of whether IQ differences between people are partly innate, which empiricism would suggest is not the case. Herrnstein (1973) argues that the differences are partly innate, and since social class differences are partly due to IQ differences, then social stratification in the United States is partly genetic. There was an enormous storm of protest.

Empiricism also was an underlying principle of Communist societies. Karl Marx held that the mind is a reflection of society, the structure of which itself derives from the underlying economic relations. The seamy side of human nature was seen as due to capitalist society. Change society and one can change human nature. Communist nations aimed to create a "new, socialist man" who would work unselfishly for the common good and take according to his needs and give according to his ability. This was a necessity for the utopian classless society. But the massive social experiment ended in 1989–91 when most of these societies collapsed. Lenski (1978) argues that they had largely failed to produce "new, socialist men," citing such evidence as existing inequality in power and wealth, rife absenteeism, four-to five-hour workdays, alienation, and resistance by the elite to Nikita Krushchev's efforts to enroll more children of workers and peasants in elite Soviet schools.

The derivational issue of just how malleable certain human characteristics are comes up time and time again. The historical evidence suggests that some traits can be partly altered on a societal basis, but only to a limited degree. For example, Communist states did produce some change in traits. Lenski (1978) argues that few in these nations in the early 1970s actually wanted a free-enterprise system back. Much anecdotal evidence from former East Germans after the 1989 reunification suggested that many disliked aspects of the new society, such as lack of community and people being money-oriented and mainly for themselves. In Japan after 1945, Douglas MacArthur largely succeeded in turning an expansionist, militaristic people into a relatively pacifist one. Such cases, as well as large cross-cultural differences in some characteristics, suggest some malleability. However, there are many human universals, such as music, dance, territoriality, division of labor, etiquette and status (Brown, 1991). Some other derivational issues are to what extent any behavioral differences between the sexes are innate and how important native talent is to skill learning. The latter is examined in Chapter 6.

However, there is now much evidence that pure empiricism is just plain wrong. Early studies with computers that learn discovered that some knowledge had to be preprogrammed to make new learning feasible. A tabula rasa computer could learn virtually nothing. Animal studies (see Chapter 2) show that animals learn some associations quickly and easily and others slowly or not at all. Humans also show much evidence of preprogrammed knowledge and propensities to learn certain things (Karmiloff-Smith, 1992). For example, commonly reported phobias are of things truly dangerous in the human evolutionary past, such as the dark, snakes, and being alone. Another example is human preferences for characteristics of a mate, which may be partly malleable but are largely innate. Buss (1989) surveyed marriage statistics and stated preferences in mate characteristics in thirty-seven cultures and found that in all males preferred younger, healthy, good-looking females, while females preferred wealthy, ambitious males a few years older than themselves. Buss argues that these preferences reflect innate programming in line with the universal mating principle of the animal kingdom: preference always reflects the best reproductive strategy. His argument goes that females have a much shorter reproductive span and need good health for a successful pregnancy. Men become programmed to prefer young females who will have more and healthier children. Male reproductive span is much longer, their health is less important, and a male a few years older is more likely to have proved himself as a provider and have social status. A wealthy man can provide more material things for the children. So, these preferences evolved because they give a big selective advantage. Indeed, there are big evolutionary advantages to building in some knowledge and propensities to learn certain things quickly and easily. This topic is discussed in more detail in Chapter 2.

Empiricism also lead to the doctrine of associationism, a philosophical tradition that aimed to discover the laws of the mind. Locke and David Hume (1711–76) were adherents. They assumed tabula rasa at birth and looked for the laws by which associations are built up, examples being frequency of pairing and Aristotle's principles (above). Associationism set the stage for the scientific study of learning.

The Scientific Study Begins

The origin of the scientific study is usually dated to 1879, when Wilhelm Wundt founded the first psychological laboratory at the University of Leipzig. Wundt favored use of the introspection method of studying the mind, which involved an observer describing what went on in his or her mind, perhaps in reaction to a stimulus or when learning a poem. William James, working at Harvard, also favored such armchair work, from which came the important distinction between primary and secondary memory (James, 1890), which is described later.

The first experimental studies were carried out by the German scholar Hermann Ebbinghaus, who was influenced by associationism and investigated how associations are learned. He began working around 1880 and in 1885 published a short monograph called *On Memory*, which reported many model experiments on a single co-operative subject: Ebbinghaus himself. He used artificial words like *zax* and *qup* (called nonsense syllables), chosen because they had few associations with real words and so memory could be studied in a situation where it was little unaffected by past learning. He examined various things. One was the time course of forgetting. He learned lists of nonsense syllables and tested his memory for them at different elapsed times by a savings method. The classic forgetting curve emerged, in which most forgetting occurred shortly after learning and then levelled off. He looked at the effects of such variables as length of material learned and whether material is best learned in one session or in several.

Around 1900, classic work on animal learning was being carried out, also influenced by associationism. In 1898, Robert Thorndike published the influential book *Animal Intelligence*, which reported various experiments. He examined, for instance, how a cat learned an arbitrary response to escape from a box (by trial and error, said Thorndike). He formulated two very influential laws. The law of effect states that responses followed by "satisfying" consequences are likely to be repeated while those followed by "annoying" ones are less likely to be. The law of exercise states that, all other things being equal, an association between a stimulus and a response will be strengthened by its exercise. In Russia, Ivan Pavlov was carrying out classic work on conditioned reflexes in dogs, published in translation in the West in 1927. The work of Thorndike and Pavlov had a great impact for the next few decades and helped form the metatheory of behaviorism.

Behaviorism

Starting around 1914, the field underwent a sea change with the advent of behaviorism. The founder was J.B. Watson (e.g., Watson, 1914; 1924), who was influenced by empiricism, associationism, and the mechanistic philosophy of René Descartes (1596–1650). Watson argued that the popular introspection method was subjective and yielded unreliable data. The field needed an observable subject matter and objective methods of study. Watson argued that behavior, which was observable and could be studied scientifically, was the proper subject matter of psychology. Watson evidently did believe that thinking exists (as subvocal speech), but only in humans, and that it could not be studied scientifically (Jenkins, 1979). But a good methodological point, that thinking is hard to study but behavior is not, was pushed to a theoretical one: that thinking could not be studied and anyway was unimportant (Jenkins, 1979). The mind did not affect behavior. As Watson (1914) put it, "There are no centrally initiated processes," which if true meant that complex mental life is irrelevant to overt behavior. Watson's argument was widely accepted, and for several decades psychology defined itself as the science of behavior. Learning was conceptualized as a change in behavior.

Behaviorism is a metatheory, an overall approach, with several variants. Here is a somewhat idealized set of its assumptions:

1. Behavior is the significant psychological event and the proper subject matter of psychology. (Today most behaviorists concede that mental processes exist but say they cannot be inferred from behavior. See Uttal, 1993.)

2. Humans and animals are machines whose behavior is completely determined by their internal and external environments. Free will is an illusion (and a dangerous one, said Skinner, 1971).

3. Almost all human behavior is learned. A neonate (newborn infant) has only a few basic inborn reflexes.

4. Learning is a change in behavior. A learner is a responder, a "behaving organism."

5. The only mechanism of human development is learning. As humans develop, their behavior becomes more complex as the behavioral repertoire increases. Complex behavioral sequences are built up from simpler ones.

6. The laws of learning are the same for all species, responses, and stimuli. Therefore, the behavior of insects, rabbits, dolphins, and humans is subject to the same laws. Human behavior can be studied by working out the laws governing a single response in a single animal species. The same laws will apply, just as principles of genetics discovered from studying the fruit fly apply to humans.

The sixth "equipotentiality" assumption is a key one. Its acceptance made the study of animal learning central in psychology from the 1930s to the mid-1950s (Jenkins, 1979). Indeed, in a presidential address to the American Psychological Association, Edward Tolman argued that virtually everything of interest to psychology will be discovered by figuring out what influences the behavior of a rat at a choice point in a maze. Research on human learning did go on in this period, but often with behavioristic concepts and principles. For instance, the verbal learning tradition that examined variables affecting acquisition of word lists (which lasted until the 1960s) was heavily behaviorally oriented (see Cofer, 1979).

In the 1930s, the neobehavioristic era began, which reached its heyday in the 1940s. There were several major theories of learning, each associated with a different neobehaviorist figure, such as Clark Hull, Kenneth Spence, Edwin Guthrie, Edward Tolman, and B.F. Skinner. They took varying positions on such issues as whether reinforcement (a reward or aversive stimulus) is necessary for learning to occur. Some also tried to construct very grand theories of learning. The archetypal example was Clark Hull. He applied the Newtonian hypothetico-deductive method to learning, setting out postulates, deriving theorems and corollaries, and describing it all mathematically. His system had units such as the hab and the pav, and concepts such as net reaction potential. His work started with a 1929 article and his most detailed statement was in *A Behavior System* (1952), which gave seventeen postulates and many theorems. Here is a sample:

Postulate VII. The incentive component (K) of reaction potential (sEr) is a negatively accelerated increasing monotonic function of the weight (w) of food or quantity of other incentive (K') given as reinforcement, i.e.,

$$K = 1 - 10^{-a\sqrt{w}}$$

Postulate VIII. The reaction potential (sEr) of a bit of learned behavior at any given stage of learning, where conditions are constant throughout learning and response-evocation, is determined (1) by the drive (D) operating during the learning process multiplied (2) by the dynamism of the signalling stimulus trace (V1), (3) by the incentive reinforcement (K), and (4) by the habit strength (sHr), i.e.,

$$sEr = D \times V1 \times K \times sHr$$

(Hull, 1952, 7)

Another neobehaviorist approach was B.F. Skinner's "atheoretical" one (e.g., Skinner, 1938; 1974). Skinner denied the value of such grand theories as Hull's and called for a "functional analysis of behavior," a description of the relations between stimuli and responses couched as laws. Researchers, he said, should try to find laws relating stimuli and responses. He also argued that there are two major types of learning: classical and operant conditioning (see Chapter 2). The Skinnerian approach is often called the "Experimental Analysis of Behavior" and is the only one that survives today.

Researchers in the 1940s and 1950s looked for crucial experiments to settle the issues on which the theories differed, such as how many types of learning there are and whether learning occurs in jumps or in small, progressive increments (Bower and Hilgard, 1981). Behaviorism in this period was never completely dominant. Some work went on outside its framework, and it was much less influential in Europe than in America. For example, Frederick Bartlett in England studied memory with a much more cognitive approach (Bartlett, 1932).

By the mid- to late 1950s, there was much dissatisfaction with behaviorism. Crucial experiments to decide the issues were hard to find, and some researchers began to believe that there were none (Baddeley, 1990). Practical applications were meager. In World War II, for example, researchers confronted with such practical problems as devising an efficient aircraft instrument panel and other performance issues found behaviorism of little help. Hull's equations did not obviously suggest solutions. So an alternative metatheory gradually became popular: the information-processing (or cognitive) framework. Some key works are Miller (1956), Broadbent (1958), Miller et al. (1960), and Neisser (1967). The approach was based on a new metaphor and involved studying the mind again rather than just behavior. The mind was viewed as working like a computer. It took in information through peripherals (eyes, ears, etc.), stored it, processed it, and output it in behavior. The approach also advocated studying humans, the argument being that the animal/human gap was so great that studies of animals told little about humans. After about 1960, the approach had gained much support, and from the late 1960s most research on humans used it. The next section describes the metatheory in detail.

The conventional wisdom is that behaviorism was swept away in a Kuhnian paradigm shift in the late 1960s and early 1970s, but this is not at all true. Behaviorism is still alive and some say it is thriving. There are many behaviorally oriented journals, several professional societies, and a division of the American Psychological Association, and behavioral principles are widely applied in education, psychotherapy, and industry. For instance, Friman et al. (1993) surveyed citation counts in leading psychology journals between 1979 and 1988 and found high citation rates for behaviorally oriented work with no downward trends, concluding that the approach had not at all been displaced. Behaviorism has evolved, however (Zuriff, 1985; Uttal, 1993). Some behaviorists now use cognitive concepts, and in 1989 the *Journal of the Experimental Analysis of Behavior* even ran a special issue on cognition and behavior.

What happened is that the learning and memory field split into two separate branches in the late 1960s, each associated with a different metatheory. Behaviorists mostly studied animal learning while cognitivists studied human learning and memory (mostly they studied memory, a standard argument being that one first needed to understand how the memory system works before understanding how knowledge is acquired). The split was almost total. As Wright and Watkins (1987, 131) put it, "The camps differ in their procedures, the questions they ask, their terminology . . . [and the] journals they publish in. . . . [C]ommunication between the two camps . . . is almost nonexistent." The split is still evident in the way learning and memory is taught in universities. Most textbooks in the field have two halves, one dealing with animal learning, usually from a behavioral approach, and the other dealing with human memory from a cognitive approach. The orientation of courses also differs greatly across universities. Lattal et al. (1990) surveyed psychology of learning and memory courses in 138 American universities and found that the dominant orientation differed greatly. About 19 percent were taught from a behavioral viewpoint, 23 percent from a cognitive one, and 31 percent from an eclectic one. The rest had other orientations, such as neurobiological.

After the split, the two approaches took different paths. The history of the cognitive half is described in the next section. The animal learning camp went through several major changes. In the late 1960s, ideas from ethology began to permeate and change practices. For instance, much evidence arose against the equipotentiality assumption, and learning came to be seen as strongly influenced by an animal's evolutionary history. Some researchers took an "ecological approach," studying how learning adapted a species to its niche and how different learning mechanisms evolved (e.g., Davey, 1989). In the late 1970s, some researchers began to see many animal species not as passive reactors to the environment but as active processors of

information like humans. Much work nowadays freely applies information-processing concepts developed from human studies to animals (see
Chapter 2). However, behaviorism is still a dominant orientation.

The Information-Processing Metatheory (Cognitivism)

There are several approaches and theories within this framework. Here
is a somewhat idealized version of its key assumptions, partly taken from
Kail and Bisanz (1992) and Massaro and Cowan (1993).

1. Psychology should study the mind. The mind is a device for representing the
   outside world and manipulating the representations. Mental representations are
   symbols for things in the world, and the mind is a program that runs on hardware
   (neurons).
2. Representations contain information and are manipulated by processes (see
   Chapter 4 for details). There is a set of representational primitives that are the
   building blocks of larger units. All cognitive phenomena can be described in
   terms of representations and processes that intervene between observable stimuli and responses.
3. A small number of elementary processes, perhaps only a few dozen, underlie all
   cognitive activity. (The analogy is to the central processing unit of a computer,
   which does a lot with only a few basic operations.)
4. Processes operate together. They can combine into higher-level routines with
   emergent properties. Several processes may combine to perform a particular
   task, and so performance results from the interaction of simpler processes.
5. Processing occurs in stages.
6. A cognitive theory is a description of how representations and processes interact
   in stages to produce performance.
7. Humans are active seekers of and selectors of information who formulate and
   act on rules.
8. Learning is constructing new mental representations or modifying existing ones.
9. Cognitive development occurs through self-modification; for example, through
   maturation, and learning.

Massaro and Cowan (1993) give a very detailed analysis of the
metatheory and also some of its problems. One, for instance, is the great
difficulty of proving a particular cognitive model of some task correct
because different combinations of representations and processes can produce the same performance.

Research in the 1960s and 1970s was heavily influenced by the computer
metaphor. Much work directly applied concepts from computer science to
the mind and explored issues suggested by the computer metaphor. Papers
spoke of registers, buffers, and filters, and key issues were whether processing is serial or parallel or whether imaginal representations (mental

images) are analogical or discrete. A landmark work in this vein was the multistore model of memory put forward by Atkinson and Shiffrin (1968), which brought together many computer-based ideas.

Figure 1.2 shows the model. It posits three main memory stores with different functions, capacities, and controlling processes. Information flows from the environment through the stores. The sensory receptors (eyes, ears, skin senses, etc.) collect information from the environment and a snapshot is briefly held in the sensory registers. Each sense has its own register, though the authors spoke mainly about the visual one. The snapshot (the visual icon) lasts up to 500 milliseconds and rapidly decays or is displaced by another icon. Strong evidence for this structure's existence is the classic research of Sperling (1960). In one experiment, subjects briefly saw a display of three rows of four letters through a tachistoscope and had to read them out. In the full report condition, subjects reported as many letters as they could and averaged four or five correct. However, in a partial report condition, a tone indicated to read only from a particular row. The tone sounded after the display had gone off, and subjects typically could get all in the row correct. Sperling's interpretation was that a nearly photographic image of the display was held in a store after the stimulus had gone off, and subjects could scan it, taking about 10 milliseconds to scan each letter. There also is evidence for an auditory register, called the echoic store. Indeed, an everyday experience of its use is hearing someone ask a question while one's attention is elsewhere, then having the query repeated, and being able to recover what was initially said. In the model, information in the registers is raw and unanalysed. A fraction of it then goes into short-term store, depending on what the individual is paying attention to.

Short-term store is related to but not identical to one's immediate consciousness. It is more than this, because material not in consciousness is still activated. Short-term store holds a little information briefly in a phonological (speech-based) code. Capacity is about eight units, based on Miller's (1956) classic limit of seven plus or minus two units. Information in short-term store could decay or be displaced by other information but was held longer than in the registers, from 15 to 30 seconds without rehearsal. The latter could keep it there longer, an example being looking up a telephone number and repeating it until dialing. Some information from short-term store then entered long-term memory (LTM), mainly by rehearsal. LTM could hold information for very long periods and used a meaning-based format, had a large capacity, and could lose information through decay or interference.

LTM stored information based on each sensory modality, as evidenced by ability to recognize stimuli in each modality, but some information might be modality-free (such as temporal information), said the authors. Information was transferred to LTM by control processes and could flow back to short-term store. Such a control process is a means of handling information,

Figure 1.2
The Multistore Model of Memory

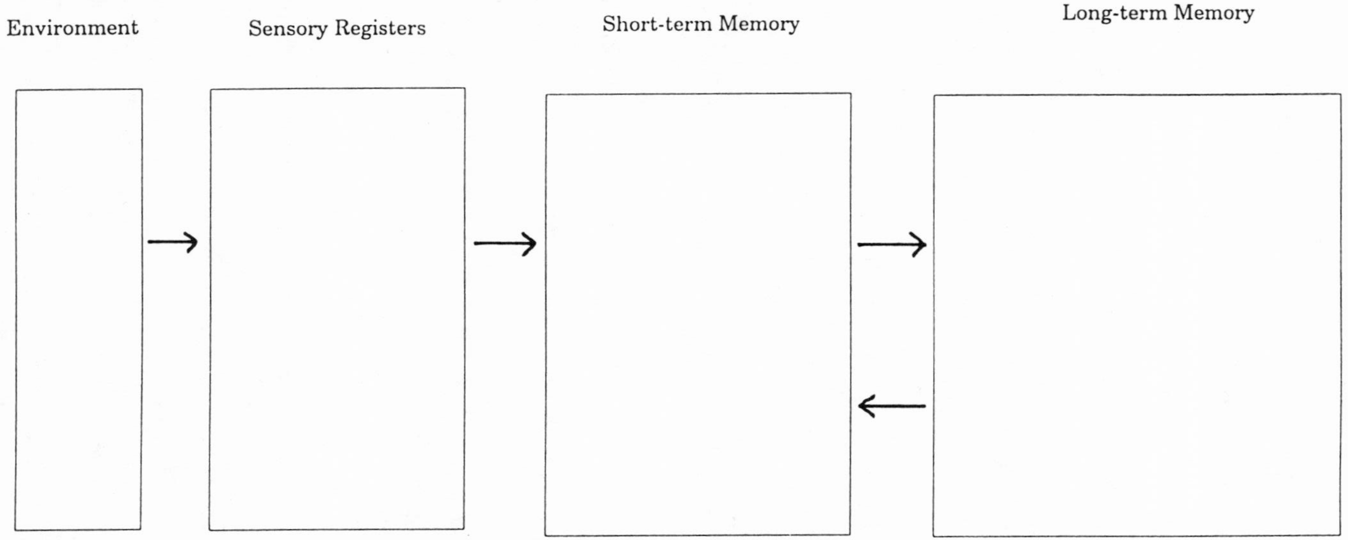

Environment

Sensory Registers

Short-term Memory

Long-term Memory

and is under the individual's control. There are many such processes and each store has its own. The registers include processes such as deciding which information to transfer to short-term store and where and what to scan within the snapshot. Those of short-term store include rehearsal, searching for a particular datum, and "chunking," grouping items into larger units and thus improving the capacity of short-term store (Miller, 1956). For instance, the digits 3-6-5-3-6-5-5-2-5-2-5-2 can be chunked into 365 365 52 52 52, so the memory load can be reduced from twelve to five units. Chunking is a learning principle of fundamental importance and will be elaborated on in later chapters. LTM control processes include organization of material and retrieval.

Atkinson and Shiffrin cited several lines of evidence for the short-term/LTM division. Among the most convincing is neuropsychological data. HM could learn little, but his short-term store was intact. The patient KF had the reverse deficit: intact ability to learn but impaired short-term memory (Baddeley, 1990). Note the strong similarity of the model to a computer at work. There are stores, charts of information flow, and mechanical processes to shuffle information about.

In the 1970s, the cognitive approach became dominant in most areas of psychology, which extensively used cognitive concepts. However, basic research was done typically in laboratories and often with very narrow tasks. At a 1978 conference, Ulric Neisser argued that more naturalistic work was needed, that memory needed to be studied in the real world (Neisser, 1982). Many researchers agreed, and in the last decade many naturalistic studies have been done. Here are some examples. Neisser (1981) did a classic study of John Dean's memory. Dean was a Watergate figure repeatedly questioned about his recall of events that could be checked against actual tapes. The comparison showed much inaccuracy, merging of episodes into one, and reconstruction of events. Dean sometimes put words into Richard Nixon's mouth. Despite the inaccuracies, however, Neisser argued that Dean basically recalled the gist of what had gone on in the Nixon White House. Schneider and Laurion (1993) looked at how information was recalled from radio news. Subjects listened to a tape and recalled news items and editorial items equally well and recalled material they were interested in best. Clark and Stephenson (1993) looked at social recall. Laboratory studies typically have individuals recall material alone, but in the real world this is sometimes done in groups. Therefore Clark and Stephenson had subjects watch a video of an interview and later recall its details alone or in a group. Social recall was more accurate and police subjects (evidently more practiced at social recall) were better than non-police subjects.

The cognitive approach lately has turned more to studying learning and is starting to connect with other disciplines, such as neurophysiology and machine learning. It also is starting to use some ideas from the animal learning tradition. One example is work on classical conditioning in causality judgments (van Hamme et al., 1993), and another is animal learning work on constraints on learning being applied to constraints on human knowledge acquisition (Gelman, 1993).

Connectionism

In the mid-1980s, an approach usually called connectionism became popular. Though the ideas had been around for some time, for various reasons the approach suddenly took off. The central idea is to simulate the brain's action with a computer system called a neural net. A neural net is composed of interconnected units roughly corresponding to neurons and can adjust the strength of connections and learn. Already there are many connectionist models of psychological functions such as memory and aspects of language learning. Some hail the advent of connectionism as a paradigm shift like that from behaviorism to cognitivism, but this may be too strong a statement. It is still too soon to see what the approach's ultimate impact will be. Chapter 7 looks at it in more detail.

To date, there are still three major approaches to studying learning and memory: behaviorism, cognitivism, and connectionism. To some extent, they complement each other, and each can be usefully applied to understanding certain aspects of learning. Each borrows concepts from one or both of the other. However, their metatheories differ. How should they be treated? When much more research has been done, it may be possible to create a synthesis of the best aspects of each or perhaps frame the whole field adequately within, say, the information-processing framework. Until then, one can use each approach according to one's purposes at the time. A useful analogy is how physicists treat gravity. There are three major concepts: Newton's notion of a force acting at a distance, Einstein's notion of a property of curved space, and the quantum mechanics view of an exchange of gravitons. Each may be useful for different purposes; for example, Einstein's for building cosmological models and Newton's for calculating spacecraft orbits.

Some Lessons of History

The above history has some lessons for researchers. Much has been achieved and a great deal is now known about learning and memory, but progress will be faster if two lessons are heeded. First, researchers need to pay more attention to integrating different areas. The field has a tendency to split into subfields that communicate little and may study some of the same phenomena under different names (Claxton, 1980). The remedy is to look more at how each subfield is linked to others, to develop a common terminology with agreed-upon meanings for terms such as *concept*, and to look for general principles that apply across the whole field. Second, researchers need to develop new ways to deal with the subject matter. Physics has been the usual model but is not always suitable. The subject matter is very complex and variable and is extraordinarily difficult to study because so many variables affect learning and memory. A slight procedural change can abolish a phenomenon. Subjects in experiments often use different strategies to perform the same task and may switch between them; grouped data may obscure what is really going on. A natural response is to simplify to make things investigable, but as Albert Einstein put it, "Things should be made as simple as possible but not more so." Sometimes researchers have oversimplified. Pure behaviorism is an extreme example, whereby many saw most human learning as being investigable with an easily studied rat pressing a bar for food. It is still too soon to say whether connectionist modeling is another example, but one can see the same wish to simplify at work (see Crick, 1989).

SOME METHODS OF STUDYING LEARNING AND MEMORY

The methods available largely determine the progress of scientific inquiry. Indeed, the history of science is full of cases in which a field advanced slowly but then very rapidly when new methods were devised. Some examples are space probes in astronomy and gene splicing and sequencing in biology. Researchers in learning and memory have developed an impressive array of methods, and this section briefly describes some major ones. Shallice (1988) and Bower and Clapper (1989) give more details.

Experimental Methods

An archetypal learning experiment has a learning phase, a retention phase, and a test phase. In Phase 1, subjects learn some facts or a skill, rest or perform some other activity, and then are tested for what they have retained (Bower and Clapper, 1989). Sometimes there is no learning phase; subjects' existing knowledge is measured in some way. There are also animal variants of the basic procedure. Here are some specific methods.

Animal learning is still often studied with the venerable "Skinner box" (Skinner, 1938). It is a small light- and sound-attenuated chamber, usually for a rat or pigeon, which has one or more manipulanda—a small lever for rats and a peckable disk for pigeons. Rewards such as food and punishers such as electric shock can be delivered. Stimuli such as lights and tones can be presented, and visual stimuli usually are projected onto the pigeon's key. The dependent variable usually is rate of depressing the manipulandum or relative rate of responding on two or more manipulanda. The setup also is used widely in psychopharmacology and animal psychophysics. For example, a rat may be trained to a stable performance and then be injected with a drug to test the drug's effect on responding. If one wanted to know the minimum angle orientation difference that a pigeon could detect, one could reward responding only when a line at one angle was present and not when another was shown and then slowly reduce the orientation difference until the discrimination broke down. There are analogous methods for humans. Infants may move a foot for a reward or university students may press a button for points or money.

There are various useful methods to study human learning. Recall tasks typically involve subjects learning a list of words and later recalling them, with dependent variables being number correct, reaction time, or order of recall. A paired associate procedure involves a learning phase in which subjects see word pairs (e.g., horse-donkey) and in a recall phase see only the first word and must supply the second. Recognition tasks usually involve presenting stimuli and then later showing them all (or a sample) and some previously unshown stimuli. Subjects must say which ones they have already seen. Dependent variables are accuracy, reaction time, the subjects' rating of confidence in their accuracy, and error patterns. Other dependent variables used in learning experiments are time or number of trials to meet a criterion, savings, and transfer of learning to performance of or learning of another task. For example, one might compare learning of gifted and average children by training them on one task and then on another, using initial performance of the second task or trials required to meet some learning criterion as the dependent variable. Concept learning methods involve showing subjects a set of stimuli (sometimes just one stimulus) which fall into categories. Subjects are trained to categorize a set and then may be shown new stimuli and asked to categorize these. Dependent variables are accuracy, reaction time, and error patterns. Bruner et al. (1956) list several variants of this basic procedure.

Several useful but expensive physiological methods have become available in recent years. There are new methods of measuring and analyzing brain waves, for example (Mosler et al., 1993). Another is positron emission tomography (PET) scans, which involve measuring glucose uptake in areas of the functioning brain. Areas active when subjects perform some task take up more glucose, and researchers can thus index what areas are involved in the task. Groups can also be compared (say, gifted and average children) while they perform a task.

Subjects' self-reports are also sometimes used. Subjects can be interviewed to determine their knowledge and its organization in a particular area, for example, or be asked why they performed as they did in an experiment. Such data are given varying weights by different researchers. Some see them as a useful addition to other data while some see them as little use. Nisbett and Wilson (1977) argued that subjects are often unable to explain why they behaved as they did and have "little or no direct introspective access to higher-order cognitive processes." An oft-used analogy is that the conscious mind trying to explain a person's actions is like a poorly informed public relations operative who is told little about company activities but continually has to explain and excuse them. In one experiment cited by Nisbett and Wilson, subjects were shown four articles of clothing in a row and were asked to pick the best one and say why it was the best. They often chose whichever one was on the far right and gave various explanations for their choice, all having nothing to do with position.

Neuropsychological Evidence

Data from brain-damaged persons has been increasingly used in recent years. Researchers may study either a single case or a group in a diagnostic category such as Korsakoff's syndrome. Such data can highlight how important some aspect of memory function is and cast light on its everyday uses, as with HM. But a patient may also provide converging evidence for a particular theory or suggest its inadequacy. A theory should be able to account for an observed pattern of deficits. Cases are useful when they show a disassociation of functions. In other words, a patient should show normal function in ability A but impaired function in ability B, rather than impaired function in all abilities. Even better is a double-disassociation, whereby one patient shows normal A and impaired B and another shows impaired A and normal B.

Shallice (1988) looks in detail at the value of such evidence and its limits. For instance, individual cases can be hard to interpret. Patients can develop strategies to compensate for deficits, and some functions recover with time. However, the data can be very useful converging evidence along with other sources.

Computer Simulation

Most fields of science now use computer simulation extensively. It is often used in cognitive psychology and also in studying animal learning. The method may be used alone or with experiments on organisms. The general idea is to devise a model of some process, write a computer program that embodies the model, and run it. One can compare computer performance with human or animal performance or just see if the model runs at all, which can be very enlightening. As Hintzman (1990, 111) put it, "To have one's hunches about how a simple combination of processes will behave repeatedly dashed by one's own computer program is a humbling experience that no experimental psychologist should miss." As well, if the program runs but does not perform much like organisms, the model can be reworked.

Simulation has some big advantages. First, the theorist must be explicit about everything. Nothing can be left vague or the program may not run. Hidden assumptions also may become evident (Eysenck and Keane, 1990), which themselves may require some thinking out. Second, the simulation can show some unexpected behavior that otherwise would have gone unnoticed and which may reveal much about one's subject matter. A classic example from meteorology is work that lead to the development of chaos theory. A computer simulation of weather change revealed that tiny differences in initial conditions could snowball and produce huge differences in later parameters, a previously unsuspected phenomenon. Third, researchers can do things to computer models that cannot be done to humans. For example, Hinton et al. (1993) devised a connectionist model of deep dyslexia and "lesioned" it in various ways to see whether the simulation reproduced the same errors as dyslexic humans.

SOME MAJOR QUESTIONS ABOUT LEARNING AND MEMORY

What are the important questions about learning and memory? Each broad framework (behaviorist, cognitive, connectionist) suggests its own questions, which may be of no interest to researchers in another framework. For example, questions from the heyday of behaviorism such as whether reinforcement is necessary for learning to occur are of no interest to cognitivists. Such connectionist issues as "What are the capabilities of various network architectures?" and "What algorithm(s) does the brain use to alter connection strength during learning?" may be of little interest to behaviorists.

A number of questions arise within the information-processing framework, which is the main approach used in this book. At a very broad level one can loosely apply the levels of analysis suggested by Marr (1982) to the memory system. Marr proposed that the visual system could be studied on three broad levels, largely suggested by the kinds of questions that a computer programmer asks before designing a large-scale system. Each level has its own questions. The broad questions on the first level are "What is the task to be done and what are its constraints?" Apply the first question to memory and the general answer is to select, store, and process information for later use so an individual can behave more adaptively. The constraints are much more complicated. The second level is "How does the system perform the task?" This involves finding out what the parts of the memory system are, what representations are generated, what processes operate on them, and how they produce performance. The third level is "What is the hardware that allows the task to be done?" The general answer of course is an incredibly complex array of neurons that can change their connection strength. The questions of major concern in this book are on the second level.

Bower and Clapper (1989) list some general classes of question from the second level. The first concerns questions about the nature of learning and of memory mechanisms. Is memory a unitary structure, and if not, what are the parts, their capacities, representation codes, and processes? Another question is what types of learning there are and what the principles of learning are. A second class of question concerns the nature of knowledge. How is it represented and organized in memory and how is it interrelated? Is there a basic unit of knowledge, and if so, what structures can it be built up into? A third class of question concerns applied matters (which may also have theoretical implications). Bower and Clapper give such examples as how learning and remembering may be made easier, how the ability to learn and remember changes with age, and how it is affected by various drugs. One can also ask many very specific questions. Neisser (1982) puts forward many: "What is retained months or years after a formal education course?" "Are there functionally different types of memory used in daily life, and if so, what are they?" "Why do some memory traces and not others come involuntarily to consciousness?" and "What happens when whole sections of the past become inaccessible, as in functional amnesias?" There are many other specific questions, such as the relation between intelligence and learning and whether prenatal learning can occur.

The hardware questions are beyond this book's scope, but some specific ones will be briefly mentioned. Much has been learned about the physiological basis of learning and memory in recent years, and it has begun to inform cognitive psychology (Phillips and Baddeley, 1989). Such evidence can help settle perennial issues not easily answered from behavioral data. An example, from Squire (1987), is the issue of whether forgotten information is actually destroyed or one just loses access to it. Physiological studies suggest that some is actually destroyed.

Dudai (1989) lists the following hardware questions. First, how are representations encoded in the nervous system? What are the codes, the computations made on them, and their neuronal realization? Second, what differentiates learning and nonlearning experiences? Not every experience results in learning at the neural level; what conditions determine this (e.g., repetition of stimuli or some essential preparatory state of the organism)? Third, is learning instructive, selective, or both? After learning, is the neuronal system involved actually reordered or modified or does input select a representation from among several endogenous variants? Fourth, is a memory trace retained in the system that learns? Is it stored in the same loci that change with learning or in a special memory store? Fifth, what are the actual molecular, cellular, and multicellular mechanisms involved in acquisition, retention, and retrieval? Dudai discusses what research has to say about these questions.

This book will address some of the above software questions and many other questions introduced in subsequent chapters.

2

Learning and Memory in Evolution and in Animals

This chapter has two major aims. The first is to briefly outline the evolutionary context of learning and memory, to examine how the ability to learn helps a species adapt to its niche. Understanding learning and memory requires seeing what problems the ability helps to solve in the evolutionary scheme of things. In the last two decades researchers into animal learning have been much concerned with evolutionary considerations, but most cognitively oriented ones have not. The computer metaphor may be responsible. Computers did not evolve to cope with our natural environment. Indeed, Claxton (1980) satirized the typical cognitive experimental preparation used to that time by saying that many researchers did not

deal with whole people but with a very special and bizarre—almost Frankenstein-ian—preparation, which consists of a brain attached to two eyes, two ears, and two index fingers. This preparation is only to be found inside small, gloomy cubicles outside which red lights burn to warn ordinary people away. . . . It does not feel hungry or tired or inquisitive; it does not think extraneous thoughts or try to understand what is going on. It is, in short, a computer. . . . (Claxton, 1980, 13)

Nowadays, however, cognitively oriented researchers are more interested in evolutionary considerations, an example being Sherry and Schacter's (1987) work on the evolution of various memory structures.

The second aim of this chapter is to survey some aspects of animal learning and memory. The chapter outlines some behaviorist concepts, paradigms, and principles, largely derived from animal studies, and modern views of such traditional notions as classical conditioning. Then follows a brief survey of the new field of comparative cognition, which applies the information-processing metatheory to animals. It investigates such issues as whether various memory structures and processes found in humans (such as short- and long-term memory stores and chunking) also occur in animals. Finally, the issue of qualitative differences in learning between different species is examined.

SOME PRELIMINARY CONSIDERATIONS

Reasons for Studying Animal Learning

The study of animal learning is now far from center stage in psychology but is still very active. It is studied for several reasons. One is intrinsic interest. A second is practical applications; derived principles have improved the welfare of zoo, domestic, and farm animals (see Chapter 8). A third is to extrapolate findings to humans, the argument being that processes occurring in humans can be studied in a simpler, more manageable form. For instance, Wasserman (1993) argues that human cognitive abilities emerge from configurations of elementary processes that can be studied in animals. Researchers can also use animals to answer such questions as "Is language necessary for chunking to occur?" Some researchers even use animal studies to test out ideas from economics. For example, Green et al. (1987) tackled the issue of the effects of a negative income tax, whereby every citizen would be guaranteed a minimum income. A standard argument against one was that subsidized wage earners would work less. Green et al. trained pigeons to peck a key for food and arranged that variable numbers of responses earned a reward, with a mean requirement. Later the pigeons got a "subsidy," occasional free food at random intervals, and the average response requirement for a reward was raised. If the animals worked as hard as in the first condition, they got just as much food. However, "subsidized" work output dropped dramatically.

Such animal-to-human extrapolation is very controversial. Many cognitive psychologists see the animal-human gap as too great and dismiss animal analogs and the applicability of principles gleaned from animal studies. Most cognitive psychology textbooks mention little animal work, aside from efforts to teach language to various species. Lachman et al. (1979, 54) exemplify the attitude: "Whenever higher mental processes are involved, we heartily disagree that human and animal behavior are necessarily governed by the same principles. . . . [H]umans and animals *may* share some cognitive abilities but it is not a foregone conclusion that they do." The human-animal gap is indeed wide, but animal research can illuminate issues concerning humans.

Approaches to Studying Animal Learning

Animal learning was studied from two quite different perspectives for much of this century. The psychological tradition mostly studied learning and in just a few species with arbitrary laboratory tasks. The dominant model was the behaviorist one of animals being reflex machines reacting to stimuli. The second perspective is of ethology, a mainly European tradition deriving from zoology. Ethologists studied many more species, looked more at innate behaviors, and studied animals in their niches. They criticized psychologists as studying abnormal (e.g., half-starved) animals in highly artificial situations, such as the Skinner box. Animals needed to be studied in their natural setting. A good illustration of data from the ethological approach is this description from McBride (1987). He watched a group of wild chickens daily traverse a familiar path. One day they came across a tree that had fallen across the path. They gave a call, clustered together, alert and alarmed, but soon moved on. For the next few days they went through the same actions on seeing the tree, but with progressively lower intensity, and eventually just moved along the now-familiar path. Another flock discovered a feral cat along a path. They went through the same routine as the first flock and repeated it on other occasions when the cat was not there, with the same intensity. McBride interpreted their learning as follows:

The birds sensed their environment continuously, comparing the sensory input with some map which told them the input to be expected. When a mismatch was detected, the individuals and their group showed orienting response behavior; during this period the birds examined the situation, evaluated it, and determined their response. In the first case, the internal maps were brought up to date, and learned; in the second case, the danger led to the place receiving continued attention, perhaps learning more and more details, so that smaller mismatches could be detected—better maps for dangerous places. (McBride, 1987, 273)

As mentioned, by the late 1960s ethology and psychology started to converge. Psychologists now freely use ethological concepts.

LEARNING AND MEMORY IN EVOLUTION

An animal in its natural environment typically faces a variety of problems: finding food and water, finding a mate and reproducing, avoiding predators, and in some species rearing young and dealing well with conspecifics. Different niches may frame these broad problems in different ways for different species. For example, the food of lions is mobile and must be hunted and caught, while that of bees is immobile but widely dispersed. Some niches vary enormously over the year in climate, food, and predator availability, while others stay relatively constant. Predator and prey species may evolve with time, becoming faster, better camouflaged, and so on.

Animals deal with such problems by gathering information about the environment and using it to behave more adaptively. Some information is stored in the genes and is used to program species-specific behaviors, and other data is stored in an individual's nervous system and is used to modify its behavior.

Species-Specific Behaviors

In every species, some behaviors (or preferences or propensities) are genetically preprogrammed because this provides big evolutionary advantages (and a purely empiricist animal could learn little). Some knowledge is much too important to leave to the uncertain, risky business of learning. The animal may need it right after birth or hatching. For instance, a tick may lie in a tree for months, insensitive to all stimuli, but may drop onto a mammal cued by the butyric acid that all mammals exude. The acid-dropping link needs to be innate because no individual animal would be likely to learn it. Bolles (1970) notes that animals have various species-specific defense reactions (SSDRs) to predators, which are too crucial to survival to leave to learning:

No real-life predator is going to present cues just before it attacks; . . . [N]or will the owl give the mouse enough trials for the necessary learning to occur. . . . What keeps animals alive in the wild is that they have very effective innate defensive reactions which occur when they encounter any kind of new or sudden stimulus. (Bolles, 1970, 32–33)

Innate knowledge may program strong preferences (e.g., for ripe versus unripe fruit), invariant stimulus-response relations, propensities to learn certain things quickly and easily, and complex behavior sequences. Genetically programmed behaviors are sometimes called "instincts," but the term is vague and is rarely used nowadays. Researchers prefer "species-specific" and "canalized." Such behaviors become programmed through natural selection. A classic example is in the gull species the kittiwake, which nests in tiny rocky ledges just inches wide. Most gull species nest on beaches, their chicks moving around a lot, but kittiwake chicks stay quite stationary. Immobility was selected because overactive chicks would tumble over the cliffs.

Ethologists distinguish between various types of species-specific behavior, of which only a few are described here. A reflex is an innate link between a specific stimulus and a specific response whereby only one part of the body moves. Familiar examples are the knee jerk to a tap and pupil narrowing to a bright light. A tropism is a change in orientation of the entire body to a stimulus, an example being a moth orienting to a candle flame. There are two major types and various subtypes of each (Hinde, 1970; Mazur, 1990). For instance, a kinesis is a tropism whereby movement is not oriented toward a specific source. Instead, a stimulus induces change in speed of movement or rate of turning. Hinde gives the example of woodlice congregating in a moist place through a tropism. They keep moving in dry places but tend to remain motionless in wet ones. As humidity rises, the proportion of motionless woodlice rises. In a taxis, behavior is oriented toward a stimulus, an example being a bee navigating by the sun's position. A fixed-action-pattern (FAP) is a fixed sequence of actions elicited by a stimulus called a releaser. FAPs are species-specific and when elicited run to completion. A good example is the egg retrieval FAP of the Greylag goose. If an egg rolls from the nest, the goose places its beak behind the egg and maneuvers it back to the nest under its breast. A female canary uses a specific weaving movement to push loose material onto her nest and may perform it on a cage floor without material. Once elicited, FAPs are independent of further environmental control and the component responses cannot be split up. If the egg is removed from a Greylag goose in mid-FAP, the FAP will continue but the taxic movements will drop out. Finally, a reaction-chain is a sequence of behaviors that can be split up. Progression from one response to the next depends on the appropriate eliciting stimulus at each stage (Mazur, 1990). An example is the complex courtship ritual of the stickleback (Hinde, 1970).

Humans have many species-specific behaviors—reflexes, preferences (e.g., for typical baby features, certain mate characteristics, and sweet tastes)—and have various propensities to learn, such as a native language and links between fear and the dark and heights.

Learning

Learning is of course the other major way in which animals deal with environmental problems. Virtually all species have at least a rudimentary ability to learn, because relying entirely on canalized behaviors can leave an animal too inflexible. This can be readily seen even in species that can learn quite a lot. They can behave maladaptively when confronted with new circumstances, like the proverbial fly trapped against a window. In the Nineteenth Century, some European swallows were taken to New Zealand. When winter came around, they instinctively flew south for the season, never to be heard from again.

Species mainly use one of two major strategies to deal with a changeable environment. The first is to rely mainly on canalized behaviors, producing many offspring with a short period between generations, as in mosquitos and paramecia. The second is to rely largely on learning, producing relatively few offspring, investing heavily in training them, and having longer periods between generations.

Adopting the second strategy makes a species much more flexible. An animal can acquire much useful knowledge and hone skills. Thus, an animal can learn such things as kin and conspecifics and their relations to itself, its place in a hierarchy, food locations, distributions, and amounts, the local landscape, safe and dangerous places, and contingencies. Some species hone and practice skills such as courtship and hunting. Lopez and Lopez (1985) describe killer whales beaching themselves to capture sea lions on shore and then wriggling back to sea. The recent British Broadcasting System series "The Trials of Life" featured some spectacular footage of such killer whales practicing their skills of capturing a sea lion at sea and then returning it alive and unharmed to the beach when finished.

Parenthetically, animals may learn from direct experience or be trained by kin. Teaching occurs in many species and is widespread in carnivores. Caro and Hauser (1992) give many examples. An adult baboon will threaten a youngster that approaches poisoned fruit. Domestic cats, when their kittens become mobile, carry live prey for the kittens to play with and recapture. Some species learn through extensive imitation, even from other species. Nagell et al. (1993) found that chimpanzees who saw a human demonstrate tool use were more likely to use the tool than chimpanzees who did not see a demonstration. Itani and Nishimura (1973) reported that when one Japanese macaque on an island learned to wash potatoes in the sea, many others followed.

Adopting the second strategy has various benefits in addition to increased flexibility. Johnson (1982) lists several. First, some important information, such as who an animal's kin are, the local landscape, and major routes, cannot be readily programmed in the genes and must be learned. Second, it allows animals to extend abilities in a short time; for example, hunting skill. Third, it gives a big selective advantage to species that live in very variable environments. Fourth, learning ability may be the only source of variation to confer a selective advantage in solving a given problem. Natural selection can only work on existing variation.

But, asks Johnson, if relying largely on learning is so adaptive, why do relatively few species do so? His answer is that the strategy exacts some great costs. First, reproduction may be long-delayed until an animal has learned enough to survive, and therefore it may have fewer offspring. And parenting and other skills may have to be learned, resulting in more casualties in the first litter. For example, young brown pelicans that reproduce have smaller clutches of young and lose more to floods because they are less likely to nest on high ground than older pelicans. Second, the young are vulnerable longer while they acquire needed knowledge. Third, parents must invest heavily in their young, protecting and training them for long periods. This reduces the number they can have and may lengthen time between litters. Fourth, the nervous system needed to support much learning ability takes much energy to maintain. Fifth, animals risk learning the wrong things, or not learning important things. For instance, rats that eat a novel food and are made ill by radiation thereafter shun that food, erroneously attributing the illness to it, as may humans who eat a certain food before chemotherapy (Logue, 1988). One way to minimize this risk is to program sensitive periods and innate dispositions to learn certain things.

Another interesting question is Which appears first in the course of evolution, species-specific or learned behaviors? The conventional wisdom is that the former do. Learning is seen as a genetically expensive adaptation requiring a complex nervous system. Primitive animals depend little on learning; their behavior is mainly canalized. Tierney (1986) summarized this view as follows:

Canalized, stereotyped behaviors are associated with simpler nervous systems. Learning requires more neurons and is associated with large, complex nervous systems. Therefore, invertebrates show mainly canalized, rigid behaviors, whereas vertebrates, particularly birds and mammals, are capable of flexible learning. Canalized behaviors are genetically programmed and evolve by natural selection in a manner identical to the evolution of morphological characteristics. The ability to learn is phylogenetically more recent than canalized behavior and emerged gradually with the evolution of large complex brains. (Tierney, 1986, 340)

Tierney argues plausibly that plasticity is a basic property of all central nervous systems and does not require more neurons or genes than strongly canalized behaviors. So behavioral flexibility may be primitive instead, and canalized behaviors may derive from plasticity inherent in all nervous systems. It is not clear if all canalized behaviors originate this way, however.

Species-Specific Versus Learned Behaviors

Most researchers no longer see these as in two dichotomous categories. Instead, a given behavior may be more or less canalized, more or less affected by genes. A knee jerk to a tap would be highly canalized while a bar press for food by a rat would be relatively uncanalized.

Biology influences what can be learned and how quickly. Here are some further lines of evidence. Breland and Breland (1961; 1966) trained various animals for zoos, circuses, and television shows using behavioral principles. After dealing with hundreds of different animals, they cataloged several cases in which the animals' species-specific behaviors began to intrude into arbitrary learned responses. For example, a hungry pig learned to drop a coin into a piggy bank for food. It learned readily but later started to treat the token as food—to root it and toss it into the air. Raccoons trained on the same task later began to rub coins together and dip them into the piggy bank without letting go. These "misbehaviors" are normal responses by these species to their food that emerged and made their actions much less adaptive. Similar problems can occur in pigeons with autoshaping (Brown & Jenkins, 1968). If pigeons are exposed to pairings of food and a lit key, they may eventually peck the key, even when this prevents them getting food. Rats can learn to associate a new taste with nausea after just one trial, even with a delay of hours between the two (Garcia, 1981). However, rats may take many trials to learn a link between a tone and electric shock and then only will with a delay of just seconds. Pigeons quickly learn to peck a key for food but only learn with great difficulty to peck to avoid electric shock. However, they readily learn to wingflap to avoid shock. A hamster can learn to dig, rear, or scramble for food but not to wash its face, mark its scent, or groom; an earthworm can readily learn to link a taste with a hot dry place but not a tactile stimulus with electric shock (Davey, 1989).

Seligman (1970) accounted for such phenomena with the useful concept of preparedness. Animals are prepared by their genes to learn some things quickly and easily and other things only with great difficulty or not at all. Some associations are prepared ones because of evolutionary pressure on a species to be able to learn them quickly and easily. It is very useful to quickly learn taste-nausea links because animals need to learn whether new foods are poisons. The food-pecking link is highly prepared in pigeons because they peck for food; that between wingflapping and shock avoidance is prepared because flying off is a natural pigeon response to pain and danger. Seligman argued that any association can be placed on a continuum from highly prepared to unprepared. Robert Thorndike actually coined a somewhat similar notion, belongingness. Associations between a stimulus and a response that belong together are easier to learn.

It is easy to think of evidently prepared links in humans, such as those between fear and the dark or being alone. Bolles (1970) also proposed that animals will readily learn an avoidance response identical to or like their SSDRs in that situation. For instance, rats quickly learn to avoid shock by exiting a compartment but have difficulty learning to re-enter one to avoid shock if they have been shocked there before. Such a contingency is very unnatural. Again, one can see nativist programming at work, genes setting a framework to be filled in by experience (Bolles, 1988).

The concept of preparedness has been criticized, however. One criticism is that it is circular. Easy associations are prepared and an association that is easy to learn therefore must be prepared. One can break the circularity by studying an animal's niche and repertoire to predict what links are likely to be prepared. Another criticism is that the notion preserves the "general process view" of learning, that there is a general process common to most or all species rather than each species having a number of specific adaptations. The general process is affected or constrained by biology (Revusky, 1977). However, the concept is very useful.

SOME SIMPLE TYPES OF LEARNING IN ANIMALS AND HUMANS

A longstanding question is how many types of learning there are. Some have argued there is just one, others say two or three, or more. Various criteria could be used to construct a classification system, such as underlying neural substrates, disassociations, and convergences, and developmental and evolutionary criteria, for example (Shettleworth, 1993). Shettleworth points out that the classification problem in animal learning has no single solution. The issue is even more complex when human learning is considered (see Chapter 3).

However, it is useful to adopt some typology of simple learning types as a working hypothesis, to be modified as knowledge of the topic increases. The following are fairly well established types of learning in animals. The first two are the simplest and are usually dubbed types of nonassociative learning. The third and fourth are more complex and are called types of associative learning because they involve learning-specific associations. Their interpretation has changed radically from the heyday of behaviorism, as will be discussed. This section also describes some associated behavioral concepts and evidence that these types of learning occur in humans.

Habituation

Habituation is generally seen as the simplest type of learning. It is ubiquitous, possibly occurring even in one-celled protozoa such as *Stentor Coeruleus* (Wood, 1973). It is defined as a diminishing responsiveness to a repeatedly presented stimulus, and occurs with reflexes. A simple example is the gill withdrawal reflex to a light touch in the sea snail *Aplysia*. After ten to fifteen touches, the response no longer occurs. After a day without the snail being touched, the response recovers. However, if the snail is touched ten times a day for four days, the response may not occur for weeks (Staddon, 1988). Another example is habituation of the orienting response, which Pavlov (1927) dubbed the "What is it?" response. He described how a dog hearing a new sound pricked up its ears, looked attentive, and oriented toward the stimulus. In humans, the orienting response involves looking attentive, orienting to the stimulus source, pupil dilation, skin resistance changes, and the alpha brain rhythm desynchronizing. After several presentations of a novel stimulus, the response declines and may vanish. A familiar everyday example is moving to a new house and initially being annoyed by noisy traffic. With time the annoyance diminishes and the sounds eventually are no longer consciously noticed. Indeed, habituation can be so complete that only the absence of stimuli is noticed, according to anecdotal evidence. In World War II, civilians supposedly learned to sleep through heavy bombing but awoke when the noise stopped. In Chicago some years ago, the police began to get many vague early morning phone calls complaining that "something funny is going on." Eventually the cause was traced to altered railway timetables. A very noisy train was no longer running, and its absence had woken people up. Human infants show habituation, and it is used to study their learning and cognitive capacities (see Chapter 6).

Various interesting phenomena may derive from habituation. One is adaptation to motion sickness after a few days and the generalized resistance to all its forms that some people develop (Crampton and Lucot, 1991). Another may be drug tolerance, which occurs as repeated doses of a drug have a diminishing effect (Baker and Tiffany, 1985). Parallels are that a repeatedly presented stimulus produces a diminished response and that cross-tolerance between drugs occurs, which may be generalization of habituation.

Thompson and Spencer (1966) list some findings about habituation. First, response decrements tend to be large at first but get smaller with further stimulus presentations. Second, a response may recover if time passes without a stimulus reoccurrence. Third, habituation is faster with less intense stimuli. Fourth, it tends to be specific to the stimulus presented but may generalize to some extent. Much work has been done on its physiological substrate. In *Aplysia*, for example, habituation of gill withdrawal occurs when neurons in the underlying reflex circuit have a decreasing tendency to release neurotransmitters (Dudai, 1989).

The ability to habituate is very useful. An animal can learn to ignore stimuli that prove harmless, rather than wasting time and energy repeatedly responding to them at full force. As Staddon (1988) put it, the animal can infer that a given stimulus is irrelevant and can be ignored. Indeed, it is hard to imagine an environment in which the ability would not be useful.

Sensitization

Sensitization is another simple type, defined as an increasing response to a repeatedly presented stimulus, or as failure to habituate (Staddon, 1988). For example, when *Aplysia* gets a noxious stimulus to the head and its gill is then touched, the withdrawal response is much enhanced. Similarly, in humans hearing repeated barking sometimes may lead to increasing annoyance. Whether a stimulus induces habituation or sensitization depends on several factors. One is stimulus intensity. A very intense stimulus is more likely to produce sensitization since it is more likely to be biologically significant. A second factor is temperament differences. People who score high on the neuroticism scale of the Eysenck Personality Inventory react emotionally to a wide range of stimuli and are more likely to sensitize than habituate to certain stimuli (Eysenck and Eysenck, 1985).

Sensitization has adaptive value. Important stimuli are likely to occur in runs. A predator may elicit a response in a would-be victim that successfully evades capture; since the predator is likely to strike again, it is useful to the prey animal to enhance that response.

Sensitization is widespread in the animal kingdom. Many primitive animals rely only on sensitization and habituation to fine-tune their behavior. It also is widespread in humans, and may underlie such effects as hyper-responsiveness to certain drugs and stressors and of the immune system to antigens in allergies (Stewart, 1991).

Classical conditioning

Classical conditioning is widespread in animals. The basic phenomenon has been known for centuries but was studied in depth by Ivan Pavlov early this century. He had been studying digestion and had a dog in a harness with a tube in its throat through which saliva could flow. Food powder was periodically blown into its mouth. The story goes that Pavlov noticed that the dog would salivate upon seeing him, because it associated his arrival with food, which Pavlov dubbed a "psychic secretion."

The basic paradigm is as follows. It applies to a reflex, such as the knee jerk to a tap. The tap is the unconditioned stimulus (UCS) and the jerk is the unconditioned response (UCR). An initially neutral stimulus (the CS) is repeatedly presented just before the UCS. After several pairings, the CS presented alone may elicit a conditioned response (CR), a knee jerk. The formula is:

$$UCS \rightarrow UCR$$
$$+$$
$$CS$$
$$\text{and}$$
$$CS \rightarrow CR.$$

The CR is often like but not identical to the UCR. It is typically much weaker, for instance.

Conditioning may be excitatory or inhibitory. In the former, a CS and UCS are paired as above, and the CS later can elicit a CR. In the latter, a CS is paired with the absence of the UCS; that is, a CS is presented and the UCS is not presented for some time afterward. The animal learns that the CS predicts the UCS's nonoccurrence. It then takes longer to turn a previously inhibitory CS into an excitatory one than a neutral stimulus, and presenting an excitatory CS and an inhibitory CS together may produce a weaker response than the excitatory CS alone (Pavlov, 1927).

Many responses can be classically conditioned. Some esoteric examples are sexual approach responses (Domjan and Hollis, 1988) and immune system responses (Rescorla, 1988). Autoshaping, mentioned earlier, once was seen as an anomaly but is now widely viewed as an instance of classical conditioning. The CS acquires the power to elicit species-specific feeding behaviors and different UCSs produce different CRs accordingly. For instance, Jenkins and Moore (1973) found that a pigeon autoshaped with food pecked the key with beak open and one autoshaped with water pecked with beak closed, mirroring typical pecks to food and water. Kamil and Maudlin (1988) found marked differences in autoshaped pecking between blue jays, robins, and starlings, each showing a different species-specific response to food. For instance, blue jays peck in bouts and move around the cubicle while robins peck continuously. Whether autoshaping occurs at all in a given setup depends on the species and its normal behavior in its niche. For example, cats autoshape to an auditory CS that signals food, but rats do not. Cats often locate prey by sound and pounce on it, while rats do not (see Davey, 1989, for an extended discussion).

Much research has examined classical conditioning. Conditioning is typically fastest when the CS precedes the UCS by about 0.5 seconds. It is still controversial whether backward excitatory conditioning, whereby the CS follows the UCS, can occur. The acquisition curve is typically negatively accelerated; increases in associative strength between CS and UCS are greatest in the early trials and then slowly level off. The number of trials needed to establish a response to a CS varies greatly with species, response system, UCS, and CS. Rats may take many trials to learn a tone-electric shock link and may not learn at all if the CS precedes the UCS by more than a few seconds. However, they can learn a taste-nausea link in one trial with a 24–hour delay. Bees can learn a color-sugar link in one trial if the CS is violet, four trials if it is green, fifty if it is blue, and 250 if it is white (Davey, 1989). Finally, CS-UCS pairing is neither necessary nor sufficient for classical conditioning to occur (Rescorla, 1988; Papini and Bitterman, 1990). Humans may show a CR without any pairings if just told of the link. Merely pairing a CS and a UCS does not guarantee conditioning will occur. An illustration is the blocking phenomenon (Rescorla, 1988). If a tone is established as a CS, and then the tone and a light are paired with the same UCS, the light may not become a CS. Its gain in associative strength has been blocked by the prior tone-UCS pairing. Whether a stimulus becomes a CS evidently depends on how well it predicts UCS occurrence and if some other CS will do so as well or better.

Rescorla and Wagner (1972) used such findings to build an influential model of classical conditioning. They proposed that the associative strength of a given CS depends on how "surprising" the UCS is, how well the CS and other stimuli predict it. Their equation for associative strength is:

$$\Delta V_A = \alpha \beta \ (\lambda - V_\Sigma)$$

Where ΔV_A is the change in associative strength to a CS on trial n,

   λ is the maximum associative strength that the UCS can produce,

   V_Σ is the total associative strength to stimuli predicting the UCS,

   α is the salience of the CS, and

   β is the salience of the UCS.

The model accounts for such phenomena as the negatively accelerated acquisition curve and various attentional phenomena such as blocking.

Classical conditioning has many interesting associated phenomena, many first described by Pavlov. In second-order conditioning, a CS is established to a UCS and then the CS is itself paired with another CS that is never directly paired with the UCS. The second CS may eventually elicit a CR. Extinction is discontinuing CS-UCS pairings; that is, presenting the CS alone several times without following it with the UCS. The CR typically diminishes and finally disappears. Spontaneous recovery occurs when a CR has evidently extinguished but briefly reappears when the CS is presented some time after the last UCS presentation.

Pavlov also studied discrimination and generalization. In the first, two CSs usually are used, one followed by a UCS and the other not, with the typical result being that one eventually elicits a CR and the other does not. In one experiment Pavlov trained a dog to discriminate between a circle and an ellipse and gradually narrowed the physical difference between them, reporting that the dog became disturbed. The study of generalization involves establishing a CS (say a 1,000 Hz tone) and then presenting similar stimuli, such as 1,100, 1,200, 900, and 800 Hz tones. The CR is often generalized to them and a common result is a generalization gradient, in which peak response strength occurs to the CS and diminishes progressively with distance from the CS. Another phenomenon is additive summation. Two excitatory CSs are established separately and then are presented simultaneously. Summation occurs when the response to this compound is greater than that to each presented alone.

Interpretation of classical conditioning has changed radically in recent years. Rescorla (1988) contrasts the old view, inherited from Pavlov, with modern views. The old view, still held by some psychologists and presented in introductory textbooks, is that classical conditioning is just mechanical reflex learning. CS and UCS are paired and the CS eventually evokes much the same response as the UCS. Pavlov held that the CS comes to substitute for the UCS. In this view, pairing is necessary and sufficient to establish conditioning, the CR is an image of the UCR, and the learning process is quite mechanical. Rescorla says that this is all wrong; instead, classical conditioning is a way that animals learn about the structure of the world. They learn what leads to what and build up a representation of the causal structure of the environment (Gallistel, 1990). The animal is not a reflex machine mechanically linking stimulus and response, but an active information processor noticing and using causal relations between events. It is a form of learning whereby animals reduce uncertainty about the environment (e.g., what UCS is imminent) and solve specific adaptive problems, such as discovering which new foods are poisonous. Rescorla makes an interesting analogy to the learning of a connectionist net, which builds up a representation of the environment and adjusts it to bring it better in line with the environment.

Several lines of evidence support this new view. First, as mentioned, CS-UCS pairing is neither necessary nor sufficient for classical conditioning to occur. Second, experiments show that the CR is sometimes not at all an image of the UCR; indeed, it may be its opposite. For example, rats jump to a CS that signals electric shock but freeze to the shock itself. Heroin addicts may develop compensatory CRs (to the CS of being about to inject heroin) that can diminish the drug's effect. Evidently, overdoses are more likely to occur when the compensatory CRs themselves are much diminished, such as when injecting in unfamiliar surroundings (Mazur, 1990). Many CRs also are sensitive to their consequences, rather than being uncontrollable reflexes. Animals use classical conditioning to allocate their time efficiently and prepare for and optimize interaction with an imminent UCS (Davey, 1989), be it a predator or a prospective mate. Classical conditioning also helps in food recognition. Chicks evidently only learn to peck for food through this process; the link is not preprogrammed (Rescorla, 1988).

Classical conditioning certainly occurs in humans. Davey (1989) summarizes several major principles derived from decades of research. Human work has favored two major preparations: an air puff to the eye, which elicits a blink, and an aversive UCS such as electric shock, which elicits the galvanic skin response (GSR), a change in skin resistance with emotion. Many phenomena found in animals also occur in humans: blocking, higher-order conditioning, and CR strength as a function of CS predictive power. However, two major differences occur. First, CS strength can be readily altered by words. Humans may show a CR just by being told about a contingency, as mentioned, and may show a greatly diminished CR if told that extinction is now in effect. Second, according to some researchers, awareness of the CS-UCS contingency seems to be necessary for conditioning to occur. Only subjects who can verbalize the link show conditioning. However, some theorists suggest that two levels of classical conditioning may occur in humans. One is primitive, autonomic, and noncognitive, and the other is cognitive and sensitive to awareness and instructions (Davey, 1989).

How widespread is classical conditioning in everyday human life? Probably it is pervasive. We learn much about the causal structure of the world from experience; that hot things burn, certain surfaces reflect more light, and so on. Many instances of emotional learning may be Pavlovian, in which people learn to attach such responses as fear, anger, disgust, and patriotic feelings to stimuli such as flags, foods, and designer goods. However, much contingency learning is from instruction.

Classical conditioning has been widely applied, in psychotherapy (see Chapter 8) and advertising, for example. Ads often aim to attach a certain emotional response to a product, service, or candidate and sometimes use a set format. A UCS is presented and then a CS, with the hope that consumers will link the two. For example, a typical beer ad presents glamorous images that may elicit positive emotions and then later presents images of beer. This in fact is theoretically ineffective backward conditioning, but it seems to work well. The UCS may be presented first to get the consumer's attention. Stuart et al. (1987) demonstrated some phenomena of classical conditioning in simulated ads. In one experiment, for example, a spurious toothpaste brand was paired with a very pleasant slide (such as a mountain waterfall scene) and in a control condition was paired only with neutral stimuli. Subjects exposed to toothpaste–pleasant slide pairings rated the toothpaste more favorably than did control subjects. Another experiment found evidence of inhibitory conditioning, whereby a stimulus first paired with neutral stimuli was later harder to establish as an effective CS than were novel stimuli.

Various interesting phenomena in humans also have been explained as instances of classical conditioning. An example is the McCullough effect in visual perception. Subjects are shown a grid of black and orange vertical bars alternating with a grid of black and blue horizontal bars, then see a black and white grid, which appears colored to them. The white spaces between black vertical bars appear blue and those between black horizontal bars appear orange. One interpretation is that color is a UCS and the lined grid in inspection is the CS. The CR is an adaptive response of the visual system (e.g., Allan and Siegel, 1993). However, this view is controversial.

Operant Conditioning

Operant conditioning involves learning a link between a response and its consequences—a contingency. It is sometimes called instrumental or Skinnerian conditioning. A technical definition is "an increase in the rate of a response as a result of a contingent reinforcer." A simple example is a rat increasing its bar pressing rate when presses earn food. The principle has been applied widely, and Skinner (1957) even proposed it is a major mechanism of language learning. It occurs in many species; in amphibians, reptiles, and fish, for instance (Davey, 1989). Invertebrates also adapt to operant contingencies, but it is often not clear whether they are judiciously learning by classical conditioning. An example of invertebrate operant conditioning is from bees learning to deal with the alfalfa flower, which has a spring-loaded club that deals the bee a hefty blow when it enters. Some bees learn to distinguish between loaded and unloaded flowers (classical conditioning) while others learn to chew through the flower's back to get at the nectar (Gould and Gould, 1982). Gould and Gould also report an experiment in which bees were trained to fly to a food source, which on subsequent trials was moved progressively further away. Soon the bees flew to the next anticipated location and waited for the food.

Here are some major concepts and principles associated with operant conditioning. Shaping is a useful method of rapidly training a response. It is defined as a progressive narrowing of the definition of a reinforced response. For instance, consider training a rat to press a bar for food. Rather than wait for a bar press to occur (which may take some time), one can initially define a response as standing in the half of the box closest to the bar. Then one can redefine it as standing in front of the bar, then touching the bar, and finally pressing. There are several types of reinforcer, which is a stimulus that increases the rate of a response it follows. A positive reinforcer is one that animals respond to get, such as food, water, warmth, and so on. A negative reinforcer is one that animals respond to avoid or escape, such as electric shock and severe cold. Negative reinforcement is often studied in a paradigm in which the animal must respond to postpone an imminent electric shock, or the shock might be present and a response then briefly turns it off. Reinforcers may be primary or conditioned. The former are innately reinforcing (e.g., food and water) and the latter become reinforcers through being paired with primary reinforcers (e.g., money). A reinforcement schedule is a rule by which reinforcers are delivered. Here are a few examples. A fixed-ratio (FR) schedule reinforces every nth response; for example, an FR 10 schedule would reinforce every tenth response. A variable-ratio (VR) schedule reinforces every nth response on average, but has a mix of requirements. For example, a VR 20 schedule might first require two responses, then twelve, and then twenty-four, but have an average requirement of twenty. A fixed-interval (FI) schedule reinforces the first response that occurs after a certain time interval. A variable-interval (VI) schedule uses the same rule but has a set of intervals with an average value. These simple schedules can be combined into more complex ones, and there may even be several reinforced responses available at a given time, each with its own associated schedule (a concurrent schedule).

Animals typically show a characteristic pattern of responding on each schedule. For example, VR and VI schedules typically produce high, constant response rates. FI schedules produce a "scalloped" pattern in which the animal pauses and responds little early in the interval but at an increasing rate as the interval goes on. When two VI schedules are available on different manipulanda simultaneously, animals typically alternate between them and allocate responses to each in proportion to available reinforcers. This relation is called the matching law (Davison and McCarthy, 1988) because animals match relative response and reinforcer rates. It is:

$$\frac{R_1}{R_2} = \frac{r_1}{r_2}$$

Where R_1 is the number of responses on manipulandum 1, R_2 the number on manipulandum 2, r_1 the number of reinforcers on manipulandum 1, and

r_2 the number on manipulandum 2. The law is sometimes generalized as follows, with k and b being constants:

$$\frac{R_1}{R_2} = k \left(\frac{r_1}{r_2}\right)^b$$

Finally, punishment is defined as a stimulus that reduces the rate of a response it follows. For example, a rat pressing a bar for food may have every press yield an electric shock, too. Response rate may then decrease.

Various phenomena of classical conditioning have operant analogs, with response rate or time allocation as dependent variables. Animals learn operant discriminations and show blocking, additive summation, and generalization gradients, for example (Mazur, 1990).

Operant conditioning is widespread in humans. People need to learn a lot of contingencies to behave adaptively, as mentioned. When humans are exposed to typical operant conditioning procedures in experiments, however, several clear differences from animal performance become apparent. First, schedule performance is often quite different (e.g., Horne and Lowe, 1993). On concurrent schedules, people show large departures from matching, and some subjects respond only on one manipulandum. On an FI schedule, humans may respond at a high rate throughout. Human performance also may be more inflexible and insensitive to changes in the contingencies. Various explanations have been proposed for the differences (Horne and Lowe, 1993). People can verbalize the contingencies and entertain different hypotheses about what they are and continue to act on them. People often think a ratio requirement is operating, for example, even if one is not. Indeed, some evidence suggests that preverbal children are more likely to show typical animal patterns while those over five years or so show adult-style performance (Horne and Lowe, 1993). Second, the reinforcers used are much weaker than those used with half-starved animals, but then response rates can be quite high, suggesting that humans' motivation is still strong. Third, perhaps a human in a cubicle pressing a button for occasional rewards is not a very useful way to study operant conditioning. As Mackintosh (1974) pointed out, it is hard to find comparable real-life situations. Subjects also know that they are in an experiment and may try to work out what is wanted of them. Some evidence suggests that more animal-like performance may emerge in more naturalistic setups. For instance, Conger and Killeen (1974) had four students at a table discuss drug abuse. One was a subject and three were confederates. The confederates on the subject's left and right delivered occasional "verbal reinforcers," such as "That is a good point," at different rates. The subject tended to match time spent talking to either confederate to rate of verbal reinforcers.

Another clear difference is in stimulus generalization, which has been extensively studied because of its importance in human learning. People generalize skills to new situations, a concept to new instances, and scientific laws to new situations. However, generalization has mostly been studied in humans using a fairly restricted paradigm (e.g., Thomas, 1974). Subjects are briefly shown a stimulus from a dimension (say a 1,000 Hz tone) and are instructed to remember it and press a button once only when the stimulus is presented. Then various stimuli from the same dimension are shown. Typically gradients occur; peak number of responses occurs at or near the training stimulus and progressively fewer occur as distance from it increases. Such findings and animal research have made the notion of a ubiquitous generalization gradient widespread. Indeed, Shepard (1987) used such data to propose a "universal law of generalization," which is that the probability of generalization decays exponentially with distance from the training stimulus. However, almost all evidence for gradients in humans is from the above paradigm. Howard (1979) argued that this paradigm does not really measure generalization; it measures discrimination and sensory thresholds because subjects are explicitly instructed not to generalize. Some work has exposed humans to an operant analog method whereby they are trained to respond to one stimulus and then are shown others and are not under instructions not to generalize. Subjects typically divide the continuum into two categories, responding alike to all stimuli within each category (Howard, 1979). Howard proposed that subjects really are learning a concept and generalizing it. The identification procedure is really just measuring their psychophysical thresholds; it is not studying generalization.

Operant and classical conditioning interact in various ways, but it is beyond this book's scope to discuss them. Mazur (1990) gives a thorough discussion.

Specialized Types of Learning

Some species show types of learning that have evidently evolved to deal with specific problems posed in their niche. They do not readily fit into the above types. However, exactly what goes into this category is a bit controversial. Taste aversion learning was once widely seen as one such type, the argument being that animals often encounter new types of food and evolve a specialized mechanism to rapidly learn if they are edible. Vertebrates learn such links in three ways (Logue, 1988). They avoid bitter-tasting substances, a natural poison sign. They observe what parents and other conspecifics eat and avoid, and they learn from hard experience after one trial. Rats, for instance, typically eat a little of a new food and then wait for a time to gauge its effect. Rapid, one-trial aversion learning has been shown in cows, coyotes, bats, catfish, and slugs, and in birds to visual cues (Davey, 1989). Is a specialized mechanism at work, however? Most researchers nowadays feel it is not. It is a form of classical conditioning, which has a more liberalized definition than it did two decades ago (Shettleworth, 1993). Research has shown that taste aversion learning has many properties of classical conditioning. Animals may generalize to other tastes and the aversion may extinguish if animals later eat the new food without becoming ill, for instance (Logue, 1988).

Parenthetically, there is much similarity between human taste aversion learning and that of other vertebrates (Logue, 1988). Most people when asked report an instance of one. Humans can acquire taste aversions with delays of up to at least six hours. People generalize (e.g., from fried chicken to other greasy foods). Extinction may occur, and there is little evidence for backward conditioning. Some stimuli are easier to link to nausea than others; tastes more than visual cues, for instance.

However, here are some examples of types of learning that do seem to have underlying specialized learning mechanisms.

Bird Song Learning. Members of many bird species need to learn a species-specific song. Knowledge of the song partly depends on experience; isolation-reared birds develop abnormal songs. A bird needs examples and feedback, and the learning seems to occur only during a narrow "sensitive" period. If the knowledge is not acquired then, it never will be. This period's duration varies across species and has two parts, a learning phase and a crystallization phase in which no further learning occurs (Davey, 1989). The learning mechanism switches off, and what has been acquired resists further change.

Evidence suggests that song learning depends on a specialized mechanism. Birds that show this learning may have specialized brain centers that are active during the sensitive period. It evidently evolved because birds reach maturity rapidly after hatching and ordinary learning processes (such as operant conditioning) are too slow for them to acquire the needed knowledge. The sensitive period often ends at normal nest-leaving time, which may prevent "misimprinting" (Davey, 1989).

Imprinting. Imprinting also is an apparently specialized form of learning that occurs in a sensitive period and whereby what is learned profoundly affects later behavior. In Lorenz's (1935) classic report, he noted that newly hatched ducklings approach and follow the first moving object that they see. This following response was learned quickly, without evident operant or Pavlovian contingencies, and appeared to be irreversible. It did not extinguish. Subsequent research has shown that birds imprint onto many objects (lights, boxes, people), but noisy ones that resemble their own species work best. The sensitive period's length is affected by rearing factors and varies across species (Davey, 1989). Mammals also may have sensitive periods. If a lamb is removed at birth and returned two or three hours later, the ewe will not accept it but will if the lamb is returned one hour later.

Language Learning in Humans? Ethics preclude experiments on possible sensitive periods in humans, but the best candidate for a specialized learning ability in people is one for language learning. Language is uniquely human, language acquisition occurs in the same sequence in all languages, and it is acquired too fast and too easily to be readily explained by general learning mechanisms. Hurford (1991) summarizes several lines of evidence for a sensitive period for language learning, which ends about the start of adolescence. First, children struck with aphasia before adolescence have a good chance of recovering and developing normal language, but adults so struck seldom do. Second, children exposed to no language at all before age thirteen never acquire a language fully, not even American sign language. Third, those who start learning a second language as children outstrip those who learn as adults. Second language learning is notoriously difficult for adults.

Why would a sensitive period evolve? Hurford points out that speaking a language well confers a big adaptive advantage, and there are selection pressures to learn one quickly and early in life. The capacity to learn one readily may switch off around age thirteen because of lack of selection pressure to acquire more words and grammatical rules or a second language once one has been acquired.

MEMORY, COGNITION, AND COMPLEX LEARNING IN ANIMALS

As mentioned earlier, a relatively new and very active research area called comparative cognition is investigating complex memory and cognitive capacities in animals (e.g., Spear et al., 1990; Roitblat and von Fersen, 1992; Wasserman, 1993). The approach involves applying the information-processing metatheory to animals. Some major questions are whether various species have separate short-and long-term stores, and if so what their capacities and representation formats are. Do animals forget, do they use such control processes as rehearsal and chunking, and what can they learn—abstract concepts, lists, a language? Another issue is the evolutionary sequence of various structures and capacities. When do separate long- and short-term stores first appear? Do fruit flies have them, for example?

Animal Memory

Here is a brief overview of some major findings to date. A somewhat speculative generalization about animal memory is as follows. Many memory structures and processes found in humans occur in various species. Indeed, human, monkey, and pigeon memory processing have many similarities and only a few apparent qualitative differences (Wright, 1989).

Memory Structures. Various species have sensory registers and short- and long-term stores. For example, O'Connor and Ison (1991) present evidence of an echoic store in rats. Pigeons evidently have a limited attentional capacity like humans; performance suffers when it is overloaded (Lamb, 1991). Animal short-term memory is often studied with a procedure called delayed choice or delayed matching-to-sample. An animal might see a sample stimulus (say, a square), which then disappears. Later, the sample and another stimulus appear and the animal is rewarded only for choosing the sample. The sample offset–choice onset interval can be varied to see how long the animal can remember what the sample was. Performance typically worsens as the interval increases, but an animal given much practice may tolerate longer intervals. Typical retention intervals are up to one minute in pigeons and two minutes in Capuchin monkeys (Davey, 1989). Pigeons can remember many types of stimuli in short-term store: colors, shapes, durations, orientations, and temporal orders (Wasserman, 1993). Animals also show serial position curves, often taken as evidence for separate stores in humans. The curve occurs when one recalls a series of items after being presented them and remembers more early and late ones. Presumably the latter are held in short-term store and the former in long-term. Rhesus monkeys also may show a von Restorff effect, whereby a middle but unusual item is recalled well (Castro and Larsen, 1992).

Several studies have examined the capacities of animal memory stores. Short-term store capacity is typically just a few items, but some species have impressive long-term memory capacities. Vaughan and Greene (1984) showed pigeons two thousand pictures in sequence and two years later tested them on a sample. They identified pictures as previously seen with about 70 percent accuracy. There was also evidence of a classic Ebbinghaus curve. The bird species Clark's nutcracker has an excellent memory for locations. It caches thousands of pine seeds every autumn in hundreds of locations over many square miles and retrieves them in spring and winter. The bird uses spatial memory to remember the cache locations and can still recall them 285 days after storing the seeds (Olson et al., 1993). The birds also show good spatial memory in laboratory tasks (Olson et al., 1993).

Animals also use various memory control processes and strategies. For example, pigeons apparently rehearse items to maintain them in short-term memory. The evidence comes from directed forgetting experiments. In one version, animals are shown a trial stimulus and then get a cue to remember or forget it. When a surprise test is given for memory of the trial stimulus, performance is far worse on "forget" trials (Wasserman, 1993). Wright (1989) presents some evidence that monkeys can adopt various memory strategies and may show maintenance rehearsal and rehearsal to add information to long-term store. Rats (Dallal and Meck, 1990) and pigeons (Terrace and Chen, 1991) may chunk items in short-term memory. Pigeons may organize a list to be learned as ordered chunks and even transfer these chunks to other tasks (Terrace and Chen, 1991). Animals also use imagery to perform various tasks and may encode spatial maps as images (Roitblat and von Fersen, 1992).

Complex Learning

What can animals learn? They can acquire some quite complex things. Early research showed that monkeys can acquire learning sets; they can learn to learn (Harlow, 1959). Typically, the animals are given a pair of objects to learn to discriminate between for six trials and then a new pair for another six trials, and so on for many pairs. With successive problems, performance on the second trial of each new set improves. Harlow found that rhesus monkeys form a set faster than squirrel monkeys and marmosets and that primates do faster than nonprimates. Animals also can learn by imitation (e.g., Russon and Galdikas, 1993).

Rules, Serial Orders, and Maps. Animals can learn these. Research shows that rats can learn and use complex rules (Fountain, 1990). Monkeys can learn serial orders of complex stimuli consisting of lists of up to eight items (Swartz et al., 1991). There is some evidence for metacognitive knowledge in chimpanzees, that they know what they do not know (Gallistel, 1990). Monkeys can learn a good representation of the web of social relations in their group, and animals can readily build up and use spatial representations (Gallistel, 1990). Bees learn and use spatial maps (Gould, 1990). Rats quickly learn them. Morris (1981) placed rats in a deep tank that had a submerged platform on which the rat could stand to keep its head above water. After learning its location, a rat placed anywhere in the tank quickly swam to the platform, showing it had a mental map of the tank. Numerous studies of rats learning their way around radial mazes show their impressive spatial learning abilities (Gallistel, 1990).

Concepts. Much research has investigated animal concept learning. Some key issues are what concepts various species can acquire and what information their concepts consist of. Concepts are of fundamental importance because the ability to categorize underlies perception and many aspects of cognition (see Chapter 4). A typical way to study animal concept learning is to use operant conditioning. Responses are only reinforced when stimuli from a given category are shown. When the animal learns this discrimination, new stimuli are shown to see if transfer to them occurs.

Studies show that animals can acquire a variety of different concepts, such as *human being* (Herrnstein and Loveland, 1964), *pigeon* (Poole and Lander, 1971), *fish* (Herrnstein and de Villiers, 1980), *oak leaf* (Cerella, 1979), the letter *A* (Morgan et al., 1976), *body of water* (Herrnstein et al., 1976), *moving object* (Dittrich and Lea, 1993), *human-made object* (Lubow, 1974), and *inside/outside* (Herrnstein et al., 1989). Pigeons can learn the concept of *same/different* but are poor at generalizing it to new stimuli. However, chimpanzees and various monkey species can (Davey, 1989).

Some species can learn the concept of numerosity and a few can even do simple arithmetic (Gallistel, 1990). The ability to count is useful in the natural environment because animals often need to count numbers of eggs, offspring, relatives, and predators and prey in various locales. An animal can judge whether to keep foraging in a certain place or move on. Some studies providing evidence of animal counting are as follows. Koehler (1950) trained pigeons to eat only a certain number of peas on a given trial; any more earned an electric shock. The birds performed reasonably well up to six peas. Davis et al. (1975) trained rats to press a bar for food and scheduled three shocks per session at unpredictable intervals. Once the third shock had occurred, response rate rose greatly. Pepperberg (1987) trained an African Gray parrot called Alex to accurately assign the numerals two to six to various collections of objects and transfer them to new sets. Boysen and Berntson (1989) taught a chimpanzee the numerals one to five and found evidence that it could add the numbers together.

What information do such concepts consist of? What is acquired that allows accurate categorization? Do animals learn abstract rules or just memorize exemplars and categorize new stimuli by analogy to them? This is still an unresolved issue about human concepts (see Chapter 4). The likely underlying principle is that people acquire what information they need to about a category for their goals at hand. If remembering a few exemplars is sufficient, they may not trouble to learn abstract rules. Herrnstein (1990, 160) suggests a roughly similar principle for animals: "Animals are remarkably good at finding whatever attributes of a set of stimuli serve their purposes in relation to the contingencies of reinforcement." They may just memorize exemplars or learn a more complex representation if need be. However, animals are not going to learn very abstract concepts like *virtual particle*. Roberts and Mazmanian (1988) compared the abilities of pigeons, monkeys, and humans to learn three concepts of increasing abstractness (these were *kingfisher, bird,* and *animal*). All three species readily learned the concept of *kingfisher*, but pigeons and monkeys had trouble with the other two. All were easily acquired by the humans.

Language? Can animals learn a language? No one disputes that animals communicate with each other in many ways. Ants use chemical signals, birds use songs and postures, apes use vocalizations, and whales use auditory signals. But such animal systems lack the complexity, power, and versatility of human languages. They have few signs, and the signs are innate with a fixed meaning. Animal systems lack the crucial feature of syntax, whereby a few symbols can be combined according to rules to make an infinite number of meanings.

Various studies have tried to teach animals human-like languages with special training. Research suggests that animals can learn to associate signs and meanings and even string signs together. The chimpanzee Washoe (Anderson, 1990) learned 132 signs and could string up to five together. It referred to a duck with signs for water and bird. Another chimpanzee put back with peers after many months away referred to them as black bugs. The gorilla Koko was asked which of two trainers she preferred and signed, "Bad question." Koko mastered four-hundred signs (Patterson and Linden, 1981). Itakura (1992) found evidence that a chimpanzee could learn personal pronouns. Animals also may pass on their knowledge. Washoe evidently taught some signs to an adopted infant.

But it is still controversial whether these animals are really learning a language. Terrace (1979) argued that they are showing only limited linguistic capacities and rarely communicate spontaneously as people do. A standard argument is that they are using abilities that have evolved for quite different purposes to perform a task for which humans have an innate ability. The systems that they learn still lack syntax.

COMPARING LEARNING AND MEMORY ACROSS SPECIES

One can ask what similarities and differences exist in learning and memory processes and capacities across species. Interspecies comparisons were common earlier this century, but most researchers later adopted the equipotentiality assumption and concentrated on just a few "representative" species. Interest has increased lately, however. A key issue is whether there are qualitative differences in learning between species. The notion that there is a general learning process that species have more or less of would suggest that there is not. However, if species evolve specialized learning abilities, then one might expect qualitative differences.

An exponent of the general process and "continuity" view is MacPhail (1987). He argued that there is no evidence for qualitative differences in learning among nonhuman vertebrates. Humans have the same basic general learning ability as nonhuman vertebrates and a species-specific language learning mechanism that leads to qualitative differences. He cites such supporting evidence as that many phenomena of learning occur in many widely spaced species (such as habituation, taste aversion learning, blocking, etc.). The preceding section presented evidence of many similarities in memory structures and processes in various species.

However, other researchers have argued that qualitative differences do occur. Bitterman (1965) reported on studies of learning in various species, including fish, monkeys, and turtles, using a variety of tasks. One was a serial reversal task. An animal learned a discrimination that was then reversed; the previously positive stimulus became the negative one and vice versa, and it was then reversed again, for many trials. Pigeons, rats, and many mammal species improve their learning rate with successive reversals, turtles do for spatial but not visual discriminations, and fish do not at all, said Bitterman. Some bird species improve faster than others.

Bitterman used such findings to characterize species as fish- or rat-like, suggesting that fish were more like Hullian stimulus-response learners and rats more like cognitive learners. However, later research showed that procedural variables may have confounded things; under some conditions fish can show reversal learning improvement (Davey, 1989). Other researchers have argued that a species may develop capacities that turn its members into a different sort of learner, as does language acquisition for humans. For instance, Povinelli (1993) recently argued that primates are a different sort of learner than other species because they can attribute mental states to others. Chimpanzees and oranguatans thus can reason about mental experiences in conspecifics, which allows them to learn more abstract things.

However, the issue is far from resolved. There is impressive evidence for commonalities in widely separated species, but also there is evidence for specialized learning abilities. One interpretation is that there is a general learning ability that varies quantitatively across species but may be affected by biology. Specialized learning abilities may evolve separately, such as language ability and the impressive location memory of Clark's nutcracker.

Another issue is whether one can construct an evolutionary hierarchy along which animals can be ranked by learning ability. The notion of such a *scalae naturae* goes back to Aristotle and still has its adherents (Jensen, 1980). It seems obvious that a chimpanzee is a member of a higher species than is a sea snail because it can learn far more and is far more flexible. However, there is little agreement on how (or even whether) such a scale could be constructed or how meaningful it would be. One problem is that the implicit assumption of biological progress from lower to higher species is faulty. The evolutionary tree has many branches (Campbell and Hodos, 1991). There are many local adaptations and not a single historical progression. A second problem is that it has proved difficult to find tasks to rank even closely related species. As MacPhail (1987) put it, apparent differences in learning capacities between species may be due to such factors as differing sensory capacities, local adaptations to a niche, or reinforcer strengths. Species *A* may perform much worse because the reinforcer used is much weaker than that used for species *B*. Slight changes in stimuli used can drastically alter learning performance because different species have evolved to adapt to quite different niches. For example, procedural changes in a reversal learning task can easily alter the ranking of animals (Mackintosh, 1987). Problems that animals face in nature sometimes are dealt with by problem-specific devices, and these may be more or less useful in solving a given laboratory problem. For example, nectar-feeding birds need to remember which flowers they have visited for nectar and are much better at learning a laboratory shift task than a stay task. Their specialized mechanism helps in one task but not in the other (Davey, 1989).

3

Structures and Processes of the Memory System

To find out how a washing machine works, one would ask what its components are, how they are interconnected, and what processes the device uses to perform its overall function. The components are, of course, a tub, a casing, electronics, and so on, interconnected with wires and pipes in various ways. Some processes are water input and output and tub agitation and spinning. Analogous questions about the human memory system are "Is there one part or several? If the latter, what are the components and their capacities, how are they linked up, and by what processes does each part and the whole system operate?" An early answer was the multistore model described in Chapter 1, which has been replaced by an updated version with more stores and processes. This chapter outlines the essentials of this model and some findings about major processes by which the system operates, such as retrieval and forgetting. The issues and findings and their interpretation are very complex and this chapter could be easily expanded into a large book. The aim is just to overview the broad terrain and some key issues.

This chapter first looks at the notion of a memory store and the development of views as to which memory stores exist. Then it presents the evolving "standard model," describing the stores postulated to date. Finally, the broad major processes are described: acquisition and storage, retrieval, and forgetting, and some subprocesses within each. A useful analogy for the whole system is to a library, with acquisition and storage corresponding to books entering the door and being shelved, retrieval to books being located and taken out, and forgetting to books being lost, destroyed, or wearing out.

MEMORY STORES

The Concept of a Memory Store

A memory store is a system for holding and processing certain types of information. The notion as it was used initially comes from computer science. A digital computer has several distinct locations in which information is held briefly or for longer. Project this idea metaphorically onto the human mind and one has the notion of a specific place that holds specific information. Memory traces are objects stored there, and retrieval is a search through the store for the location of a given trace.

However, the metaphor should not be applied overenthusiastically; it is just a useful way to think about memory. It is not perfect for several reasons. Eysenck and Keane (1990) point out that human memory is much more flexible than a store of objects such as a library. We can rapidly sort the things that we know by a variety of different attributes if need be; for instance, animals by size, color, habitat, ferocity, evolutionary taxa, and so on. A conventional library organizes books by content and would be hard pressed to suddenly list all its red books or those over ten inches high. Human memory operates in a different way than the store metaphor would suggest. We often know whether we know something before retrieving the exact information (e.g., what Albania's capital is) and know very rapidly whether a question even has a sensible answer (What was Napoleon's telephone number?). It is hard to explain such facts with the idea of searching through a storehouse until finding an object. However, the metaphor is useful.

Reasons for Expecting Memory to Have Separate Components

There are several arguments for expecting memory to have separate stores. First, an argument for separate short-and long-term stores is that an organism needs to hold some information active to use it but would be overwhelmed if all that it knew was active at one time. Second, there is much evidence that the brain has specialized systems for storing different sorts of information (Tulving, 1985). Information about an object's location and its identity are stored separately, for example. Such data suggest that different systems have evolved at different times to deal with various environmental problems. (Tulving also suggests that different systems may emerge at different times in an individual's development, though McKee and Squire, 1993, present some evidence against this idea.) Third, Sherry and Schacter (1987) marshal some evolutionary arguments for the existence of separate stores. They say that one would expect qualitatively different stores to evolve (instead of one store that gets more complex) because of "functional incompatibility." This means that the nature of a structure that serves one function is such that it cannot be adapted to serve another at the same time. Nature may produce a particular specialized memory system, then additional memory capacities that evolve must be underpinned by quite different structures. Examples that they cite are systems that underlie song learning, imprinting, and spatial location in birds. The first two strictly limit what information can be stored and the periods for learning it. How could they be adapted to serve spatial learning over a lifetime? Instead, a new structure needs to evolve. However, Sherry and Schacter point out that some memory systems are not so specialized and may be adapted to new purposes.

Some researchers find such arguments unconvincing. They see the stores notion as almost quaint and argue that memory may retain but a single memory trace that is accessed by different processes (Roedinger, 1990; Shiffrin, 1993). For instance, rather than short-term memory being a separate store, it may just be the part of LTM currently active (Crowder, 1993). A variant of this general approach is Craik and Lockhart's (1972) "levels of processing approach," discussed later. This complex issue is still unresolved. However, the view taken here is that the notion of many separate stores is a good working hypothesis supported by much converging evidence.

Early Work on Memory Stores

The study of memory stores goes back at least to the last century. In 1883, Francis Galton made a distinction much like the modern one between short- and long-term memory by describing the former as a "presence-chamber in which full consciousness holds court" and the latter as an "ante-chamber full of . . . ideas [and] . . . situations just beyond the full ken of ideas." William James wrote of primary and secondary memory, the latter holding information not currently in consciousness (James, 1890). Introspection indeed strongly suggests this distinction, and doubtless many laypersons make it. Indeed, Ericsson and Polson (1988) describe a waiter with no formal study in psychology but excellent memory skills who had abstracted out the distinction himself.

Such ideas were brought together in the multistore model, which was a useful organizing framework but soon met several problems. First, there were problems in the details. For example, it proposed that information could only go into LTM by rehearsal. However, we often learn incidentally (without rehearsal), from conversations or reading magazines, for instance. Second, knowledge in LTM can influence what comes into short-term memory. As mentioned in Chapter 1, existing knowledge affects what can be learned. Another good illustration is the oft-published Roald Dahl sketch which at first glance looks like a random series of inkblots (see Howard, 1987, page 38). But when one is told that a dalmation dog is depicted, the object and background emerge. One's knowledge affects what is perceived. Third, evidence turned up for more stores than the model proposed. In a retrospective, Shiffrin (1993) acknowledged that the model was too simple.

The Levels of Processing Approach

Dissatisfaction with the multistore model in the early 1970s lead Craik and Lockhart (1972) to propose a quite different approach to studying memory. They argued that postulating memory stores had its problems because estimates of capacities, coding characteristics, and forgetting rates of hypothesized stores varied according to the paradigm used. Rather than postulate more stores to account for new data, they argued, we should instead examine the learning processes that make certain stimuli more memorable. They did not actually dispute that short- and long-term stores exist, but they downplayed their importance. Memory is better seen as a series of processes. A key factor influencing memorability of material is the "depth of processing" of a stimulus. For instance, a word can be processed at various levels; its typeface, its sound, and its meaning, for instance. Each can be seen as a progressively deeper level. The deeper and more elaboratively a stimulus is processed, the better it is recalled.

Some evidence for the above generalization is a robust phenomenon from an incidental learning paradigm (Craik and Lockhart, 1972). Words are presented singly, and subjects answer one of three types of questions about each: "Is it in capital letters?" "Does it rhyme with_____?", and one which queries its meaning, such as "Is it a geographical feature?" When all words are shown, subjects unexpectedly are asked to recall them. Typically they recall few associated with the capitals question, more associated with the rhyme question, and many associated with the meaning questions. Craik and Lockhart argued that answering a meaning question induces deeper processing than one about capitals or rhyming, and deeper processing produces better recall. The same effect occurs with other types of stimuli. For example, Bloom and Mudd (1991) manipulated depth of processing of faces by asking questions about the sex or "niceness" of various faces. Evidently niceness judgments induce deeper processing, as those faces later were recognized better.

Craik and Lockhart also distinguished between maintenance and elaborative rehearsal. The first aims to keep information current until it is used (e.g., a phone number looked up until it is dialed) and the second involves deeper processing and long-term storage. As mentioned in Chapter 2, animals also may show both types.

The 1970s saw hundreds of studies testing out this framework. However, it met with many criticisms, summarized by Lockhart and Craik (1990) in a retrospective. First, the levels notion is circular; there is no obvious independent measure of depth of processing other than memory performance. Second, the framework neglects retrieval processes. Third, studies showed that surface aspects of stimuli (such as words being in capitals) are not necessarily forgotten as quickly as the framework implied. Instead, given a particular task, subjects may just attend to certain information more than other information. Indeed, subjects in the above-mentioned incidental

Figure 3.1
The "Standard Model" of Memory

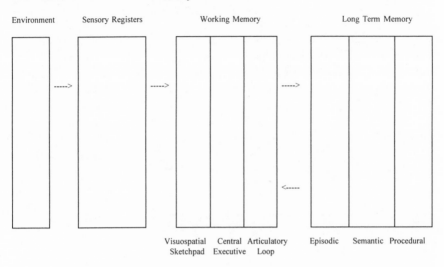

learning experiment sometimes said that they just looked to see if capitals were present, rather than reading the word at all. Fourth, evidence accumulated for a multiplicity of stores. Lockhart and Craik noted that their own ideas had altered since 1972.

However, the principle that memorability is improved by extent of processing is well established. The notion of levels has been applied to many areas, such as reading, child development, selective attention, and even pharmacology (Lockhart and Craik, 1990).

THE "STANDARD MODEL" OF VARIOUS STORES

The "standard model" of memory derives from work of many researchers, a few notable ones being Endel Tulving (e.g., Tulving, 1985), Alan Baddeley (e.g., Baddeley, 1986; 1990), and those whose work led to the multistore model. There may be many more stores than those listed here, and some researchers see the evidence for some stores as problematical. Neurological patients with particular patterns of deficits are a major source of evidence for various stores, but as Crowder (1993) points out, sometimes it is unclear whether their deficits are due to problems in a store or in coding.

Figure 3.1 presents the model. The three basic stores of the multistore model have been elaborated and one has been renamed. Here is a brief description of each.

The Sensory Registers

The sensory registers are conceptualized much the same as in the multistore model. However, a recent view is that the registers represent a series of stages of initial information processing rather than a single store (Greene, 1992). They store incoming information for analysis, and storage evidently occurs in a number of stages. Unattended material seems to be lost in about five seconds. The distinction between registers based on different senses is still made; visual (iconic), auditory (echoic), touch (haptic), and so on. Little is known about any but the first two, partly because they are the most important and partly because the others are so hard to study.

Are the registers important? Haber (1983) questioned whether they are, arguing that they may just be a laboratory curiosity of no real importance to normal perception. However, most researchers disagree. Coltheart (1983), for instance, pointed out that the icon is created at stimulus onset and is important because perceptual and memory processes then work on it. The registers allow more time to process stimuli.

Working Memory

The term *working memory* replaces the term *short-term memory*, although Atkinson and Shiffrin did refer to STM as a working memory. Working memory is seen as a collection of stores and processes that hold and process information briefly so that it can be used to deal with current problems. Some samples of such problems are deciding if a sheep is larger than a goat, whether *horse* rhymes with *course*, doing mental arithmetic, completing the analogy "point is to space as ——— is to time," and understanding speech. The system processes information taken from the environment and/or LTM. Baddeley's latest model of working memory has three main parts, the central executive and two slave systems—the visuospatial sketchpad and the articulatory loop.

The Central Executive. This part is analogous to the managing director of a corporation. It controls the flow and processing of information in the memory system. For instance, it would determine what information goes from the registers into working memory and then to LTM. Baddeley (1990) suggests that it operates more like an attentional system than a memory store. However, relatively little is known about it.

The Visuospatial Sketchpad. This store briefly holds and processes visuospatial information. Figure 3.2 presents some examples of tasks that evidently involve its use. Some others are answering such questions as these:

1. Which of Texas, Alaska, and Florida is shaped most like California?
2. Which of Paris, London, and Rome is closest to Berlin?

Figure 3.2
An Example of a Task that Involves Using the Visuospatial Sketchpad. Are the Figures Identical?

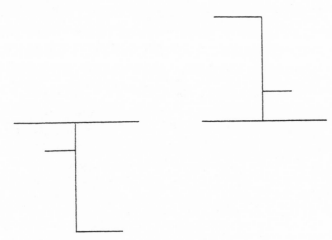

3. Which of famous faces X,Y, and Z is most like A?
4. How many windows does your home have?

Persons given such tasks or questions without external aids typically report visualizing objects and manipulating them or comparing them. This is the visuospatial sketchpad at work. In daily life, it is evidently used for such tasks as orientation, navigation, and answering questions that require use of visuospatial information. Architects and visual artists evidently rely on it heavily to do their work, or at least they did before computer-aided design became widespread. Ability to use the sketchpad varies widely (see Chapter 4). Some persons are very adept, and others are not. This ability has at least two aspects, vividness of the images and prowess at manipulating them, which may be independent (Lohman, 1988). The sketchpad's capacity is unknown. However, it can improve by chunking, as in the example of recall by chess experts of positions, mentioned in Chapter 1.

An obvious question is whether equivalent stores exist for information from other modalities. One would certainly expect so. Everyday experience suggests that there is one for auditory information; most people can mentally play over a melody. Ludwig van Beethoven composed some of his finest works when deaf and must have been using a working memory store to hold and manipulate auditory images. Schab (1991) presents evidence for a short-term store to remember odors.

Hanley et al. (1991) present some interesting evidence for the sketchpad's existence and importance in daily life. They describe a patient who suffered a stroke in 1985. Subsequent neurosurgery left some intriguing deficits: though her general intelligence and most cognitive functions stayed intact, apparently her sketchpad was impaired. She reported various problems; she could not recognize the faces of persons who had become famous since 1985 or learn new routes around town or around new houses that she visited, and she reported having no dreams since 1985. Tests showed various deficits: impaired performance on mental rotation tasks (whereby subjects see a complex figure and answer questions about how it would look from other orientations), in standard mental imagery tests, and in using mnemonic devices based on visual imagery to learn word lists. However, she had no trouble retrieving images from LTM (e.g., faces of persons famous before 1985). Evidently, the deficit was just for dealing with new material. The exact interpretation is still unclear, however. Perhaps only part of the sketchpad was damaged or just one link between it and some other structure was severed. Hanley et al. suggest that there may be two sketchpads, one for incoming information and one for material retrieved from LTM.

The Articulatory Loop. This slave component is a short-term store for speech-based information. An example task involving its use is digit span or recalling a telephone number. Baddeley (1990) suggests that it has two parts. One is the *phonological store*, which holds information in an abstract phonological code. Its capacity is limited to what can be articulated in one-and-a-half to two seconds. A useful analogy is to a tape recorder with a short tape that runs about two seconds and can only hold what can be spoken in that time. Recently, there has been a reconceptualization of Miller's classic short-term memory limit of about seven units. The argument goes that the average is about seven not because the store has seven slots but because most westerners can articulate only about seven digits in two seconds. Chinese digits take less time to articulate and Chinese speakers have a longer average digit span. Indeed, articulation rate correlates with digit span across a variety of languages (Hulme and Mackenzie, 1992). Digit span may rise so reliably with age (from around four digits at age five, six at age ten, to the adult seven) because the loop's "length" grows; the tape can run longer. Words can enter the loop through inner speech, auditory presentation, or from LTM. Items in it can be lost easily through noise or distraction.

Exactly how chunking fits into this scheme is still unclear. It has been known for some time that the idea of seven slots regardless of the unit's nature is not right because the type of material chunked affects capacity; it is seven digits, six letters, and five unrelated words. It may be that articulation rate is the key variable. But a simple thought experiment suggests that span for any sort of material could be increased by training people to use rapidly articulated symbols, to associate these with items, and to group items into larger chunks, themselves labeled by rapidly articulated symbols.

The other component is the *articulatory process*, which "refreshes" the loop; it keeps the tape running. For example, say that one wanted to briefly remember a seven-digit phone number. The articulatory process keeps placing the digits onto the loop again after each two-second run through, analogous to resetting and replaying a tape. Thus, such "refreshment" can maintain the digits indefinitely. Without it, information may stay up to 10 seconds and possibly as many as 20 (Longoni et al., 1993). Longoni et al. also suggest that the apparent two-second limit is a limit of the control process rather than due to decaying traces in the store.

There is much evidence for the loop's existence. First, some neurological patients evidently have severely impaired loops but are otherwise intact. For instance, they may have a digit span as low as one but no other major problems (Hanley et al., 1991). The patient "PV" (Baddeley, 1990) showed poor short-term recall but only for auditory stimuli, which required the loop's use. Baddeley (1993) describes "SR," who had an impaired store with a digit span of just four. He was poor at recognizing and recalling names, but his vocabulary and reading skill were normal. Baddeley also has used an articulatory suppression method, whereby subjects intone something verbal continually (such as "blah, blah, blah") and simultaneously perform another task. The rationale is that suppression blocks encoding of information onto the loop. This suppression greatly impairs performance of tasks that involve the loop, such as digit span, but does not affect others (Hulme and Mackenzie, 1992).

Some information from the working memory stores then may go into LTM, either through explicit rehearsal, incidental learning or some other process. It is still unclear whether information must go through working memory to get into LTM, or whether it can pass directly from the registers. Current thinking is that factual information cannot (Eysenck and Keane, 1990) but procedural knowledge (knowledge of how) may. For instance, "HM" could readily acquire new skills and even learned to do the Tower of Hanoi problem, which involves transferring disks from one peg to another to make a certain configuration.

Long-Term Memory

LTM holds all of an individual's knowledge. Its capacity is virtually unlimited, allowing the average adult to store the vast amount of knowledge needed to support daily activities. An interesting demonstration of its great capacity is a study by Standing (1973). He showed subjects a series of ten-thousand pictures, each for a few seconds. Later they were shown a sample of the ten-thousand, each paired with a picture that had not been shown, and had to pick out the previously seen one. Accuracy averaged 73 percent, showing that they had retained something about most of the pictures.

Implicit and Explicit Memory Systems. There is much evidence that LTM holds at least two major types of knowledge, evidently mediated by two different brain systems. They are called implicit and explicit memory. One view is that the implicit system deals with procedural knowledge (knowledge of how) and explicit with declarative knowledge (knowledge that) (Squire et al., 1993). Information in implicit memory is unconsciously held, resists forgetting, shows little transfer beyond training stimuli and is acquired through practice. This system holds information that underlies habituation and classical conditioning, motor skills, and performance of tasks such as stem completion priming (Schacter, 1992). In this task, subjects study a word list and then complete stems consisting of three letters (e.g., *Cal___*with *Caller*). Subjects who see the list are more likely to fill in the stems with words from the list than are subjects who see no list. The word list primes their performance, though they report being unaware of it. Priming also can occur when subjects are briefly shown a stimulus and try to identify it. They more accurately identify items that have been recently exposed to them. These priming effects may persist for months (Berry and Dienes, 1991). Another task involving the implicit system is artificial grammar learning (e.g., Reber, 1989). Subjects study letter strings generated from a system of rules that defines permissible strings. Then they are asked to categorize new strings. They typically perform better than chance, though they cannot verbalize the rules. One interpretation is that they are unconsciously abstracting them out. Performance on such implicit memory tasks is not affected by amount or type of study.

Information in the explicit system is consciously available, is prone to forgetting, and does not need practice to be learned. One view is that this system evolved later than the implicit system (Schacter, 1992). There is much evidence for the two different systems from disassociations in task performance with normal and neurological patients (Squire et al., 1993).

The systems involve different learning processes. In some situations implicit learning is faster and leads to better performance. Turner and Fischler (1993) compared the performance of subjects in a speeded task who implicitly learned some rules with those explicitly taught them and found that the former performed better.

Parts of LTM. LTM evidently has several parts, though exactly how many and how they are interrelated is still unclear (Squire et al., 1993). Tulving (1985) argued for at least three major parts, as follows. Procedural memory holds knowledge of skills and habits (possibly mediating the implicit system). Episodic memory (sometimes called autobiographical memory) holds knowledge of events; what one did yesterday, where one vacationed last year, and so on. Tulving argued that the classic verbal learning experiments of the 1950s and 1960s, in which subjects learned lists of familiar words, tapped episodic memory. Since subjects knew the words already, they were just learning that they had re-encountered those words in the laboratory at a certain time. Semantic memory holds knowledge of words and their meanings and grammatical rules for stringing them into sentences. Tulving suggests that these three parts are hierarchically interrelated. Procedural memory is at the base, with semantic memory above it as a single specialized subsystem. Above semantic memory is episodic memory, in turn a specialized subsystem of it. Each has its own capabilities but is supported by the system below it. Only procedural memory can operate independently.

Tulving proposed that episodic and semantic memory hold different sorts of knowledge. However, the two types of information may not be so distinct, and it is not clear if there are actually separate stores. Probably the question will only be answered from physiological data. Semantic knowledge may derive from adding together traces in episodic memory that become divorced from their context. For instance, the generalization "Dogs bite" stored in semantic memory may derive from many experiences of being bitten, which have been forgotten. As well, memory traces in episodic memory may blend together, as found in Neisser's (1981) study of John Dean's memory.

Researchers speak of many more memories; recognition memory, odor memory, face memory, and so on (e.g., Schwartz & Reisberg, 1991). And Paivio (1986) argued that there are separate but interconnected memory systems for verbal and imagery-based information. It is still unclear if these represent different stores or whether there is one store that holds many types of information.

LTM holds an enormous amount of knowledge that is well organized and is accessible through different retrieval paths. The complex topic of knowledge organization is covered in Chapter 4, but here are a few words about views of its content and organization in episodic and semantic memory.

Knowledge in Episodic Memory. We store a vast amount of knowledge about events in our own past and about historical events (such as wars and recessions) that we live through. Event knowledge may include information about people involved, emotions experienced, goals met, and so on. Some obvious questions are how accurate our recall is of such details, how the information is organized, how much we forget, what makes certain events particularly memorable, and what cues activate recall.

Several interesting studies cast light on such issues. Neisser's (1981) study of John Dean's memory showed much inaccuracy of recall of details and merging of episodes. Wagenaar (1986) examined his own episodic memory in action. Over four years, he recorded various life events on cards, for each filling in details about what happened, where, who was involved, and when it happened. He also rated each event for salience, his emotional involvement, and its pleasantness. After four years he tried to recall the events by cueing himself with one or more of the what, where, when, and who details and trying to fill in the others. Recall was very good. Forgetting rate had been very slow, making quite a contrast to the almost complete forgetting of nonsense syllables after 31 days that Ebbinghaus had found. The "what" cue was a powerful way to retrieve a memory trace while "when" was almost useless. The probability of recall rose with the number of these cues given. Pleasant events were recalled better overall. Wagenaar also found evidence for the intriguing phenomenon of telescoping. Here one underestimates the time elapsing from a salient event. Events on average occur further off in time than we believe. His estimate of the date of various events on average was 73 days more recent than they did occur.

Several recent studies have suggested that knowledge in episodic memory is hierarchically organized (e.g., Anderson and Conway, 1993). The top level has abstract knowledge covering lifetime periods (e.g., "when I was in high school," "when I was in the army"). These in turn index general events, which themselves index more specific ones. The top level also may have thematic information (e.g., general goals at the time such as getting a degree, significant other persons such as Crystal to whom I was married). These also can index general events.

Brown (1990) looked at the organization of knowledge of news events held over several years and found a similar sort of structure. (All of us are bombarded with descriptions of news events all day long. Most descriptions are probably ignored or quickly forgotten, but knowledge of some is retained.) Brown found evidence for the following model of its organization. The basic unit is knowledge of an event, which itself is composed of components as listed by Wagenaar: where, who, and so on. Knowledge of an event also may be linked to concepts in semantic memory (e.g., the killing of John Lennon in 1980 may be linked to the concepts *prominent killings* and *terrible crimes*), and hence to other knowledge. Event knowledge may be stored in a "narrative structure," which is built up further as more details about an event are acquired. The narrative structure may be a web of causal relations. Brown gives the example of the 1983 assassination of Benito Aquino in Manila. There are links between it and events such as the popular unrest it caused, President Ferdinand Marcos later calling an election, and the 1986 revolution. Another level of organization is the historical period. Event knowledge seems to be stored under period headings. In U.S. history these are often the terms of individual presidents. Thus, the Johnson years from 1963–69 are coded as a different period from the later Nixon years. Brown found that political events were more likely to be embedded in narrative structures with such headings than were nonpolitical events. Some events, such as the 1963 assassination of John F. Kennedy, were remembered very vividly. These may form mental landmarks, which can cue retrieval of other information.

Knowledge in Semantic Memory. Semantic memory information seems to be organized into separate but interconnected networks of words and con-

Figure 3.3
A Fragment of Semantic Memory Knowledge in Teachable Language Comprehender Notation

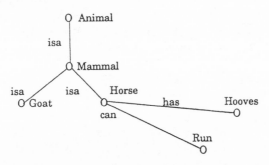

cepts (their meanings). A word is a symbol, and a concept is a word's meaning, as evidenced by the fact that the same word can label many concepts (e.g., form) and the same concept can be labeled by many words (e.g., the concept of *end* by the words finish, terminate, conclude, and so on.) The basic unit of knowledge can be regarded as the concept (see Chapter 4).

A variety of network models of semantic memory were proposed in the 1960s and 1970s. Quillian (1969) proposed one called the Teachable Language Comprehender. In it, semantic memory knowledge was organized taxonomically with nodes corresponding to concepts and labeled pointers as relations between concepts. Figure 3.3 gives an example. The network is expansible in all directions. The model was implemented as a computer program and could answer questions like "Is a robin a bird?" by activating nodes for robin and bird and determining if they were linked.

The model was updated into the "spreading activation" model of Collins and Loftus (1975). It assumed separate but interconnected word and concepts networks but did not organize concepts taxonomically. Figure 8.1 gives a fragment of semantic memory organization according to the model. It answers questions like "Is a robin a bird?" by assuming that nodes are activated (e.g., by hearing the concept name), and activation then spreads along links from activated nodes, analogous to vibrations from a tuning fork. The system then determines if the waves of activation intersect at some node. Another network model is ELINOR, which uses a somewhat different notation (Norman and Rumelhart, 1975).

Network models have been criticized, however. Kintsch (1980) reviewed work on semantic memory and concluded that research had not produced a great deal of information. Johnson-Laird et al. (1984) said that network models in general are too powerful and fail to connect semantic memory to the environment. However, the models are still generally presented in textbooks, and the notion of spreading activation is used to account for priming effects, for example. The models give a useful notation for representing knowledge on paper (which is widely applied in education) and in an AI system.

Mathematical Models of LTM. A variety of mathematical models of LTM have been proposed. Some use semantic network principles and others use connectionist principles. Raaijmakers and Shiffrin (1992) review some of these efforts, which are beyond this book's scope to cover.

And now the major processes can be described.

ACQUISITION

Acquisition usually refers to taking information from the environment and storing it in LTM. Here the term is defined more broadly; a learning process is any process that adds to or alters existing knowledge. Thus, acquisition also refers to acquiring new arrangements of knowledge by manipulating existing knowledge. Consider a computer that stores the name and address of every resident of a town. The system actually holds much implicit information—who lives with whom, average household size, and so on. The processes that make such implicit knowledge explicit are best termed learning processes. A more clearcut example of the necessity to call them learning processes is Albert Einstein deriving the entire special theory of relativity from just two assumptions, that the speed of light is constant and the laws of physics are the same in all frames of reference. The theory was implicit in what Einstein already knew, but his working it out is best described as involving complex learning processes. In practice, most instances of learning probably involve both. Existing knowledge is used to select and alter information taken from the environment. An example of a process involving both is explanation-based learning (described in detail in Chapter 7), which involves learning a concept from a single presented example and manipulation of a rich knowledge base.

Many processes can and have been called learning processes. Churchland (1986) includes imprinting, learning by imitation, one-shot aversion learning, bird song learning, place learning, learning a language, learning mathematics, learning social skills, and learning to lower blood pressure (say, by biofeedback). One can add habituation, classical and operant conditioning, implicit artificial grammar learning, tadpoles injected with a chemical as eggs preferring that chemical after hatching, and the complex learning processes involved in scientific research. There is no comprehensive list or generally accepted taxonomy of categories of learning processes. Several authors have proposed relatively small-scale ones. For instance, Gagné (1970) lists eight types of learning. Bedford (1993) presents a taxonomy with three major subdivisions: representing new information about the world (an example being classical conditioning), correcting internal malfunctions (e.g., prism adaptation), and matching internal states to internal states of others (e.g., language acquisition). Each has various subcategories.

But such classification is an important early step in a field's development. Most sciences early on develop a working taxonomy of their subject matter to interrelate phenomena they deal with, often revising the system later. Such classification is difficult because there are many possible bases and categories that cut across each other. For example, animals can be classified in many ways: carnivore/herbivore/omnivore, land/sea/amphibious, dangerous to humans/not dangerous, domestication-liable/not domestication-liable, and so on. These cannot be interrelated in a single taxonomy because they overlap. Instead, researchers often develop a variety of categories and taxonomies to serve different purposes. One taxonomy may become "primary" because it includes many useful categories and has great organizing and predictive power (Sneath and Sokal, 1973). For example, biologists may use the categories above and two primary taxonomies, one based on evolutionary history and the other on morphology. A field's primary taxonomy may evolve under the pressure of research and theorizing, an example being the American Psychiatric Association's taxonomy of psychiatric disorders. The bases used also may change. Physicists used to classify subatomic particles by weight (e.g., into leptons, hadrons, etc.) but now do so by isospin. The best strategy is to list many useful categories, propose a primary taxonomy as a working hypothesis, and let it evolve with further research.

This section applies this general approach to classifying learning processes. First, some major categories proposed over the years are listed, followed by a taxonomy that interrelates some major ones. A preliminary primary taxonomy is much better than none at all, despite its limitations.

Some Major Categories of Learning Process

Here are some useful categories, some mentioned earlier. It is far from exhaustive.

Implicit and Explicit. Implicit learning involves such tasks as stem priming and artificial grammar learning, and occurs unconsciously and through practice. Explicit learning evidently involves just declarative knowledge and occurs consciously, and the information acquired is prone to forgetting.

Empiricist and Rationalist. Empiricist learning is acquiring information from the environment, and rationalist learning is from manipulating one's knowledge base.

Prepared and Unprepared. Prepared learning is facilitated by genetic predispositions (e.g., taste aversion learning). Unprepared learning is not (e.g., a rat learning to press a bar for food or a student learning quantum physics). In practice, these are two ends of a continuum.

Verbal and Nonverbal. Verbal learning involves learning words; nonverbal does not.

Associative and Nonassociative. Associative learning involves learning an association, and nonassociative does not.

Supervised and Unsupervised. Supervised learning involves a teacher who may arrange stimuli and experiences to make learning easier or to direct it in other ways, and unsupervised learning is learning on one's own.

Strategic and Incidental. A strategy is a consciously applied scheme to improve learning. Strategic learning is effortful. A simple example is using rehearsal or chunking to remember a word list. Incidental learning is learning without consciously employing a strategy or even trying to learn at all, as when idly reading a newspaper and picking up information about the number of spelling errors without intending to. Hasher and Zacks (1979) made a related distinction between automatic and effortful learning processes. Automatic processes occur without effort. Hasher and Zacks cite the example of frequency encoding, whereby people learn about event frequencies without trying to.

Rote and Meaningful. Rote learning is acquiring information verbatim, as it is, without necessarily understanding it. Examples are memorizing a short quotation, poem, or picture. One can see rote learning as a strategy, one that students may use when time is short or material is very difficult or dull. Meaningful learning is learning of material that makes sense, that can be understood. The learner may just take in the gist or take it in verbatim but also understand it. An obvious question is what makes it possible to learn some material meaningfully. What does it mean to understand certain material? One view is that material is meaningful if it can be plausibly related to one's existing knowledge (Skemp, 1979). A good example is the washing clothes passage mentioned in Chapter 1, which becomes more meaningful when given a title that allows one to assimilate it to existing knowledge.

Assimilation and Accommodation. Jean Piaget made this useful distinction between general processes. Assimilation is adding information to existing knowledge structures without altering them or doing so very little. For example, say a person encounters a new breed of dog and adds knowledge of it to her concept of *dog*. The existing concept is little changed by the experience. Accommodation is a major restructuring of existing knowledge structures, induced by encountering anomalies to them. For instance, a firm believer in a flat earth on venturing into space might restructure his concept of the earth as a cosmic body to account for what he sees. An example from geology is the change to plate tectonics in the late 1960s, which restructured geologists' concept of the earth.

Discrimination and Generalization. These can both be seen as learning processes. Discrimination is learning to tell stimuli apart or to make different responses to stimuli one can already tell apart. Generalization can sometimes be an active process whereby a learner acquires knowledge in one situation and tries it out in another. For example, knowledge of how to behave acquired in a psychotherapy room may be generalized to various outside situations and revised according to experience.

A Preliminary Taxonomy of Learning Processes

The above dichotomies overlap with each other to some degree and cannot all be fitted into a single taxonomy consisting of mutually exclusive categories. However, some of the above and some others can be organized into a taxonomy, which Figure 3.4 presents. The taxonomy has its flaws and is presented mainly for organizing and heuristic purposes. Several different bases are used, such as physiological considerations and the type of knowledge acquired.

The major division is between implicit and explicit learning processes. Implicit processes subdivide into conditioning, perceptual–motor skill learning (at least simple forms), learning that results in repetition priming, and artificial grammar learning. Conditioning divides into associative and nonassociative. Explicit learning is divided into two major types. Rationalist learning is by manipulating an individual's existing knowledge base and empiricist by partly or completely taking in information from the environment. Rationalist learning is subdivided according to the type of representation used, purely symbolic, purely imaginal, or both. The first does not involve mental imagery manipulation; for example, if one knows that $a=b$ and $b=c$, then one infers that $a=c$. An example of the second is constructing a new image from existing ones; for example, seeing what one's lounge would look like by imagining a new set of furniture in it. Most common would be using both types, as in answering "How many windows does your home have?" Albert Einstein reported using imagery (as well as mathematics, of course) to construct the special theory of relativity; for example, by imagining himself traveling at the head of a beam of light. Purely verbal information (which is known already or acquired from experience) can alter an image. For instance, Vosniadou and Brewer (1992) and Nussbaum (1979) looked at the development of children's knowledge of the earth as a cosmic body. An early notion was of the earth as a plain. Then children must have heard that the earth is round and altered their image to a disk.

Empiricist learning is divided into incidental and effortful/strategic. Strategic processes are divided by the type of strategy used. An example of an imagery-based one is from Bower (1970). He showed that subjects who linked words by an image in a paired-associate procedure showed much better recall. A purely verbal method would be making up a rhyme to link a list of abstract words. Some mnemonic devices involve both. For instance, the keyword method is useful for learning vocabulary in a native or foreign

Figure 3.4
A Taxonomy of Learning Processes

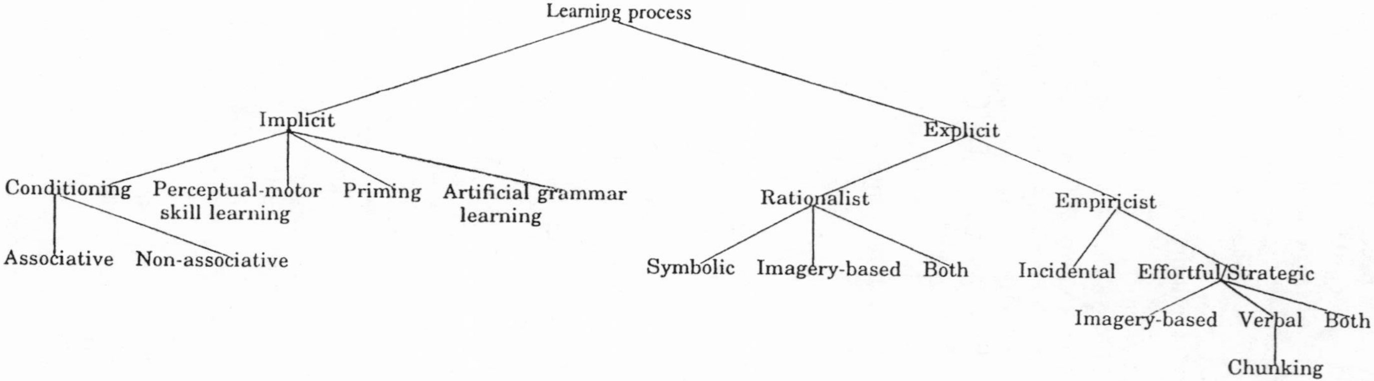

Learning process

Implicit

Conditioning Perceptual-motor Priming Artificial grammar
skill learning learning

Associative Non-associative

Explicit

Rationalist Empiricist

Symbolic Imagery-based Both

Incidental Effortful/Strategic

Imagery-based Verbal Both

Chunking

language. It involves taking part of a new word and forming an image that links the stem with its meaning. For example, to learn the meaning of *poteen* (an Irish whiskey), one takes part of *poteen* as the key word (say, *pot*), and links it with an image of, say, a bottle of whiskey in a pot. Encountering the keyword then triggers the image and the meaning. The method works well (Levin et al., 1982).

Some effective learning strategies involve both or either of these types of representation. Two examples are elaboration and organization (e.g., Anderson, 1990). Elaboration involves adding information to material to make it more memorable. Organization is grouping items to be recalled. For example, to recall a list of words, one could group them into categories such as flowers, animals, and boats. The category may aid retrieval. Indeed, people seem to adopt this strategy spontaneously (e.g., Puff, 1979). Bousfield (1953) gave subjects a single hearing of a long list of words and asked them to recall the words. They tended to recall words in clusters from a category rather than in order of presentation.

A very important and oft-used organizational strategy is chunking, which as mentioned earlier is a way to improve recall by grouping items into larger units. Chunking occurs with many types of material—digits, musical pieces, chess positions, and even procedural knowledge. For instance, in learning a skill such as typing, movements are chunked into larger movement units (see Chapter 5). Acquiring expertise in an area largely is learning to organize material into larger chunks and learning to use them adeptly. Chunking evidently underlies some impressive memory feats. For example, Chase and Ericsson (1982) had a subject practice two hours a day for months at a digit span task. His span rose to an astronomical eighty digits, partly because he organized them into chunks. Buschke (1976) highlighted the importance of chunking (though perhaps overstating it) by saying, "Learning is organized by chunking."

Some types of learning sometimes considered to be a single process may involve several processes from this taxonomy. For example, concept learning may involve various types. One may learn a simple perceptual concept incidentally by forming a prototype from instances or use strategies to learn a textbook concept like *virtual particle*. One can learn a concept purely by manipulating a knowledge base. Physicists derived concepts of various subatomic particles from theory long before instances were observed. Similarly, such processes as language learning may involve many processes used at different times.

Some Factors Affecting Acquisition

Many factors may affect learning. Such variables as age, intelligence, and preferences are covered in Chapter 6, and a few others are mentioned here. First, spaced learning is usually more effective than massed learning, a finding first reported by Ebbinghaus. Second, strong emotion may make certain events much more memorable. An example is the interesting phenomenon of flashbulb memory. Ask someone of a certain age where they were when they first heard of the 1963 Kennedy assassination (or 1986 Challenger disaster or start of the 1991 Gulf War) and they often can say where they were, what they were doing, and give many details of the situation. Such emotion-laden memory traces seem very vivid and evidently resist forgetting, as though a snapshot had been taken. Brown and Kulik (1977) dubbed these "flashbulb memories" and postulated a special brain mechanism that is activated under great emotion and says, so to speak, "Now Print." Encoding is automatic. However, subsequent research suggests that no special mechanism is at work. Flashbulb memory traces are vivid but vary in quality and are subject to forgetting (Pillemer, 1990; Weaver, 1993). Weaver suggests that an individual's undue confidence in their accuracy makes the traces seem unique among memories.

Another factor is generation. This occurs when subjects learn lists of words either supplied by the experimenter or self-generated. They may recall the latter words better, constituting the generation effect (Slamecka and Katsaiti, 1987).

RETRIEVAL

Learning would be pointless without some way to retrieve stored information. Human memory excels at retrieval. The system can retrieve data very fast (and determine beforehand if a fact is known or even exists) and can readily sort items by different schemes. For example, one can quickly list many known green objects, large objects, girls' names that begin with C, and events that occurred or objects that were invented in 1977. Computer data base systems with good organizational schemes, cross-referencing, and efficient search processes still cannot match the versatility of human memory.

Retrieval from Short-Term Memory

Much research has examined retrieval of information from short-term memory, based on a paradigm devised by Sternberg (1966). Subjects are given between one and six digits on each trial and then must decide if an additional probe digit is one of them. For example, a subject might hold the set 6–4–5–3–9 in short-term store and then be asked if 8 is in the set. The major finding is that time to so decide rises linearly with the number of digits in the set, a result found with many sorts of stimuli (Greene, 1992). Sternberg proposed that the digits are stored at locations in short-term memory and the probe is checked against each location in turn. The search process is serial and exhaustive. To retrieve any digit, one must go through the entire set in order, and the search only finishes when all digits have been checked.

However, there is much evidence against Sternberg's model. In an extensive review of data from the basic paradigm, Greene (1992) suggested that a model proposed by Ratcliff (1978) fits the results better. This model proposes that digits are stored as separate traces consisting of features. The probe makes contact with similar traces and is compared with them in parallel as the subject tries to find a match. Ratcliff uses a tuning fork analogy; the probe is like a rung fork that seeks resonances from similar traces. Greene (1992) discusses the issues in depth.

Retrieval from Long-Term Memory

Retrieval from LTM also has been extensively studied. First, here are some useful distinctions. One can distinguish between retrieval of symbolic information and of imaginal information, which would evidently go into different working memory stores. Second, one can distinguish between recognition and recall. Recognition generally is much easier; one need only identify a given stimulus as one previously encountered. The Standing (1973) study mentioned earlier shows just how good human memory is at recognizing pictures. Odor identification is also quite good (Schab, 1991). Recall is digging out information that is not also externally present, such as answering "What is the capital of Uruguay?" rather than "Is Montevideo the capital of Uruguay?" Recall can be voluntary or involuntary, a distinction made by Ebbinghaus. The first is suddenly recalling something automatically, such as a name or an event. The second is effortful recall; one consciously tries to recall something. The distinction is not absolute, however.

The Relation between Recognition and Recall. There is some debate over the exact relation between recognition and recall. Some have argued that they are essentially the same process, and others that they are quite different. An early view was that recall is a two-stage process involving recognition. One first retrieves information and then determines if it is familiar. Recognition is easier because it only involves the second (familiarity) decision. A more recent view is that retrieval depends on closely matching information encoded with that currently available. Recollection is better according to how well one can reinstate features of the learning event, which is discussed later.

Some Findings about Recall. Recall often is easy. Some desired facts (such as the capital of Mexico) can be retrieved almost instantaneously. Again, such speedy retrieval is necessary to deal with an environment in which events occur quickly and needed information must be rapidly accessed. Sometimes, however, one must search hard to dig out information. The process is more like problem-solving. An oft-used analogy is to perception;

retrieving a certain memory trace is like hunting for a figure buried in a complex field. An illustration is a classroom demonstration in which students are asked, "What were you doing at 2:30 P.M. on Monday, February 1, 1993?" People first look blank but if pressed try to generate landmarks that point to the information: "In 1993 I was still in high school. That would be second semester, and my timetable on Monday was. . . . " Sometimes a memorable date nearby, such as a birthday, may help pinpoint the trace. Sometimes a person will report recalling exactly where they were and what they were doing at that time. Thus, there are several retrieval processes and recalling certain information may involve one or more. Indeed, there is physiological evidence for this point. Rosler et al. (1993) found that different brainwave patterns occurred when subjects were asked to retrieve different sorts of information from semantic memory.

Recall of even well-known information occasionally fails, and it is still a puzzle why the marvelous retrieval mechanism sometimes does not work. An illustration is the famous "tip-of-the-tongue" phenomenon, which occurs when one cannot quite recall a word and which Brown and McNeill (1966) described as "mild torment, like being on the brink of a sneeze." Sometimes the sufferer generates the word's first letter, number of syllables, and similar sounding words. People average one such instance a week and increasingly more with age. About half are resolved in a minute, but about 4 percent never are, and proper names are most commonly involved (Brown, 1991). Why does this phenomenon occur? One account is that the brain stores words separately from their meanings and with age and disuse the links between the two may weaken and on occasion may not be activated (Burke et al., 1991).

Memory traces retain the gist, the meaning of material and may systematically change over time. Human memory is typically approximate, "good enough," rather than verbatim like a computer. Recall may be reconstructive, and traces may become increasingly inaccurate with time. A classic illustration is a study by Carmichael et al. (1932). Subjects saw a set of figures and were told that they represented different things. For example, one figure was two circles linked by a line, and some subjects were told that it was a pair of eyeglasses and others that it was a set of dumbbells. When the subjects were later asked to draw the figures from memory, recall was biased toward what they had been told; those told the figure was eyeglasses drew a figure that looked like eyeglasses. Bartlett (1932) found similar reconstructive biases when subjects read and later recalled a rather strange American Indian story called "The War of the Ghosts." The story departed somewhat from western story conventions, and their recall was biased toward a more traditional tale's framework. Indeed, a common everyday experience is revisiting a house lived in many years before and finding the reality very different from the recollection. The memory trace is distorted with time.

This characteristic of systematic bias can cause problems. One is in giving eyewitness testimony, where people are likely to report only what they believe they saw, which can change over time or be altered by clever questions from police or lawyers. A good illustration is a study by Loftus and Palmer (1974). Subjects saw a film of a car crash and then were asked how fast the vehicles were going either when they "hit" each other or when they "smashed into" each other. Those given the "smash" wording estimated higher vehicle speeds and were more likely to report having seen broken glass, though the film showed none. This bias may even snowball over successive recall episodes, making a trace held by one person or many increasingly inaccurate, as in the child's game of gossip. Vicente and Brewer (1993) showed that scientists may unintentionally make this error. Authors of research papers and textbooks often rely on secondary sources rather than looking up the originals. Then their work may become someone else's secondary source, and so on. Quite large errors can accumulate from successive reproductions. An example they cite is Benjamin Whorf's 1940 report that Eskimos have several words for snow. How many? Whorf said three and hinted at as many as seven. In the succeeding literature, numbers given are much higher; one author has up to one hundred. A second example Vicente and Brewer cite is the Watson and Rayner (1920) study of Little Albert, a baby who was classically conditioned to fear a white rat. The story on successive reproductions was altered, as writers gave different accounts of the study. Vicente and Brewer say that the details of studies are typically altered or lost, and the bias is often toward the author's own views.

Several other phenomena of recall are worth mentioning. Hypernesia is an improvement in recall with repeated testing (e.g., Burns, 1993). Subjects learn, say, a list of words and then repeatedly recall them. Performance on later trials is sometimes better than on earlier ones. Reminiscence is a related phenomenon that occurs when subjects recall items on later test trials that they did not recall on earlier ones (e.g., Madigan and O'Hara, 1992).

Finally, recall often is greatly helped by retrieval cues, which are stimuli that point to information stored in memory. Indeed, this theme is sometimes used in films. Baddeley (1983) cites the classic 1950s detective film plot in which a crime occurs, a witness cannot quite recall something crucial, but near the film's end, a cue triggers the memory trace and the case is solved. A striking demonstration of the phenomenon is in a study by Godden and Baddeley (1975). Divers learned a word list either submerged or on a beach and then were tested for recall in either situation. Recall was about 40 percent better when test and learning environments were the same. Evidently, the former acted as a cue pointing to the memory trace of the word list. Indeed, the apocryphal tale of the drunk returning home, placing his car keys somewhere, and only recalling where when again drunk is true. The state of being drunk serves as a cue pointing to the memory trace.

Such findings lead Tulving (1983) to propose the encoding specificity principle. This states that the likelihood of retrieving a target bit of information is a monotonically increasing function of the overlap between information present at retrieval and the information sought. In other words, something is more likely to be recalled in the presence of cues close to those present when it was learned.

FORGETTING

Forgetting is losing information from memory. By necessity, forgetting from the registers and working memory stores is rapid. They need to be able to rapidly clear space for incoming information. An enduring issue is whether forgetting from working memory is due to simple decay (weakening of the trace with time) or interference (the trace being disrupted by other stimuli). The evident answer is both (Baddeley, 1990).

Forgetting from LTM has been extensively studied. As mentioned, traces in implicit memory resist forgetting. One can still readily perform a skill such as typing or bicycle riding many years after learning it, with little or no intervening practice. However, declarative memory traces often are forgotten quickly, unless overlearned (like childhood nursery rhymes), frequently used, or linked to very strong emotion (as in flashbulb memory). However, autobiographical information also may resist forgetting, as mentioned earlier.

Virtually everyone has cursed his or her fallible memory at some stage. However, its proneness to forgetting is now recognized as a strength. It is a useful way to prevent memory being cluttered up with useless information. Computer systems that learn can soon become overloaded and dysfunctional if they cannot delete unneeded information. An interesting question is whether the ability to forget evolved as a useful adaptation or is a fortuitous property of declarative memory.

Forgetting often follows the negatively accelerated curve discovered by Ebbinghaus. Several studies have found a similarly shaped curve over very long intervals. For example, Bahrick (1984) tested memory for Spanish words learned in school up to fifty years before (subjects were of different ages). As Figure 3.5 shows, most forgetting occurred in the first few years and then leveled off. Bahrick suggests that some words go into a "permastore," never to be forgotten. Some other research has looked at forgetting over very long intervals. Bahrick et al. (1975) tested the ability of 392 subjects to recognize faces of high school classmates and to recall their names. The time span since finishing high school ranged from about 3 to 570 months. Recall declined steadily with time and very precipitously at 570 months. Recognition was much better; about 90 percent on average for the first 180 months, but it then declined rapidly. Squire (1989) asked subjects details about one-season television programs that had gone off the air between one

Figure 3.5
Long-Term Retention of Spanish Vocabulary in Bahrick's (1984) Study

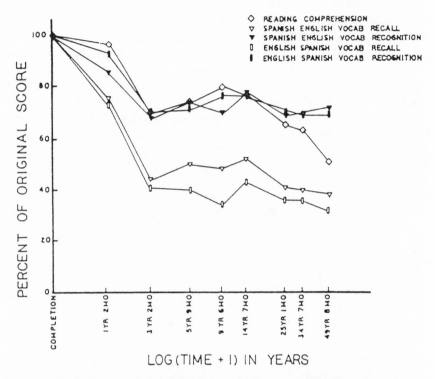

LOG (TIME + 1) IN YEARS

Copyright © 1984 by the American Psychological Association. Used by Permission.

and fifteen years previously. Subjects were tested annually for nine years. Recall declined steadily over the years, and eight years after a program had gone off was down to chance level. Thus, various patterns of forgetting seem to occur. Which one does occur in a given circumstance may depend on many variables—how well material was learned, its emotional significance, type of material, and so on. Studies are needed to work out which variables are significant.

However, there is evidence that some sorts of material are much better recalled than other sorts. Conway et al. (1991) tested recognition and recall of material learned in a cognitive psychology course up to ten years previously. Most material was forgotten in the first three years according to a recall test, but much more was retained according to a recognition test. Concepts were remembered better than names, suggesting that knowledge structures acquired during the course were better remembered than details. Indeed, this accords with anecdotal reports of what can best be recalled after a course; the major themes, principles, and concepts linger while the minor details are quickly forgotten. Memory is best for gist. Interestingly, subjects in the study often were not aware how well they remembered much course material over such long periods. Finally, subjects who had gotten higher grades tended to forget less.

One way to retard forgetting of declarative knowledge is to overlearn it. Another is to review it periodically (Bahrick and Hall, 1991).

Some researchers once believed that material is never really forgotten; people just lose access to it. It remains stored in some corner of memory that one no longer knows how to access. One apparent source of evidence was the dramatic findings of the neurosurgeon Wilder Penfield (e.g., Penfield and Perot, 1963). He operated on over a thousand patients and during the operations stimulated the surface of the cortex of conscious patients with electrodes. Subjects sometimes reported a long-forgotten memory trace; for example, a patient remembered overhearing a certain telephone conversation between his mother and his aunt, another recalled the sights and sounds of a certain baseball game. However, the memories had a dreamlike quality. One interpretation is that the memories were localized and were all still there. However, several critical analyses of the data suggest otherwise (Squire, 1987). For example, one cannot be sure that the reported events actually did occur or were just reconstructions. Second, only a few subjects actually reported such memories. Third, there is evidence that the unused memory traces may be destroyed (Squire, 1987). It is very unlikely that all we have ever known is still stored.

Causes of Forgetting

Forgetting has several causes in addition to decay. One is interference. If subjects learn some material (such as a word list) and then learn other material later (such as another word list), learning the second list may interfere with recall of the first. The more similar the material, the more interference there is. Exactly why interference occurs is still unclear; Bower and Mann (1992) list some possible explanations. They also found that interference could be reduced if, before subjects were tested, they were instructed to reorganize and simplify the material that caused interference. Another cause of forgetting, at least forgetting of details, is schema effects (see Chapter 4). A schema is a knowledge structure that consists of organized slots that are instantiated with details. Memory traces can become biased toward schemas over time.

A final possible cause is repression, an active motivated forgetting of unpleasant material. The term originated as a Freudian defense mechanism designed to protect a person from anxiety. It is a cornerstone of psychoanalysis. Freud held that a prime reason for neurosis is traumatic experiences, memories of which have been repressed but which nevertheless continue to affect behavior. An aim of psychoanalytic therapy was to uncover the repressed memory trace and bring it to consciousness, which would make the symptoms disappear and, as Freud pessimistically put it, "convert neurotic misery into everyday unhappiness." This general notion was used in several Alfred Hitchcock films. In *Marnie*, the heroine was a kleptomaniac who repeatedly took secretarial jobs, gained her employer's trust, and then absconded with the safe's contents. This behavior was eventually traced to a traumatic event in her childhood, which when uncovered stopped her stealing.

Does repression actually occur? Studies suggest that it possibly does. As mentioned earlier, more positive than negative memories are recalled, suggesting that negative ones are repressed. There is some experimental evidence that motivated forgetting occurs (Baddeley, 1990). In addition, some rare psychiatric syndromes evidently represent extreme cases of repression. For instance, the fugue syndrome typically occurs after an individual undergoes a period of stress. He then suddenly loses his memory for hours, days, or even years. He may suddenly get it back, realizing that he is in a strange place and wondering how he got there, having amnesia for the entire fugue period. Sometimes the individual disappears, to be found years later with a new family and no evident memory of his previous life. Kopelman et al. (1994) describe a woman who had a seven day fugue state and still complained of almost complete loss of autobiographical memory for a year afterward. Extensive tests differentiated her problem from organic syndromes and suggested her memory loss was partly simulated. They suggest that patients with psychogenic amnesia may have varying levels of awareness for differing memories. The rare multiple personality syndrome also may involve repression. The individual may develop several distinct personalities, with memory for one or more of them inaccessible to the other personalities.

4

Knowledge

The term *knowledge* can be used in at least two major senses. The first is of facts about the world that are true and may be stored in books, computers, and human brains. Philosophers often use this sense and a definition such as "justified true beliefs." They ask such questions as what knowledge is and how we know facts to be true. The second sense is the information that a given individual holds in his or her mind—information about American history, African geography, past life events, quantum physics, one's spouse, and so on. These senses differ because not all of an individual's knowledge will be "true facts." Much is bound to be inaccurate, patchy, incomplete, or false (e.g., that whales are fish and that there is a worldwide conspiracy to hide data about UFO landings). Sometimes the senses are used interchangeably, but they need to be distinguished. For instance, a researcher might ask, "How should knowledge be represented in a computer system?" typically using the first sense; another might ask, "How do children represent knowledge of lifeforms?" using the second. This chapter is concerned with the second sense. Knowledge will be defined as representations in LTM that consist of information.

This chapter's first section examines some facts about human knowledge and then discusses the nature of representation and some postulated types of mental representation. Then it considers what the unit of knowledge is and the constraints on what knowledge humans can learn.

SOME FACTS ABOUT KNOWLEDGE

An Individual's Knowledge is Variegated

The knowledge that an average adult has is evidently very variegated; it comes in many forms, and parts may be interrelated in different ways.

For example, a person's knowledge of trees may include information about the parts of trees and their interrelations, images of specific trees, information about childhood experiences of climbing trees (and associated sights and feelings), information about their uses for humans, and procedural knowledge of how to chop one down. Indeed, Graesser et al. (1993) suggest that people can hold the following five types of knowledge about a concept like *tree*.

1. *Taxonomic*: Definitions of words and relations to other concepts.
2. *Spatial composition*: How objects are laid out, what parts they have, and how these are laid out.
3. *Sensory*: How something looks, feels, and so on.
4. *Procedural*: Related actions, plans, and goals.
5. *Causal*: How events and states are causally related; for example, information about contingencies.

These types of knowledge may be integrated with each other. An example Graesser et al. give is the concept of *musical instrument*, which might contain much information. Taxonomic knowledge would be of the subordinate categories of brass, woodwind, string, and percussion instruments and their various subtypes and interrelations. Spatial composition would include how the parts of, say, a trumpet are interrelated; sensory how an instrument looks, sounds, and feels; procedural how to hold and play one; and causal how such things as air flow (e.g., in a trumpet) produces sound and how manipulating parts can change pitch.

Knowledge is variegated, and there is no general agreement on what types exist. Researchers speak of many types: abstract, exemplar, implicit, semantic, procedural, and so on. Indeed, Alexander et al. (1991) found that many knowledge terms are used in different disciplines. Some terms were *conceptual, content, domain, metacognitive, tacit, sociocultural, strategic, world,* and *task*. They found overlap and even contradiction in terms used. An important task is to develop a consistent set of terms and to interrelate them into a taxonomy.

The Average Adult's Knowledge Base Is Huge

People know a lot and need to in order to support many everyday activities. Several researchers have tried to estimate how much the average western adult knows. (Their assumptions may be disputed, however.) First, some have estimated vocabulary size. Charness and Bieman-Copland (1992) discuss various estimates, one being about 80,000 words for a high school graduate and another being between 50,000 and 200,000 for a university graduate. Working the estimates and expanding to include proper names of people and places, they estimated as many as 200,000 words on average. Using different assumptions, Landauer (1986) estimated that the average Stanford undergraduate knows about 100,000 words.

Landauer (1986) tried various ways of estimating the number of bits of information in LTM that an average adult acquires, which he dubbed the "functional information content." He assumed various learning rates (e.g., 1.2 bits per second from reading) and forgetting rates, which suggested that the average thirty-five-year-old has acquired about a billion bits (1.0×10^9). Landauer also tried to estimate the maximum capacity of LTM from synapse numbers, assuming that each synapse corresponds to two to ten bits. With 10×10^{13} to 10×10^{15} synapses, the capacity may be one thousand to a million times that actually used.

Much Knowledge Is Left Computable

As mentioned previously, a lot of knowledge is left computable, either to save space or because of no prior need to make it explicit. Processes can extract additional knowledge if need be. Here are two additional computer examples of such extraction. Supermarket checkout counters now routinely record items bought by each customer. The machine can process it to yield buyer profiles and what products are likely to be bought together. Francis Narin of CHI Research in Haddon Falls, New Jersey, recently placed patent information in a computer. The U.S. patent office issues about three hundred new patents a day, which name the inventor(s) and other details. Processing these data can tell which individuals and companies are most productive, how important a given patent is (indexed by the number of citations in subsequent patent applications), and nationality relativities of holders (such data showed that Japanese companies filed more applications than U.S. companies for the first time in 1985).

Deriving new knowledge from old is called inference making. Much research has examined human inference making and its flaws. There are two major types of inference. Deduction is inferring a firm conclusion from premises according to the rules of formal logic; for example, if $a=b$ and $b=c$, then $a=c$. Induction is going from a single fact or two to a generalization; for example, if one has seen a single white swan, one might induce that all swans are white. There are many types of inductive inference (Evans, 1989). One is imputing probable causes of events (e.g., that one's cold was probably caught from one's spouse), and another is generalizing (e.g., that all swans are white). Humans are prone to various inferential errors, even when taught formal logic (Evans, 1989; Maddox, 1993). For example, many people say that erroneous syllogisms such as the following are correct.

Some Fosterites wear yellow buttons.

No Wallyites are Fosterites.

Therefore, at least some Wallyites do not wear yellow buttons.

Some researchers now say that human inference making is sometimes quite irrational.

Knowledge Is Essential to Support Many Everyday Functions

Knowledge is needed to perform many everyday activities. An example mentioned earlier is learning. Another is perception; the brain uses input and existing knowledge to build up representations of the outside world (Epstein, 1993). Visual perception depends on knowing that objects appear smaller when they are further away and that coarser-grained objects are likely to be closer, for example. Persons blind from birth and given sight as adults never see properly, partly because they have not built up the necessary knowledge to perceive patterns well. The role of world knowledge in everyday tasks may only become clear in special circumstances, such as when trying to program a robot to do a simple task. An illuminating example from AI's early days is an effort to get a robot to pile up blocks into a tower. The robot always started by placing the top block in midair. Human commonsense knowledge of gravity prevents such an error.

Here are some more cases.

Understanding Language. A huge knowledge base is needed to understand even simple sentences. One needs to know the word meanings, how they vary with context, and grammatical rules to extract the overall meaning. Often the listener must read much between the lines, using existing knowledge. Consider the sentence "The quick brown fox jumped over the lazy dog." The listener needs to know what foxes and dogs are, what jumping is, that dogs chase various animals, and so on. An amusing example of the importance of world knowledge in comprehension comes from the early days of efforts to program computers to translate from one human language to another. If one translated a sentence from English to another language and then back to English, the result was sometimes comical. Thus, "The spirit was willing but the flesh was weak" might return as "The alcohol was wanting but the meat is not strong," or "Out of sight, out of mind" as "Invisible idiot." Effective translation requires understanding, which depends on a large knowledge base. Indeed, human translators say it is difficult to translate complex technical material. Effective translation may require cultural knowledge, too. When the James Bond film *Dr. No* premiered in Japan, the title was mistranslated as *We Do Not Want a Doctor.*

Coping with Environmental Diversity. Humans can deal effectively with many environmental problems through being able to fall back on other models of reality if one does not work. Again, this flexibility depends on a large base of world knowledge. Computer systems to date are "brittle" because they lack a human-like knowledge base, at least beyond narrow domains. Lenat and Guva (1990) give many examples of computer brittleness. Expert systems may perform well in a narrow domain but typically fail when the domain is widened a little, and they often cannot cope with spurious input that humans quickly see as faulty. For instance, computers may miss odd input like a 103-year-old pregnant woman, a nine-year-old grandmother, and a twenty-year-old who has worked in a mine for twenty-two years. An expert system that diagnoses skin disease was fed details about a 1969 Chevrolet. It asked, "Are there spots?" The answer was yes. It then asked, "What color are they?" The answer was red. It eventually diagnosed measles.

Lenat and his colleagues are trying to build a computer system that has human-like commonsense world knowledge. They are implanting knowledge laboriously by hand but hope that the system eventually will learn from books as easily as people do. The system also can learn by making inferences. Sometimes it is left running overnight, manipulating its knowledge base. Some inferences are interesting and plausible:

"Nations with the same religion belong to the same international organizations."

Some are wrong but understandably so:

"Most people are prominent."

(Most persons that the system has been told about are famous.) Some are just silly:

"When a man shaves with an electric razor, he is not a person because he has electric parts."

Humans quickly recognize whether many such inferences are valid. Eventually, the system may know enough to do so itself.

THE NATURE OF REPRESENTATION

The term *representation* is used in two major related senses. The first is as something that stands for something else. A portrait is a representation of a face, a map of a territory, the word *horse* of a class of animals, and a mathematical model of aspects of the physical world or an economy. The second sense is of a relation between two things, such that one in some way stands for the other. (In mathematics, representation means an isomorphism between two things, which exists when there is a procedure that maps entities, relations, and operations in the represented system into entities, relations, and operations in the representing system. A requirement

Most ideas in this section come from Palmer (1978), Paivio (1986), Rumelhart and Norman (1988), and Gallistel (1990, Chapter 2).

Figure 4.1
An Illustration of the Nature of Representation

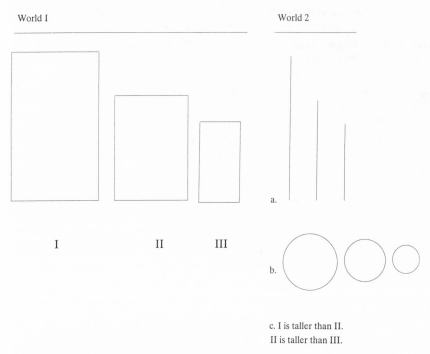

c. I is taller than II.
II is taller than III.

Adapted from S.E. Palmer (1978), Fundamental aspects of cognitive representation. In
Cognition and categorization, ed. E. Rosch and B. B. Lloyd. Hillsdale, NJ: Erlbaum.

is that the relation between two or more entities within the represented
system has a corresponding relation between their representatives in the
representing system. See Gallistel, 1990.)

Figure 4.1 illustrates these and other key ideas. The figure shows two
worlds, world 1 being the represented world and world 2 the representing
world. The objects in world 2 represent those in world 1 in various ways. The
objects in part *a* stand for the height of each rectangle, the objects in part *b* for
their width, and those in part *c* stand only for the rectangles' relative heights.
The objects in world 2 are representations of the objects in world 1, and
representation is the relation between world 1 and various objects in world 2.

Representations have a content and a format. Content is the actual
information that a representation holds and format is the form in which it
holds it. The same content can be held in different formats and the same
format can hold different contents. In part *a* in the figure, the content is
information about the rectangles' heights, in *b* it is about their widths, and
in *c* only their relative heights. *A* and *b* use the same format while *c* uses a
different one. Another example is the information in the sentence "The bird

flew the coop." It could be held in many formats: on a record, a compact disk, magnetic tape, paper, in a computer, and so on. The content is the same, but the format is different. Similarly, a format such as magnetic tape can hold many different contents.

Two major types of format are analog and analytic. Analog representations in some way resemble that which they represent, as in *a* and *b*. Further examples are a landscape painting, a map of a nation, and a phonograph record of a concert. An analytic representation bears only an arbitrary relation to that which it represents; it represents by stipulation. For example, the word *cat* represents a class of animals but does not resemble an actual cat. Any other word would do. Most words are analytic representations, with a few exceptions such as *hiss* and *boom*. Paivio (1986) argues that this analog-analytic distinction is better seen as a continuum than as a dichotomy. Some representations may use both formats. A map may represent a territory's shape in analog format but land elevation by arbitrary colors, an analytic format. Finally, a representation may hold only part of the information in what it represents. *A* in Figure 4.1 holds only information about heights and *b* only about widths. A mathematical model of an economy holds only some information about some of its entities and relations.

Another useful distinction mentioned in Chapter 1 is that between a representation and the processes operating on it. A representation is an entity and a process is something that affects it (e.g., adds to it, divides it, or just shifts it from one store to another). A good analogy is to carpentry, in which the entity worked on is wood and the processes that operate on it are sawing, nailing, planing, and so on. A representation is useless without processes to operate on it (Palmer, 1978). The information-processing framework, as mentioned in Chapter 1, seeks to explain human performance by models consisting of representations and processes.

Biological representation is a relation between the outside world and the inside of an organism. The term can apply on two levels. One is the neural level; Dudai (1989) says that the fundamental question in neurobiology is the nature of the neural representation of knowledge. For instance, how does the primitive nervous system of *Aplysia* represent a stimulus-response association? By a change in neural connection strength in a particular locale? How does the human brain represent an abstract concept like justice? As a particular pattern of neural activity, a single "grandmother" cell, or otherwise?

The second level is the mental one; representation is a relation between the outside world and the mind. The mind can be seen as a device for representing the world and operating on those representations. A simple example is a mental map of a town, which holds information about part of the world. One can use it to navigate and infer where new shopping centers are needed, for instance. When people are asked to draw their mental maps, they are often inaccurate but usually suffice for their purposes. Another example is the intriguing ability of some chessplayers to play "blindfold," a form of chess played without sight of the board. The players call out each move and keep track of the changing positions of many pieces on sixty-four squares. A few can play more than one game at a time, the world record standing at an astronomical forty-five, set by Miguel Najdorf in 1947. The blindfold player must mentally represent each board and use various processes to find good moves. How the neural representations give rise to the mental ones is a very old problem, still unsolved.

TYPES OF MENTAL REPRESENTATION

There are several major questions about mental representations. If the mind is metaphorically likened to a container with entities in it that correspond to things in the world, what is the nature of these entities? Is there one type or many, and what are they? Is there a single primitive, an atomic unit that cannot be further subdivided and from which larger structures are built? What representation formats does the human mind use? These questions are very difficult to answer. Indeed, Paivio (1986) dubbed the problem of mental representation as possibly the toughest in science. For instance, throughout the 1970s, a debate raged as to whether mental images are analog or analytic, a question that is still largely unresolved. Anderson (1978) argued that behavioral evidence alone could not answer it because any finding could be explained by some mix of representations and processes. However, much physiological evidence now suggests that at least two types of format exist, as discussed later.

Various representational entities have been proposed. Paivio (1986) and Rumelhart and Norman (1988) give extensive reviews. This section briefly describes the major ones.

Features

Features are units that combine to form larger bundles. A view that dates back to Aristotle is that concepts (word meanings) consist of bundles of elementary features. For example, the concept of *square* consists of such features as "has four sides of equal length," "is a planar figure," "is a closed figure," and so on. The concept *bachelor* might be represented by such features as "is male" and "is unmarried." Such features may, however, themselves consist of more elementary ones. Features come in various types (Howard, 1992). For instance, perceptual features (such as blue) are those obvious to the senses, functional features refer to use (e.g., can be used to drill holes), and relational features refer to a relationship (e.g., a cousin is the child of one's aunt or uncle).

Propositions

A proposition is an abstract entity (not tied to any particular sensory modality) that makes a statement and is true or false. Examples are "Birds have feathers," "The sky is blue," and "Swans are purple." Propositions are discrete, analytic representations that many researchers believe are basic building blocks used to construct larger representational structures (Paivio, 1986). A sentence can be broken down into one or more propositions.

Propositions can be expressed in a notation called predicate calculus, which is useful for programming knowledge into a computer. The two things of concern (the arguments) go in brackets and the relation between them (the predicate) goes outside. For example, "The horse is on the plain" can be expressed as:

ON (Horse, plain).

Schemas

The philosopher Immanuel Kant coined the term *schema*, and Bartlett (1932) brought it into psychology. Much research was done on schemas in the 1970s and 1980s (Mandler, 1984; Howard, 1987). A schema is an abstract mental structure that consists of slots organized in a certain way. The schema is matched to sensory input and the slots are filled in with data to create an instantiation. A simple example is the schema of a human face, which has slots for two eyes, a nose, a mouth, and so on, arranged in a certain way. A given human face instantiates the schema because the slots can be filled in with specific eyes, nose, and so on. Schemas vary in abstractness from specific ones such as face to very complex ones such as nation and scientific theory. They also may embed within each other. For example, parts of the face schema can be seen as schemas embedded within it (e.g., eyes, nose) and the face schema itself is embedded within the human body schema.

Schemas can be divided into several types. There are schemas for objects such as face. There are schemas for events, which are often called scripts because they prescribe sequences of actions. For example, the typical restaurant script has slots for the actions of sitting down, examining the menu, ordering, eating, paying the bill, and exiting. When entering a restaurant, one usually retrieves this script and uses it to guide actions. A specific visit (say to Joe's Diner on March 17) is an instantiation. There are also schemas for actions, which consist of procedural knowledge (see Chapter 5).

One view (e.g., Rumelhart and Norman, 1988) is that LTM contains numerous schemas that we continually retrieve and match to input to guide behavior and understanding. For example, a detective investigating a murder has some stock schemas (such as jealous husband, burglary gone wrong) which he or she matches to details to try to solve a given case.

Humans have schemas to handle most situations they encounter and may be disturbed when expectations prescribed by a schema are not met. Australian comedian Garry McDonald used to interview celebrities and violate the usual television interview schema by appearing nervous and asking very strange questions. Some interviewees appeared very disturbed. Another reaction is laughter; much humor is based on violating schema-given expectations. For example, a Monty Python sketch features a television quiz show with four major Communist figures competing for a lounge suite by answering trivial questions; instantiations of our quiz show schema usually have quite different contestants.

Schemas can be learned or may evolve in three major ways. First, knowledge may be added to them, as in Piagetian assimilation. Second, the schema may be restructured to account for anomalies, as in Piagetian accommodation. Third, it may be learned from scratch from one or more instances, which is probably the hardest way (Rumelhart and Norman, 1988).

Mental Images

How many windows does your home have?
How would that sofa look in your living room?
Which is larger, a sheep or a goat?

As mentioned in Chapter 3, most people say that they answer such questions by visualizing the objects and "inspecting" the images. Mental images are analog representations because they resemble the actual objects in some way and to some degree preserve the relations between their parts.

The study of mental imagery has a long and sometimes controversial history. Aristotle held that all thought takes place in images. In the Nineteenth Century Francis Galton conducted studies of differences in imagery vividness, and the Betts scale of imagery vividness was devised in the early Twentieth Century. However, the topic went under a cloud in the behaviorist heyday as "mentalistic." In the late 1960s, research on it again grew popular. One aim of studies around that time was to experimentally demonstrate its existence and use. An example is the Bower (1970) study mentioned in Chapter 3, which showed the effectiveness of an imagery-based mnemonic device. Another oft-cited demonstration is from the "mental rotation" paradigm (e.g., Metzler and Shepard, 1974). Subjects are exposed to pairs of complex block figures consisting of cubes. Members of each pair are either the same but at different orientations or are mirror images. Subjects quickly say if the figures are identical, and time to do so increases with angular difference between them. One interpretation is that the subjects visualize and mentally rotate one figure to match the other, and time to do so rises with angular disparity. However, some researchers have argued that subjects may just follow the experimenter's demand characteristics to produce such results. Other studies show that common visual illusions occur with imagined stimuli and that mental practice may improve athletic performance (Finke, 1989). In this case, athletes practice a task such as a golf swing in the imagination.

Much is known about mental imagery, and here is a brief summary. First, there evidently is imagery for each sense, though most work has studied visual imagery. Most people say that they can conjure up images of a melody, an odor, or a sensation of falling. There is also experimental evidence. For instance, Carrasco and Ridout (1993) had subjects rate the similarity of sixteen odors (such as leather and chocolate) either directly perceived or imagined. Multidimensional scaling of judgments showed similar underlying dimensions of similarity (such as fruitiness, strength, and familiarity) for perceived and imagined odors, providing evidence for olfactory imagery. Second, mental images evidently are not identical to actual perceptions; they have a meaning component and may be distorted in various ways. Third, as mentioned in Chapter 3, people differ greatly in imagery vividness and ability to manipulate their images. Some say that they do not experience images at all (Kosslyn, 1980). (Indeed, I was told by a student that she had vivid imagery but her mother had none, and the mother always thought that the daughter's imagery was unique.) The best known case of a vivid imager is S.V. Shereskevski, a Russian journalist described by Luria (1968). His imagery was so vivid that it interfered with normal vision. He reportedly slept late sometimes because his image of his alarm clock showing an early time was more vivid than the actual sight of the clock. His prowess at imagery gave him excellent recall but made him an ineffective person. Indeed, most people report images less vivid than actual perception, very useful because otherwise images and percepts would be confused (Symons, 1993). Very vivid dreams and hallucinations, which evidently involve the same system as imagery, typically occur only when someone is in an abnormal state; e.g., fevered, drugged or psychotic (Symons, 1993). Fourth, imagery apparently involves both brain hemispheres and appears to use the same brain mechanisms as perception (Farah, 1988). Brain imaging studies show that similar regions are active when subjects conjure up images and perceive in that sense. Like visual percepts, visual images have separable spatial and identification aspects. Good and poor imagers may differ physiologically. Charlot et al. (1992) measured cerebral blood flow of good and poor imagers at rest and when conjugating verbs and using mental imagery. The differences were striking. The poor imagers showed an increase in blood flow to the whole cortex when doing both tasks, while good imagers only showed regional increases, such as in the visual association cortex.

Finke (1989) adeptly summarized many findings about imagery with five principles:

1. Images may hold implicit information. (An example is the number of windows in one's home.)
2. The spatial layout in an image corresponds to the way in which actual objects or parts are arranged in space.
3. Image transformations follow the same laws of motion as those in actual objects. (For example, if one rotates a mental image of a given shape, the same laws apply as if one were rotating the actual object.)
4. The structure of an image corresponds to that of actual objects.
5. Imagery is functionally equivalent to perception. (As mentioned above, they evidently involve the same brain mechanisms.)

Kosslyn (1980; 1983) proposed the most detailed existing model of imagery. He has modified it at times to account for new findings, and so some have criticized it as ad hoc. However, it fits much data quite well. The model proposes that visual imagery takes place on a template that has a grain (like a photograph), and images are most vivid in its center. The template only holds so much material; visualizing a large elephant may mean that parts "spill out from view." Once established, the image fades quickly. Images are generated from underlying propositional representations, analogous to the way in which analog television images are generated from discrete information. There are files for propositions and images. Various processes operate on images. For example, one process creates an image from the underlying propositions (over time and piece by piece). Another looks for things in an image (e.g., in answering whether a lion has whiskers) and scans across the image at a limited speed. Another process performs transformations on an image. Subprocesses of that process are zoom, scan, pan, and rotate. For instance, zoom works like a zoom lens on a camera, moving all points of an image out from the center. Some evidence suggests that the efficiency of these processes may improve with practice (Wallace and Hofelich, 1992).

The ability to form and store images evidently evolved from the ability to perceive. It is very useful to be able to hold percepts for a time and work on them. Humans today put this ability to many everyday uses. An interesting example mentioned earlier is blindfold chess. Saariluoma (1991) examined how blindfold players manage this feat. Studies suggested that the image of each board is stored in LTM and brought into the visuospatial sketchpad when needed, and the images have meanings. The players evidently used chess-specific chunks of knowledge to construct the images and reported that the meaning "or sense" of each position is central to recalling it.

Prototypes

A prototype is a representation of a category, usually defined as knowledge of a highly typical or an idealized category exemplar (Howard, 1992).

For categories with very concrete exemplars, the prototype might be a mental image; for example, a prototype bird might be an image of an archetypal one that flies, gets around early in the morning, and looks like a robin. However, prototypes for categories with abstract instances might consist of sets of features. For example, a prototype representing the category of totalitarian states might consist of knowledge of such features as "has a dictator," "has a secret police," "has government control of the press," and so on.

Mental Models

Craik (1943) coined the term *mental model*, and much research has recently been done on them (Johnson-Laird, 1983; 1989). The notion is a bit vague, however. Johnson-Laird defines one as a model of some part of the world that is constructed from primitive symbols (e.g., from world knowledge). The model may be completely analog (e.g., a visual image) or partly analog and partly propositional. Therefore, a mental image is a special case of a mental model. A mental model is not a schema because it has no slots to be filled. The model's elements are images and/or abstract relations between them. An example is a model of an internal combustion engine. It might consist of images of the parts and the relations between them and abstract knowledge of how the machine works. Another example mentioned in Chapter 3 is the mental models that children have of the earth as a cosmic body. An early model was of a plain, and later models reflected the integration of analytic information. For instance, the model became a flat disk or one in which the world was round but the ground was a cross-section of the planet. This example also shows that mental models may be wrong or partially inaccurate. Norman (1988) illustrates with the example of mental models of a refrigerator thermostat. The actual machine can only be on or off; temperature switches only alter the proportion of time it is on. However, many persons' mental models assume that the switch directly varies temperature.

Models can be manipulated to see what various operations might do; they allow "mental simulations" (Rumelhart and Norman, 1988). For example, a billiards player can use a mental model of the table and knowledge of the laws of physics to simulate consequences of a shot. Mental simulations allow one to discover knowledge implicit in the representation. Rumelhart and Norman give the further example of deciding if a salt shaker could be a chair: Can one sit on it? Yes, if people were a few inches tall or a salt shaker were three feet tall.

Mental models can be acquired in various ways—from analogy, from direct experience (as with an engine), or even from text. People can readily build up a partly analog model from words alone, or from text and diagrams. Hegarty and Just (1993) looked at how people build up a mental model of simple pulley systems from texts and diagrams. The study suggested that subjects first try to understand both the text and the diagrams and integrate the information in bits corresponding to several clauses of text. They construct models in parts and then combine these into a global one.

Production Systems

This is a format for procedural knowledge. It consists of knowledge of actions to be performed if certain conditions are present. For example, part of the knowledge underlying car driving might be represented as follows.

1. If car is a manual transmission, to change gears, depress clutch and shift gear lever.
2. If you wish to stop, then depress brake pedal.

Computer expert systems typically use this format.

Chunks

Chunks are groupings of information into larger units. These were discussed in Chapter 3.

Discussion

Do all these types actually swim in the representational sea? The mind may well use several formats. Certainly, there is much evidence for at least analytic and analog types. Paivio (1986) suggested that there are separate but interacting analog and analytic systems related by referential links. There is much evidence that people often use both analog and analytic formats. Use of external analog representations is widespread in every culture—in maps, art, and so on. External analog representations are easy to learn and use, and many of our metaphors are visual ("I see what you mean" and "He shed some light on the issue"). Use of analog information is needed to perform some tasks. Glenberg and McDaniel (1992) point out that languages usually have just a few prepositions for the very large number of spatial relations that humans can learn, and so there must be analog representations for these. Waddill and McDaniel (1992) point out that analog information often promotes understanding. Diagrams greatly help people organize and understand textual information.

People can readily switch between the two formats. Many studies suggest that people can readily form an image from purely verbal descriptions and that such images have similar properties to images formed in other ways. For example, Denis and Cocude (1992) asked subjects to construct a mental map of an island from a verbal description, which said, "The island is circular with a harbor at eleven o'clock, a beach at four o'clock . . . " and so on. Times to scan across the resulting images increased with distance across the island, as occurs with images constructed from actual pictures. Denis and Zimmer (1992) found similar spatial priming and mental scanning effects in images generated from text. McNamara et al. (1992) had subjects learn a fictitious map and then told them facts about its cities. Experiments showed that these facts were readily integrated into their representations.

However, more research needs to be done to work out if all these formats exist. It is too soon to judge.

THE UNITS OF KNOWLEDGE

A fundamental question posed in most fields is "What are the units?" For example, what are the units that natural selection works on, and what are the units of matter? One can ask this question at two levels. First, what are the fundamental units, basic in that they cannot be decomposed further but can be combined into larger structures (Estes, 1988)? Second, what are the functional units, if any, which may subdivide but function as units at some level of analysis? An illustration is with matter. Quarks may be fundamental, indivisible units, but atoms are functional units at the level of chemistry.

One can ask the same two questions about the units of knowledge. Early researchers considered the unit to be the association or the memory trace (Estes, 1988). However, what criteria should be used to evaluate candidates? Anderson (1980) defined a unit of knowledge as a "package of data that processes treat in an all-or-none fashion" and suggested two criteria. First, if one element of a structure is encoded into an associative structure, then all parts of it are. Second, if one element of a structure is taken into working memory, then all are. Anderson considered several candidates, such as the proposition and the schema, and suggested the schema as a unit.

Elementary Units

One would expect there to be an elementary unit and a set of rules by which it can be combined into larger structures. Fodor's (1983) language of thought hypothesis holds that there is an elementary meaning unit from which larger representations are constructed, just as an infinite number of meanings can be constructed by stringing together a few words. Schank (1981) argued for the following conceptual primitives out of which concepts are built (see also Mandler, 1992). He proposed eleven primitive acts (e.g., propel, move, and ingest), several primitive states (e.g., anger, hunger, and health), and primitive roles (e.g., actor, object, and direction). Complex concepts are built up by combining these. Lakoff (1987) suggests a primitive image/schema as a basic unit. However, there is yet no general agreement on what the elementary units are.

Functional Units

There probably is no single functional unit of knowledge that operates at all levels because of the ubiquity of chunking (e.g., Estes, 1988). Units used at one level during learning or performance may be grouped into larger units or split into smaller ones at another stage. A person may also switch between different functional units according to his or her purposes. For example, in reading, the early elementary units arguably are letters. As the student's skill increases, the unit may become syllables, words, and perhaps whole phrases. In Morse code learning, the initial units are individual dots and dashes but become letters (patterns of dots and dashes) and syllables. In musical performance, the elementary unit for plans for performing may be the note. However, different circumstances may induce persons to use different units. Palmer and van de Sande (1993) found that in some contexts the unit was the note and in others the chord.

However, it is useful to regard some knowledge structure as a functional unit. The concept is a good candidate because it meets Anderson's criteria, it is a building block of larger structures such as principles and taxonomies, and much evidence suggests that information in LTM is largely organized around it. Let us examine more closely what concepts are and some facts about them.

THE CONCEPT AS THE FUNCTIONAL UNIT OF KNOWLEDGE

Concepts have been studied since the Ancient Greeks, and several disciplines study them today, including psychology, linguistics, philosophy, cognitive science, education, and AI. However, there is no universal agreement on a definition of *concept*, and different disciplines tend to use different ones. Cohen and Murphy (1984) list several definitions—a definition of a term, a set of things, and a cognitive representation of a category, for instance. However, a popular and useful definition is the last one above, the information that an individual has about a category. A category can be defined as a set of things in the world and a concept as the information that an individual has about it. Thus, my concept of *dog* consists of all I know about them; that they bark, have four legs, bite, are mammals, and come in various types. The category is the set of all dogs. The concept has many uses: making inferences, relating the category to other ones (such as animal and lifeform), and making sense of the world (Howard, 1987). Another useful distinction is between an individual and an expert concept (Howard,

1992). The latter is the most developed one in existence for a given category and is held by experts (e.g., physicists' concept of *subatomic particle* and doctors' concept of *measles*). An individual concept is that which a given person has of that same category (e.g., my limited concepts of *subatomic particle* and *measles*). It may be the same as an expert concept (if the individual is an expert), or contain much less information. When people speak of *the* concept of something, usually they mean the expert concept.

Some Important Findings about Concepts and Categories

Work starting in the 1970s turned up some interesting findings about concepts (see Mervis and Rosch, 1981). First, instances of a given category may vary in typicality, in the extent to which they are good, clear examples. Robins and sparrows are usually judged as better examples of birds than penguins and ostriches. Subjects even judge 4 as a better example of an even number than 8, itself judged a better one than 106 (Armstrong et al., 1983). Typicality variation is implicitly acknowledged in daily life. For instance, in a criminal trial, a jury determines guilt but the judge determines typicality. An example of murder such as a premeditated contract killing may be judged as more typical and deserving a longer sentence than one judged atypical, such as a mercy killing.

A second, related finding is that category boundaries are often vague and may be changeable. It is sometimes unclear if a stimulus is in or out of a given category and some persons may say it is and others that it is not. For example, McCloskey and Glucksberg (1978) gave subjects pairs such as "apple-fruit" and asked if one was an instance of the other. Subjects were tested twice, one month apart. There were wide individual differences in categorization of some pairs. Some subjects placed a stimulus in a category and others did not, and the same person might categorize the stimulus differently on subsequent testing. It is easy to find similar category boundary disputes in science. Scientists dispute whether viruses are lifeforms and whether computers are intelligent beings. Sometimes a precise definition is imposed to make a firm boundary. Economists define a recession as a downturn in which gross national product declines in two successive quarters and a person as unemployed if he or she is actively seeking work and has worked less than an hour in the past week. Courts also may impose category boundaries (e.g., whether capital punishment is an instance of cruel and unusual punishment or a genetically engineered organism is an instance of patentable object). Imposed boundaries also may be moveable. A government may alter the border of drunk driver from a driver with a 0.08 blood alcohol level to 0.05 to reduce accident rates or to 0.1 under pressure from the liquor industry. Category boundaries also may be extended by using a concept metaphorically (Lakoff, 1987). For example, the border of lion can be extended to include some people ("George is a lion").

The Information That Concepts Contain

Concepts consist of information, but what information? What knowledge do people acquire when they learn a concept that enables them to categorize, to relate the category to other categories, and make inferences? There is still a major debate about this question, which dates back to Aristotle. He held that people acquire knowledge of common (defining) features of the category's instances that are singly necessary and jointly sufficient to categorize all exemplars. People categorize stimuli by seeing if they have all the defining features. Any stimulus must have them all to be an instance.

However, this view has problems. First, children have great trouble learning defining features but may still categorize well (Howard, 1987). Second, many concepts have no obvious defining features but can still be used to classify, some examples being *justice* and *truth*. Wittgenstein (1953) illustrated the problem with the concept of *game*. What features do chess, football, bridge, solitaire, and charades share that are singly necessary and jointly sufficient to categorize all games? There are none, said Wittgenstein; those games only tend to share features. Chess has some features in common with football, which in turn has other features in common with soccer. Games have a family resemblance structure. The features that they tend to share are called characteristic features.

So some new views were proposed, which were summarized by Smith and Medin (1981). They dubbed the defining features theory the "classical view" and considered two other ones, the exemplar view and probabilistic (or prototype) view. The former holds that people retain information about one or more specific instances and categorize new stimuli by analogy to these. For example, one might represent the category of dogs by a few known ones: one's pet, Lassie, and Rin Tin Tin. If one encounters a new animal, one determines if it is a dog by seeing if it is similar enough to the stored exemplar representations. The concept of *Pandora's box* might be represented by knowledge of the original Greek myth and stimuli categorized by analogy to it. The format might be analogical, propositional, or both. Several mathematical models have been developed that assume people just learn exemplar representations (see Hintzman, 1986; Estes, 1993).

The probabilistic view holds that people learn a very clear, typical example or a set of characteristic features and categorize with these. A given stimulus might be classed as an exemplar if it is judged sufficiently similar to the representation.

A debate raged throughout the 1980s over which view is correct, which still has not been resolved. However, some researchers now believe that asking which is correct is a poor question. People are not likely to learn any single type of information about a category. Knowledge is variegated, and people are likely to learn different things about a category according to their existing knowledge, purposes in learning, the nature of the category, and other factors (Howard, 1992). Categories vary enormously in size, complexity, and whether instances actually do share common features (Homa, 1984). Squares do, and people can readily learn a defining feature concept of squares, while instances of *surrealistic artwork* do not. As well, our needs in acquiring a concept may differ. One may just need to remember a few instances of *subatomic particle* to pass an exam but may need to learn abstract defining features to do scientific research. A stroll through an art gallery may induce one to form a prototype of *impressionist artwork* or just remember some examples but still be unable to specify defining features. An individual may even have a mix of types in a concept. A doctor may know the defining features of *measles* (infection by a virus) but rely on characteristic features to diagnose cases. Landau (1982) gives the example of *grandmother*. An individual's concept may include information about the abstract relational defining feature but also of a prototypical grandmother, with gray hair, wrinkles, bifocals, and so on. Anyone who could only represent categories by exemplars or by defining features would be severely handicapped.

The likely principle underlying human concept learning is much like the one that Herrnstein proposed for animal concept learning: people acquire what information they need to about a given category. Concepts are likely to contain many different types of information, and some may be left computable. An entire concept also may be implicit in existing knowledge and only made explicit if the need arises. Knowledge contained in a concept may include features, schemas, mental models, procedural knowledge (e.g., of emotions), and relations to other concepts.

Barsalou (1987) took this view even further. He argued that concepts are not fixed entities at all but are assembled in working memory from knowledge in LTM when the need arises. He gives examples of ad hoc categories such as foods not to eat on a diet and ways to escape being killed by the Mafia when they have a contract on you, which indeed fit this idea. However, the truth is likely to be somewhere short of this extreme. Ad hoc concepts may be assembled (although they may become fixed if repeatedly used), but other concepts are probably quite fixed. Many others may be in between; partly fixed, but with much more knowledge about them able to be computed from the knowledge base if the need arises.

Therefore, different people are likely to have quite different information about the same category. A small child is likely to have a less rich concept of *dog* than a biologist or a dog breeder, and a layperson less about *schizophrenia* than a psychiatrist. Some persons will have no concept at all about a given category (e.g., most Trobriand Islanders about *quark* and pre-1900 physicists about *black hole*). Concepts develop. The knowledge that they contain may increase and be reorganized with experience. How then can we talk of *the* concept of *square* or *black hole*? Again, as mentioned, *the* concept of something is the expert concept.

This view resolves some problems in this area and much evidence supports it (Howard, 1992). For instance, Piaget's early studies showed that children have quite different concepts of *life* than adults. Initially, the concept is quite narrow, excluding from the category fish, insects, and plants. With development, more knowledge is added, and eventually the category may include seeds and bacteria. The Nussbaum (1979) study mentioned earlier showed that children have quite different concepts of the earth. Finally, many studies in the last few decades have examined what information people have about such scientific concepts as *gravity* and *motion* (Howard, 1987). Quite often laypersons' concepts are very different from expert ones. People will say that gravity derives from air, that a bomb dropping from a moving plane will fall straight down, that antibiotics work on the human body rather than on bacteria, and that natural selection operates by changing an individual during its lifetime, who then passes that trait on to offspring (Howard, 1987). These "misconceptions" often greatly resist change. People hold them because they seem to derive directly from experience and indeed may have been held by scientists in previous decades. Howard (1992) reviews more evidence for the above general view.

A Taxonomy of Concept Types

People may hold many types of information about a category. Some obvious questions then are what types concepts typically consist of and what factors determine whether a given individual represents a particular category with a particular type or types. Howard (1992) proposed a large-scale taxonomy of concept types. The taxonomy has over thirty types and will only be described briefly here.

The major dimension is nonmetaphorical/metaphorical/mixed metaphorical and nonmetaphorical. The notion of a metaphorical concept comes from Lakoff and Johnson (1980). They argued that some very complex concepts may be partly defined by metaphorically projecting one or more other concepts. For instance, the concept of *time* may be learned by projecting a spatial metaphor. *Time* is conceived of as a line with future in front and past behind, as evidenced by use of *long* for both length and duration. Concepts such as *mind* may be defined by several metaphors: a container ("I cannot get that tune out of my mind"), a brittle object ("His mind just snapped"), and a machine ("My mind is not working today"). *Anger* may be partially understood by such metaphors as heat ("He turned red with anger") and volcano ("He exploded with rage"). In the taxonomy, metaphorical concepts are based on such metaphors while nonmetaphorical ones are not. Mixed concepts combine the two types (e.g., a defining feature set and a metaphor). Other types are exemplar and idealization concepts.

Many categories may be represented by one or more of these types, and the type used may change with experience. For example, a child initially might represent the category of fathers with a single exemplar (her own), then shift to characteristic features (a male of a certain age who lives in a house with children and maybe a wife), and finally shift to one based on the abstract biological defining feature.

Concept Learning

Concepts may be learned in many different ways. Some ways are through instruction, through abstraction from one or more instances, through hypothesis testing, by processing existing knowledge, by explanation-based learning, and by memorizing exemplars (see Howard, 1987). These ways and others may be combined in a given instance.

Why People Learn the Concepts That They Do

An oft-asked question is why people hold some concepts and not others. One reason is that some concepts are innate, examples being *blue* and *red*. However, given that a set of stimuli can be partitioned into a virtually infinite number of different categories, why do people learn some concepts and not others? There are doubtless many reasons. First, some things are so obvious to human senses that people are likely to form a concept of them, such as *sun* and *star*. Second, people are likely to form concepts that are useful, solve problems, allow useful inferences, and promote their well-being. Concepts such as *poison* and *predator* are so useful that people are likely to learn them but not useless concepts like *bush with pinstripes*. Third, many concepts are explicitly taught. A person is induced to form an individual concept of a given expert concept that the culture deems important, even if the individual does not. An example for a student would be *ion* and *subatomic particle*. Lakoff (1987) gives the example of an Australian aborigine tribe with a cultural concept representing a category that contains women, fire, and dangerous things. Members of that culture are induced to learn it. Fourth, some concepts may be acquired because existing knowledge strongly predisposes a person to learn them. Theories about the world (described later) affect what can be acquired. For instance, an African tribe has a single category for misfortunes; members do not distinguish between accidental and inflicted misfortunes because their theory of the world holds that all misfortunes are due to witchcraft. Westerners hold other theories about the world and so form two concepts instead of one.

KNOWLEDGE STRUCTURES

Concepts are functional units that can be interrelated to form larger knowledge structures such as taxonomies and schemas. For instance, a schema such as *face* consists of several component concepts (*eyes, nose,* etc.), which themselves consist of concepts. A taxonomy (such as of animals) consists of such component concepts as *mammal, reptile,* and *bird.* A complication is that each conceptual structure can be seen as a schema or a concept, depending on one's purposes at the time (Howard, 1992; Skemp, 1979). Here is a brief description of some major structures consisting of concepts.

Principles

A principle consists of two or more interrelated concepts. Examples are "Evergreen trees do not shed leaves in autumn," "Coup d'etats are more likely to occur in nations where the government is distant from the people," and basic scientific laws such as Boyle's or Ohm's. The simplest type of principle is a basic proposition.

Taxonomies and Partonomies

As is well known, a taxonomy is a structure in which concepts are interrelated by class inclusion. A partonomy is similar except that the relation is part-whole. A simple example is human body–arms,–legs,–torso,–head, and so on. The latter concepts are parts of the body and themselves subsume component concepts. Concepts may be interrelated into much more complex structures, such as *food chain.*

Taxonomies are very important. They allow people to interrelate things by tracing through the structure (e.g., to see how *seed* and *horse* are related), they allow inferences (that a canary has skin), and they allow one to make sense of phenomena. Children start learning taxonomies early, and as mentioned, taxonomies are of fundamental importance in science.

A final useful distinction is between an expert knowledge structure and an individual one, analogous to the expert/individual concept distinction made above. The expert one is defined as the most developed in existence, and an individual one as the one that a given individual actually has of that expert structure. The latter may be nonexistent in some individuals (e.g., many Trobriand islanders for *subatomic particle*), fragmentary, or virtually identical (if the individual is an expert). Of course, an individual's structure may be inconsistent with the expert structure.

Taxonomies and partonomies may have a basic level, a level of abstraction that is commonly used for thinking and talking about the structure's referents (Mervis and Rosch, 1981; Howard, 1987). Consider the lifeform taxonomy. One could use categories at various levels of abstraction for many purposes. One could call a given dog a beagle, mammal, animal, lifeform, and even an entity. But when speaking of a particular dog, one typically uses the abstraction level of *dog*. Saying, "Here comes a four-year-old, black, Arizona-born beagle" or "Here comes a black entity" would sound silly in most circumstances. One level seems too specific and the other too abstract. The oft-used level of *dog* is called the basic level. Concepts on the basic level often are the first that children acquire, and their taxonomic knowledge may grow upward and downward from there (Anglin, 1977). Mervis and Rosch (1981) also argue that the basic level is the most abstract level for which one can visualize a prototype. However, experts may sometimes use a more specific basic level than nonexperts because they need to make finer distinctions; for example, marine biologists of *fish* and wine tasters of *wine*.

Domains

The term *knowledge domain* has several different meanings but here will be defined as a relatively circumscribed area of knowledge. Examples are the domains of chess, quantum physics, courtship and marriage customs, bacterial diseases, and dinosaurs. Domains can be very large (e.g., physics) or very small (e.g., sewing) and a domain itself may consist of component domains. For example, physics divides into particle physics, solid state physics, and so on. Some domain boundaries are clear (e.g., chess), but others may shade into each other. An individual may know nothing, a little, or a lot about a given domain. Again, one can distinguish between an expert's knowledge of a domain and a given individual's knowledge of one. Expert knowledge of a domain evidently consists largely of interrelated concepts (see Chapter 5).

Domains may differ from each other in several ways. They may be structured differently and may contain concepts of quite different types. For instance, domain knowledge of artifacts and living things seems to differ (Keil, 1986; Atran, 1989). Children see objects in the latter domain as natural kinds with an underlying "essence" but not those in the former. Knowledge of some domains may be innate or at least strongly affected by innate predispositions to learn certain things (e.g., colors, human nonverbal communication), while others are not (e.g., quantum physics). The types of concept that a given domain has may differ. Mathematical concepts are typically well defined and are clearly related to others (at least for experts), while those in art and history are much more ill defined, such as *surrealism, impressionist artwork, revolution,* and *totalitarian society*. Atran (1989) quite plausibly argues that different domains may require different sorts of processing of information. For example, chess playing requires looking for familiar patterns, applying domain-specific principles (such as "push passed pawns"), and calculating myriad variations of possible moves. Art requires different processes. Some strategies that work well in one domain may not work in others, though some general strategies may work well in most or all (such as chunking and means-ends analysis).

There is much evidence that knowledge in LTM is encapsulated in domains. First, there is a good logical argument. Doing so is an efficient way to deal with a domain. The most striking illustration comes from early efforts to build artificially intelligent computers. No one could build a system that solved problems well in many domains. The proficient programs are expert systems that use much knowledge of a narrow domain. Second, some neuropsychological patients have brain damage that affects only one domain. Warrington and McCarthy (1988) describe a patient with a selective impairment for names of artifacts, and Sartori and Job (1988) describe one with a deficit for names of living things. Third, studies of prodigies and experts show that skill is typically domain-specific (see Chapter 5). Few people become expert in more than one complex domain (such as chess), and strong performance in one domain usually does not transfer to others. Prodigies typically excel in only one domain. The famous chess prodigy Samuel Reshevsky could beat most adults at an early age but showed no other strong talents and a below-average IQ score. Chi and Koeske (1983) describe a four-year-old with proficiency in the single domain of dinosaurs, who performed well at tasks in this domain.

How do people acquire knowledge of a new domain? People often start by using domain-general strategies (Anderson, 1990), ones that work in most or all domains. Examples are means-ends analysis and general strategies such as "Note important concepts and relations." Later they may learn domain-specific strategies. A second way is to use analogies from one or more other well-known domains. An analogy projects knowledge of a familiar domain onto an unfamiliar one to highlight similarities or predict aspects of it (Clement and Gentner, 1991). For example, the domain of electricity may be learned about partly by projecting a water flow analogy, or the domain of atoms by the miniature solar system analogy. Some features and relations are likely to apply but others are not, and a person must learn which. People use several constraints to do so (see Clement and Gentner, 1991). Analogies vary in quality and never fit exactly, of course. The failure of an analogy's predictions may spur further learning.

Indeed, analogy use is pervasive in human learning (Keane, 1988). The language is full of analogies and their cousins, metaphors. Proverbs in one domain are frequently applied by analogy to many others (e.g., "He who has only a hammer sees nails everywhere"). Analogies are used extensively in education. For example, fractions are often taught with a pie analogy. The history of science is full of examples of new knowledge gathering about a domain being guided by a useful analogy. The computer analogy is used extensively to understand the mind and even how DNA works.

Knowledge of a domain also develops as a person goes from being a novice to an expert at it. The expert domain may develop with time, too. New concepts may be formed, deleted, or rearranged, and the whole domain structure may change in a conceptual revolution.

CONSTRAINTS ON KNOWLEDGE

There need to be constraints on what knowledge can be acquired. A given situation may have countless possible things to learn, and a learner may only acquire useful knowledge if biased to (Medin et al., 1990). And some things cannot be readily learned without constraints. As Keil (1990) put it, "No known learning procedure can learn rules or categories without constraints." One example is from Quine (1960). He asked how someone could learn a foreign language by interrogating a native speaker. The learner points to a rabbit and the speaker says, "Gavagai." Most persons would assume that *gavagai* means "rabbit," but the word could mean a virtually infinite number of things; undetached rabbit part, a species found only in that glen, any object that is pointed to, and so on. Without shared constraints on word meanings, it would be impossible to learn a language. A second example is from chess. A given position may have many possible legal moves and an exponentially increasing number of possibilities with subsequent moves. Yet a chess expert typically considers just two or three (Holding, 1985). His or her knowledge severely constrains what moves are examined and what is learned about them. Chess-playing computers still lack that knowledge and must play by exhaustively searching countless possibilities.

Several questions arise. What types of constraints are there, how much latitude do they allow, and is all knowledge acquisition constrained? Is *constraint* the right word? Would better terms be *predispositions, enablers,* and *permitters*?

Types of Constraint

There are several types of constraint, not yet all enumerated or interrelated into a taxonomy. First, some constraints are genetically programmed, examples being the type of object a duckling is likely to imprint on and a human to associate with fear. Markman (1990) lists some constraints on the meanings that children are likely to assign to a new word. They are predisposed to associate words with whole objects (rabbit instead of paw for *gavagai*). Children expect words to be related taxonomically instead of thematically and for each object to have just one label (e.g., an object cannot be both a chair and a table). This of course does not always hold, as Markman points out. Beagles are dogs and animals. Another constraint is that they expect words to refer to object categories. Spelke (1990) lists some constraints on object perception. Infants divide perceptual arrays into units that move as wholes, that move separately, and that tend to maintain their size and shape during motions.

A second type of constraint is maturational (Newport, 1990). A child's developing nervous system may allow more things to be learned or things to be more easily learned at older ages (see Chapter 6). For instance, speed of processing and working memory capacity increase with maturation.

Some constraints may be learned. When one acquires knowledge in a domain, that knowledge may constrain what more can be learned. For instance, constraints from religious knowledge prevent some people accepting the theory of evolution as knowledge. Albert Einstein deeply held the assumption that the universe is static, and when his general theory of relativity predicted it is expanding, he could not accept it. He introduced a mathematical "fudge factor" to stop the theory so predicting. His deeply held beliefs about the causal nature of the universe also meant he later could not accept the strange account of physical reality that quantum mechanics gives. The history of science is full of cases in which scientists rejected new findings because they were inconsistent with existing scientific knowledge. An example from psychology is early work on taste aversion learning, initially rejected because it did not fit the equipotentiality assumption (Garcia, 1981).

Various studies have looked at how prior theories about the world affect and constrain what can be acquired (e.g., Carey, 1985; Murphy and Medin, 1985). The term *theory* in this context is vague, however. A better word might be *principle*. Knowledge of many domains is built on first principles, which constrain what is acquired (Gelman, 1990). She says that some such principles are general (e.g., that all events have causes) and some are specific (that animals move by themselves but artifacts do not).

Here are some examples. The psychiatric taxonomy, at least in its early versions, is based on a major underlying principle derived from a physical disease metaphor. The idea was that mental disorders are analogous to physical ones and have signs, symptoms, time courses, treatments, and so on. This principle partly constrains what concepts are formed and how they are structured. Gelman (1990) argued that children's developing biological knowledge is based on first principles, such as that living things move on their own, have structured insides, and so on. These constrain further knowledge and inferences. Children will say, for example, that mammals can go up a hill by themselves but statues cannot. Another example is the tale of cargo cultists of the South Pacific in World War II. Islanders observed that cargo-laden planes sometimes landed in airstrips and believed the planes were sent by the spirits. They built their own airstrips, with huts like those they had seen, and waited patiently but futilely for planes to arrive. Westerners' knowledge of how such goods came to be there would prevent them acquiring such beliefs as the cargo cultists, whose own beliefs about the spirit world predisposed them to acquire them. Interestingly, the islanders could not be dissuaded from their beliefs, even when taken to western cities and shown how goods were manufactured.

This notion of constraint by first principles may also explain why some concepts seem more natural than others; why, to quote Komatsu (1992), the category "things that are either more than a second long or weigh less than a ton" seems unnatural while "things that have feathers and fly" seems natural. The latter category would be more useful in daily life but also derives from underlying principles about lifeforms and physics (that feathers aid flight, for instance). No underlying principles would suggest why the two things belong in the category in the former example.

An important principle of knowledge acquisition therefore seems to underlie a variety of phenomena. The principle is that what can be acquired is constrained by various factors, and it can explain why fields such as quantum mechanics and set theory are so hard to learn about (they go against natural constraints), why many students have "misconceptions," why many scientists have trouble accepting some new ideas, and why things such as a native language and the rules of social behavior are relatively easy to learn.

---------------------------- **5** ----------------------------

Skills and Expertise

This chapter surveys the areas of skills and skill learning and the study of expertise. The two are closely related, because an expert is someone with a highly developed level of skill in some domain. Skills involve procedural knowledge. Some highly over-learned skills, such as typing, may consist almost entirely of procedural knowledge while others, such as computer programming and carrying out scientific research, involve a mix of procedural and declarative knowledge.

SKILLS

Definition of Skill

The term *skill* is a bit vague, with several technical and everyday meanings. Indeed, some researchers suggest banning it. However, Holding (1989) offers a useful general definition: a skill is a co-ordination of perception and action. For example, a skilled typist looks at written words and reproduces that text easily with rapid, deft strokes. A skilled tennis player perceives his or her own position and the opponent's position and posture, anticipates the likely direction of a returning ball, and acts appropriately.

Virtually every human activity has been called a skill, even thinking (Bartlett, 1932). Traditionally, the study of skills in psychology has focused on relatively "simple" ones such as typing and tracking (which is continuously co-ordinating sight and a compensatory response, as in steering a car between lines in a lane). However, the term *skill* also is applied to very complex activities involving the co-ordination of many perceptions and actions, such as reading and chess playing. Researchers also speak of "social skills," which involve perceiving others' needs, desires, traits, and so on and acting appropriately.

Performance of a given activity is skilled when it meets several criteria (e.g., Holding, 1989). First, the performance gains a goal with a minimal use of time and energy and so appears almost effortless. Examples are a person easily tossing a basketball into a hoop, a bus driver adroitly navigating through heavy city traffic while conversing, and an intelligence analyst readily identifying a missile silo from grainy satellite photos. Second, performance is almost errorless and further practice improves it very little. Third, performance is nearly automatic. It requires little or no conscious attention. Fourth, the individual can readily focus on what is important to performance and ignore what is not.

A useful distinction is between the performance and the learning of a skill. The latter is the long and often difficult acquisition process, and the former is the actual execution of a skill. Performance can be affected by fatigue, drugs, aging, stress, and handicap; indeed, the breakdown of a skill due to such factors may provide clues to help understand it. Learning may be affected by many factors, too, such as those above and spacing of practice, intelligence, and so on.

Importance of Skills

Skills are very important in daily life, and it is a very adaptive characteristic of humans and other species that they can be acquired. Everyone has a wide range of skills, from largely innate ones such as walking, to highly prepared ones such as speaking a native language, to unprepared ones such as reading, driving, and playing bridge. Some skills are so important that most citizens of technological societies acquire them (such as reading and driving), while others are less crucial and are so difficult to learn that few do (such as computer programming and doing scientific research). People vary widely in their ability to perform some skills. Some chess players attain a high skill level, others a moderate level, and some never get much beyond the "woodpusher" stage, for various reasons.

Much everyday human learning involves skill acquisition and improvement. Schools teach many basic ones such as doing arithmetic, more complex ones such as reading, and "abstract thinking skills" such as reasoning. Industries train employees in such skills as adeptly using new technology, performing the tasks of new jobs, and dealing with customers. The military trains skills such as basic weapon use, battlefield planning, logistics, and so on.

History of the Study of Skills

The scientific study of skills began in the Nineteenth Century. Holding (1989) lists a few studies of motor memory carried out in 1880, of Morse code use in 1897, of repetitive timed movements in 1899, and in 1903 a study that examined whether a skill learned on one hand transfers to the other (it does). But research was relatively sparse until World War II, when psychologists suddenly faced many practical problems for which the then-current behavioristic theories were inadequate. They needed to learn how to quickly train pilots, design easy-to-use equipment, keep a radar operator alert for long periods, and so on. There was much interest in the skill of tracking, which is involved in many military activities such as anti-aircraft gun firing. To help solve these problems, psychologists borrowed ideas from engineering. One idea was the notion of a skilled person being like a servo-mechanism, who acts and then adjusts actions according to feedback, like a thermostat. A later such development was the notion of a human as a limited-capacity information processor (Broadbent, 1958), also borrowed from engineering. These analogies migrated into the rest of psychology, later helping to dethrone behaviorism. Ironically, however, the skills area later became more behavioral itself; information processing ideas only became widely used in the 1970s and 1980s.

The skills area has been a subfield largely separate from the mainstream study of learning and memory. Until recently, most textbooks in learning and memory and in cognitive psychology barely mentioned the study of skills and even such well-established and important generalizations as the power law of practice (described later). However, the skills subfield and the mainstream increasingly interact and eventually may completely integrate.

Today much is known about skills and skill learning, but there is no widely accepted general theory. The subject matter is very complex. Researchers in the field deal with such issues as how skills are organized and learned, what role feedback has, and how much transfer occurs and in what circumstances. A major practical issue is how to teach particular skills.

Some Types and Dimensions of Skills

Human skills vary along many dimensions and fall into various categories. There is no universally agreed-upon taxonomy. However, there are some useful categories and dimensions. A useful classification is into perceptual, motor, and cognitive skills. In practice, the boundaries between them are vague and most actual skills have elements of each, varying in their relative proportion (Holding, 1989). Perceptual skills involve no complicated actions. They involve detecting whether a given stimulus occurred, for instance identifying a complex stimulus in noise. A simple example is radar screen monitoring, where the task is to determine whether a blip occurred and, if so, what object it represents (e.g., bird or plane). Howe (1988) describes a technician with the uncanny perceptual skill of identifying vague objects in a video game screen. He had thousands of hours of practice at preparing visual stimuli for experiments and could identify stimuli on the screen accurately in about one third the time it took others.

Motor skills involve body movements. These can be relatively gross, as in weightlifting and high-jumping, or very fine as in complex ballet routines and the work of skilled sculptors. Motor skills can be serial (involving a fixed sequence of actions as in a dance routine) or not, discrete (with a distinct start and end, perhaps repeated again and again, as pitching a baseball) or continuous (as in swimming or tracking) (Schmidt, 1991).

Cognitive skills involve complex decision-making; much thinking may go on between initial perception and resulting action (Colley, 1989). Examples are reading, disease diagnosis, and chess-playing. Each has perceptual input (a printed page, a set of symptoms, and a series of board positions, respectively) and actions in response (deciphering the text's meaning, diagnosing measles or some other ailment, and playing rook takes knight). Much thought may go on in between. Some cognitive skills are quite complex. For example, metacognitive skills involve the ability to monitor and control one's own information processing. Problem-solving skills can be complex, too, and may be domain-independent or -specific. Welford (1976) noted that most important human skills are cognitive ones, but they have been extensively researched only in the last two decades or so (Colley, 1989).

Colley and Beach (1989) and Holding (1989) list some major dimensions of skills, which overlap with some of the above categories. First, skills can be placed along a perceptual-to-motor continuum, with, say, radar scanning at one end and weightlifting at the other. Playing a video game such as "Space Invaders" would be somewhere in between. A second dimension is open versus closed. Open skills involve continuously gathering information from the environment, while closed skills involve little or none. Open skills depend heavily on external feedback, while closed ones do not. For example, playing tennis requires continually monitoring ball position and speed and the opponent's position, intentions, and fatigue level. One's own actions are continually adjusted accordingly. Lifting weights or executing an Olympic dive requires little or no attention to feedback other than that from one's own body. Somewhere in between is a skill like baseball pitching. A third dimension is controlled versus automatic. The former involves a skill whose performance takes much attention (as in chess-playing), while the latter involves a skill that takes little (e.g., typing when highly skilled). Performance of a skill at the early stages of learning may be controlled but with much practice may become automatic. A final dimension is simple to complex. Simple skills involve uncomplicated actions, such as pushing a button to signal the presence of a radar blip. Complex skills involve complex actions, such as playing a violin or executing a difficult ballet sequence. Holding (1989) proposed a classification system of skills based on some of the above dimensions. He placed two broad dimensions (simple to complex and perceptual to motor) as a pair of orthogonal axes and proposed that various skills can be located at points in the four quadrants. At the origin is sailing, at the extreme of simple on the axis is sorting, and at a point between the extremes of perceptual and complex is air traffic controlling.

Analyzing Skilled Performance

Much research has investigated the structure of skilled performance. Various experimental methods have been used, and as mentioned, study of the breakdown of skilled performance under stress, fatigue, sleep loss, or drugs can give clues about the skill's organization. It turns out that perceptual-motor skills are very complex. Many actions may have to be co-ordinated in time and space, and the execution may depend on much external and internal feedback. It is far beyond this book's scope to delve deeply into this complicated topic but I will illustrate the complexity of a seemingly simple skill, typing. Salthouse (1991) argues that typing is a good candidate for the study of skills because the actions required fall into discrete categories (keystrokes) and the skill involves an interaction between perceptual, motor, and cognitive processes. The task itself is easy to describe and errors are easy to detect. There is no generally accepted model of typing performance, however, though several models have been proposed (Gentner, 1988).

Salthouse notes that several robust phenomena of typing constrain models of the skill. First, skilled typists perform very quickly what is essentially a choice reaction-time task. This suggests that the processing operations involved overlap in time; they seem too fast to occur in strict sequence. Second, typing is much slower than reading and typing speed does not relate to understanding of material typed. So reading and typing involve different processes. Third, typing speed is about the same for random words and meaningful text, but it slows down progressively as the material degrades from actual words to random letter assortments. This suggests that the typist's unit is at least several letters long. Indeed, when material is shown one letter at a time (so that when one letter is typed, the next appears), performance slows down dramatically. This suggests that typists look several letters ahead of the one actually being typed. Research also shows that typists apparently commit a finger to a particular character about three characters ahead of the current keystroke; excellent typists may commit to seven characters ahead. Errors typically fall into several distinct categories. One is transpositions, whereby two letters are reversed (*teh* instead of *the*), and another is substitutions (*thr* instead of *the*). Many errors involve adjacent keys.

Salthouse (1986) proposed a fairly broad four-component model of typing, which gives some notion of the task's complexity and how skilled typists manage to perform it. The first part is input, which involves converting text on a page into chunks (letter groupings, which Salthouse suggests are smaller than a word). The second is parsing, decomposing the chunks into ordinal strings of characters. Third is translation, converting the characters into movement specifications. Fourth is execution, actually moving the hand and fingers to strike the keys. The skilled typist has a representation of the keyboard linked to the appropriate movements for each character. Salthouse also suggests that increasing skill involves circumventing normal human processing limitations. For instance, typists expand eye-hand span to process up to seven characters in advance and learn to overlap processing of successive keystrokes. Thus a discrete serial task can be converted into a continuous one. Adams (1987) reviews much more work on the performance of such motor skills as typing.

Skills often are hierarchically organized. A wide range of discrete movements may be organized into units through chunking. For example, a skill such as hitting a golf ball may be composed of many discrete small action units organized into larger ones and into the overall swing. Different functions and properties may be assigned to different levels of the organization. Researchers also have proposed a variety of representational concepts for the knowledge underlying skills. For instance, the notion of a motor program dates back to Karl Lashley (Summers, 1989). The idea is that the brain stores a program that contains all information needed for movement patterning. Once elicited, the sequence is smoothly and precisely executed without requiring peripheral feedback, like a computer program or a fixed action pattern that runs to completion. The schema notion is also used (Newell, 1991). An individual may have an idealized version of the movement class with interrelated slots organized in a certain way. The slots can be filled with specific actions in an instantiation.

Finally, task complexity relates to skilled performance in a way that can be described with a simple equation known as Hick's law (Hick, 1952). To illustrate, say that a subject must quickly decide which of several light bulbs has just flashed. As the number of bulbs that could be flashed increases, time to decide rises as follows:

$$T = k \log (n + 1)$$

Where T is time to respond, k is a constant, and n is the number of alternatives (in this case, bulbs). Another version is:

$$T = k \log (n \, C/E + 1)$$

Where E is a measure of the strength of each stimulus (in this case, a bulb flash) and C is a measure of the requirements for speed versus accuracy.

Skill Learning

Much research has tackled the difficult question of how skills are actually acquired, how humans manage to learn the complex co-ordinations of many perceptions and actions involved in complicated skills. Several issues concern the exact course of skill learning and whether it is broadly the same for all skills, the role of feedback, and when and to what extent transfer occurs.

Some similar learning processes seem to be involved with many skills. One is learning to attend to relevant cues, to sort out wheat from chaff. Chess players learn to see the few good moves on the board, novice car drivers to attend to the car's controls and the important objects ahead, such as traffic signs and lights, other cars, and road conditions. With many skills, the right movements must be acquired. The learner must first acquire the ability to perform them and then to co-ordinate them. For instance, the novice driver learns to depress the clutch and the brake pedal to the right level, to shift gears, to turn the steering wheel the right distance for a given turn, and so on, and then to co-ordinate these actions. For very complex skills, many muscle units need to be co-ordinated. Chunking is ubiquitous in skill learning. Drivers learn to group actions into larger units, chess players to group pieces into perceptual chunks, and satellite photo interpreters to group fragments into patterns.

The Three-Stage Model. The very broad pattern of skill learning seems to be remarkably similar for a wide range of perceptual, motor, and cognitive skills. Fitts and Posner (1967) proposed that skill learning occurs in three stages (which later became the basis for more specific models). In practice, the stages overlap; it is often hard to distinguish where one begins and the next ends. Learners may go through them at a rate that depends on the nature of the skill and other factors such as intelligence.

In the first (cognitive) stage, the learner gathers facts needed to perform the task and tries to understand what is required. The needed declarative knowledge may be taken from an instructor or a manual, or be worked out by analogy and/or trial and error, as in learning to use a computer program without any help. The learner determines what actions are needed, their sequence (if any), and where to look for feedback. An example is learning to swing a golf club. First the learner needs to learn how to hold the club, what postures to adopt in a swing, where the club should touch the ball, and so on. A novice chess player learns the moves of the pieces, the goals of each player, various other rules, and some simple strategies.

In the second (associative) stage, the learner actually tries out the movements (or looks or listens for things if it is a purely perceptual skill). He or she practices the task and gets feedback on actions. Practice and feedback are very important. No one can ride a bicycle perfectly with just declarative knowledge. A cognitive skill such as using a word processor requires much trying out of actions and an effort to grasp how the machine works. During this practice phase, declarative knowledge is converted into procedural knowledge (Anderson, 1987), though it still is not clear exactly how. With extensive practice, declarative knowledge may drop out from use and be forgotten. For instance, a novice driver may initially use self-directions ("Now, to change gears, I push the clutch and . . . ") but after much practice no longer needs them. Indeed, eventually the learner may have little or no declarative knowledge of how a task is done. A skilled typist, asked where p or c is on the keyboard, typically goes through the motions of typing them and watches where the fingers go. Fine performers are sometimes poor teachers of driving, guitar playing, or using a word processor, because they are no longer sure how they perform the task. The length of the associative phase depends on the task's complexity and how similar it is to others that the learner has mastered.

The third (autonomous) stage is the phase of high skill attainment. Actions are fast, smooth, effortless, accurate, and largely removed from awareness. Performance typically needs little conscious attention, so that the learner may be able to perform other tasks simultaneously (e.g., drive while conversing and listening to the radio). Over the course of learning, the learner may need to pay less and less attention to task demands. (However, some skills still require some conscious attention to perform, no matter how highly practiced, such as chess playing.) This ability to auto- mate performance, chunk components, and free up consciousness greatly improves human ability to deal with the environment. Skills when autono- mous also greatly resist forgetting. No one ever really forgets how to type or ride a bicycle. Some skills may deteriorate a bit more than others if not practiced, however. Concert pianists must practice many hours a day to keep their skills honed. However, many skills evidently deteriorate little. For example, Hill (1957) reported how he learned to type as a student at Columbia, did not touch a keyboard for twenty-five years, and then took just a day of practice to recover his previous typing speed.

The Power Law of Practice. The power law of practice is a relation over the learning period between time to perform a task and amount of practice. The amount of practice can be measured as time spent practicing or number of practice trials. The law is:

$$T = a P^{-b}$$

Where T is time to perform the task, P is the number of trials (or time spent practicing), and a and b are constants. The relation is represented graphi- cally in Figure 5.1. It shows that practice improves performance mostly in the early stages of learning and progressively less so with further trials. Continued practice eventually reaches a point of diminishing returns. However, performance still improves indefinitely, although at a very slow rate. The classic example is from a study of cigar factory workers who improved their speed of rolling cigars over ten years (Anderson, 1990).

The power law holds with many skills, such as mirror tracing, recalling facts, using a computer text editor, checking proofs, and playing solitaire

Figure 5.1
**The Relation between Practice and Performance that Constitutes the Power
Law of Practice**

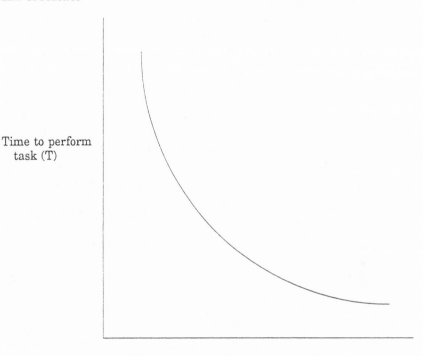

Time to perform
task (T)

Number of trials (P)

(Newell, 1990). Newell suggests that the relation holds because of chunking. The learner builds progressively larger chunks of actions, and their use improves performance. However, the chunks may become less useful with practice because the situations in which they are helpful occur less often. Newell simulated this idea with a computer system called SOAR, which learned by chunking and whose subsequent performance was consistent with the power law.

Some Variables That Affect Skill Learning. Many variables affect skill learning. One is timing of practice. Spaced practice (e.g., with rest and intervals between practice sessions) is typically more efficient than massed practice (one or a few long sessions). Anderson (1990) cites some illustrative studies. In one, learners acquired Morse code use as quickly with four hours of practice a day as did a group who practiced seven hours a day. In another study, retention of use of algebra rules was better after spaced practice than massed. Possible reasons are that fatigue and boredom may reduce attention in long sessions and that learning may need time to consolidate. Another variable is part/whole learning of actions. Is it better to learn a complex skill in parts and then practice the whole skill later or learn all actions at once? It apparently depends on the task. If the task requires much co-ordination of many actions for successful performance, it may be better to learn it as a whole. Anderson (1990) contrasts two studies that illustrate this point. In one, subjects learned to type simultaneously on two different typewriters, one hand on each. It was more efficient to learn to type on each one with a single hand and later integrate the two sets of actions. But for a superficially similar but far more complex task—playing the piano—it was better to learn to use both hands together. Mane et al. (1989) suggest that if some parts of a skill are much harder than others or there is too much knowledge to grasp initially, it may be best to learn the task in parts. They illustrated with skill at playing a certain video game.

Much work has investigated the role of feedback. There are several types of feedback, and Holding (1965) presented a simple taxonomy. It has two broad categories, intrinsic (generated by movements themselves) and artificial (e.g., feedback from an external source, such as someone saying that the learner has hit a target). Artificial divides into concurrent (feedback given continually during performance, as in tracking) and terminal (given at the end, as in learning whether a just-fired cruise missile has hit its target). Feedback is critical to skill learning and maintenance. It dramatically improves learning. Evidence is mixed as to whether learning can occur without external feedback (Salmoni, 1989). Some skills may rely mostly on intrinsic feedback (such as a dive sequence), with artificial feedback given only at the end. Some skills depend on feedback throughout (e.g., tracking).

Anderson's Model of Skill Learning. Anderson (1983) proposed a large-scale model of skill learning, partly descended from Anderson and Bower's (1973) HAM model. Newell (1990) hails it as the first unified theory of cognition. It has evolved over the years and only parts have actually been implemented as a computer program. The version called ACT* has an architecture consisting of a declarative knowledge memory, a procedural knowledge memory, and a working memory that operates like a blackboard. Declarative knowledge is represented in a semantic network, and procedural knowledge is represented as production rules. A highly practiced skill is represented as production rules that fire according to given conditions. Skill learning proceeds as in the three phases given by Fitts and Posner. Initially, task-relevant declarative knowledge is gathered and stored by using domain-independent methods such as means-ends analysis and analogical reasoning. Then knowledge is compiled, converted from declarative semantic net-formatted representations to production rules, by several major processes. One is proceduralization, which is creating specific production rules and reducing the amount of declarative knowledge that needs to be held in working memory. Another is composition, which is collapsing several production rules into a single one (a form of chunking). A learning mechanism used in the autonomous phase is tuning, whereby productions are altered slightly to fine-tune the learner to the environment. Anderson lists two quite familiar examples of tuning. Generalization is increasing the generality of a rule to cover more stimuli, so that more *if* conditions trigger a *then* response. Discrimination is reducing the number of *if* conditions that trigger a given *then* response. A third tuning process is subsumption, building new schemas out of old ones or elaborating existing schemas to apply to new things. ACT* was altered to a model called PUPS (Anderson, 1989). PUPS uses more knowledge, can generalize by analogy, and can make causal inferences.

Anderson has applied the ACT* framework to help understand several complex skills; notably geometry proof problem-solving and learning to program in the computer language Lisp. Studies with these skills show that the model is a good fit to how subjects acquire them. For instance, Anderson (1982) described a subject who learned two geometry postulates declaratively and used them to solve a series of problems. According to a protocol analysis, eventually he could apply the postulates virtually automatically. A similar shift was shown in learning Lisp programming. Indeed, Anderson set up a computer tutor based on ACT* to teach Lisp at Carnegie-Mellon University, one which teaches well but not quite as well as a human tutor.

However, ACT* has its problems. Gilhooly and Green (1989) note that it has no executive processes directing the overall system and cannot easily account for the invention of new actions. However, it is a useful framework for thinking about skills learning.

Holland et al.'s Induction Paradigm. Holland et al. (1986) proposed a general framework for understanding skill learning that is based on production rules. In the system, knowledge is represented as one of three types of rule: empirical (derived from experience), inferential (derived from altering empirical rules), and system operation rules (which function like an executive, like metacognitive rules). The last may, for example, be used to resolve a conflict over which of several competing rules should fire at a particular time. The system works in parallel. Given a stimulus, a number of rules may be activated and then the strongest one may be selected and used to decide how to respond.

Transfer of Skill

Transfer of skill occurs when knowledge of one skill affects learning and/or performance of another. Positive transfer is where the knowledge helps, and negative transfer is where it hinders. Negative transfer is relatively rare. The usual example cited is the einstellung phenomenon, in which a person solves a series of problems with one strategy and then takes much longer to solve a problem that needs a different tack than someone who comes to it fresh. Transfer can be measured in several ways. One way is savings in time or trials to learn a second skill to some criterion, and another is performance on a second, related task. For example, one may train subjects to fly on an aircraft simulator and then test their performance in flying an actual aircraft. However, as Hammerton (1989) points out, the latter method is sometimes a poor measure of transfer, as performance may improve radically after initial problems in adjusting to the second task.

Transfer is very important. Life would be very difficult if it did not occur. One would have to learn to write again with every new pen or pencil, for example. There was an anecdotal report about a neuropsychological patient who could drive his own car but could not transfer this skill to other cars. Transfer is very important in practical training situations. Trainers may ask how much transfer does occur from aircraft simulators, for example, or to what extent educational programs that try to train general thinking skills and learning strategies really promote transfer beyond the training stimuli. Belief that they do was once widespread. The old formal discipline theory, now discredited, advocated training in the classics as a way to strengthen the mind generally. There are many such general programs, examples being Edward de Bono's lateral thinking programs and Reuven Feuerstein's Instrumental Enrichment program (e.g., Gilhooly and Green, 1989). Skills learned in such programs may transfer to some extent (see Gilhooly and Green, 1989).

A generalization from much research is that transfer does indeed occur often, but it is typically small and restricted to tasks quite similar to those trained on. For example, transfer of motor skills is usually small and occurs when tasks have common movements (e.g., tennis and squash) and similar strategies (Schmidt, 1991). However, there is little or no transfer of abilities such as speed of performance of some task (Schmidt, 1991). An archetypal example is Chase and Ericsson's (1982) subject who learned to increase his digit-span to eighty. This skill did not transfer to letters at all; his letter span was just seven. When mentally retarded children are taught a learning strategy such as rehearsal, their performance often improves but does not transfer beyond the training stimuli (Howard, 1991). The expertise literature (see next section) shows that expertise rarely transfers from one domain to another. For instance, Gick and Holyoak (1987) found that subjects rarely transfer solution methods across domains. For instance, subjects given the famous two rays problem (in which one has to destroy a tumor without damaging surrounding tissue and does so by concentrating weak X-rays at the tumor site) rarely apply the general solution methods to another domain such as war. The method might be applied by concentrating two attacking forces at a particular defensive point, for example. Most subjects fail to transfer the solution method even after doing the tumor problem first. However, Holyoak (1991) cites some evidence that explicit instruction may help people to transfer.

It is still unclear why transfer occurs when it does. Relatively little work has been done on transfer in the last two decades (Salmoni, 1989), but some old notions are still used as explanations. For instance, Thorndike (1903) proposed the still-used identical elements view. Learning task A can help on task B only if there are common elements of performance (e.g., holding a tennis racket like a squash racket). However, relatively little is known about transfer and the stage of skill learning at which it occurs when it does occur (Salmoni, 1989).

EXPERTISE

In everyday parlance, an expert is a person with a highly developed skill in some domain. Example domains are engine repair, wine, hunting, soccer, Japanese history, military science, and even the study of expertise. Almost everyone becomes an expert in some domains, such as speaking a native language and dealing well with others. Relatively few do in other domains, such as bridge and quantum mechanics. Even then, some domains have many more experts than others. Bridge and typing have a lot while Icelandic studies has few. An archetypal example of a rare expert is Chase and Ericsson's subject mentioned above.

Experts are very important in daily life. They are essential in running a technological society, which relies on them to do many tasks: to diagnose and repair ailments of humans, animals, and machines; to run large organizations; to build and operate complex machinery; to teach children; and to forecast trends. Quine (1977) points out that we rely on experts for much of our categorization; for instance, of metals into exemplars and nonexemplars of gold and jewels, and houses and artworks into monetary value categories. Of course, expert systems now can do some of these expert functions. Performing such tasks well requires much experience and knowledge, and no one has the time to acquire and keep up with expanding knowledge in more than a few complex domains. Indeed, it takes an estimated ten years to become an expert in a complex domain, and so most people could only become proficient in one or two domains unless extremely motivated (Howard, 1991).

The study of expertise has become a very active subfield in recent years, for several reasons. First, analysis of expert knowledge and performance can cast much light on the nature and learning of skills. For example, the study of pattern recognition in chess experts mentioned in Chapter 1 shows that chess expertise partly depends on learning and using recurring patterns. Studies of expert typists show that they look further ahead than novices, which suggests that typing processes run in parallel. The study of expertise can help show how knowledge develops over a long period in interaction with the environment. Second, there are good practical reasons. Much education aims to turn students into experts, or at least put them on the path to expertise. One can use a model of expert knowledge in a domain as a goal of instruction. An example of this approach is the "intelligent tutor" used to teach Lisp programming mentioned in the last section.

Some major questions in the field are as follows. First, in what ways do experts and novices in some domain differ in their skills and their knowledge organization? What is the nature and structure of their knowledge? Under what conditions might expertise transfer from one domain to another? How does expertise develop? What factors push it along, and what is the pattern of development? Are there distinct stages, for example? Finally, are there principles of expertise common to most or all domains? Already, there is a reasonable picture of the likely answers to these and other questions.

What Is an Expert?

Unfortunately, it is not always clear who exactly is an expert in a given domain. An everyday definition (say, someone who knows a lot and adeptly solves problems in a domain) does not always help determine this. A more technical definition is someone with good declarative and procedural knowledge in a domain that can be readily accessed and used and who has superior self-monitoring and self-regulation skills (Chi et al., 1988). It is still much harder to identify experts in some domains than others. In chess and tennis it is easy. Each game has an international ranking list with numerical ratings based on current performance. Strong performers earn titles, such as grandmaster in chess. But it is harder to determine and rank experts in physics. Should one use possession of an advanced degree, number of publications, or prestige of employing institution (e.g., Salthouse, 1991)? Even then, persons who rank high on such criteria may still perform relatively poorly in their domain. In complex domains such as economic forecasting, persons labeled as experts often perform little better than novices and worse than simple linear mathematical models (Camerer and Johnson, 1991). This definitional problem crops up in studies of expertise. Different experimenters use different definitions and selection criteria, sometimes making it difficult to compare findings across studies.

One useful approach is to see experts as persons on an extreme of a distribution of skill (Salthouse, 1991). The exact cut-off may be variable, however. Thus there may be gradations of expertise rather than just an expert-novice dichotomy. It may be difficult to pick the point during acquisition when someone suddenly becomes an expert. Patel and Groen (1991) suggest the following categories along a continuum from novice to expert. The first two categories refer to novices and only the fifth to an actual expert.

Layperson: has only commonsense or everyday knowledge about the domain.

Beginner: has prerequisite knowledge about the domain but little else (e.g., knows the rules of bridge but little more).

Intermediate: knows more than a beginner but less than a subexpert. (This is a default category. Examples would be a club player at chess or a second-year medical student.)

Subexpert: Has generic but not specialized knowledge of a domain. (An example is a medical doctor in general practice with a generic knowledge of, say, pediatrics).

Expert: Has specialized knowledge (e.g., a chess grandmaster or specialist pediatrician).

Types of Expert

Experts can be classified in various ways. Various researchers have proposed several typologies of experts, though none is generally accepted. Patel and Groen (1991) speak of generic and specific experts, the former being like subexperts (above) and the latter like experts. They also speak of domain-independent experts, persons who are adept at using domain-independent heuristics and can rapidly acquire knowledge about a new domain. They only consider such a type as a possibility, however. Holyoak (1991) distinguishes between routine and adaptive experts. Both types are good at quickly and easily solving familiar problems in a domain (e.g., diagnosing medical ailments or automobile faults). The adaptive experts also are adept at solving novel types of problems and inventing new methods and concepts in an area. An illustration might be the difference between a run-of-the-mill general medical practitioner and a top-flight medical researcher and practitioner who has contributed much to the discipline.

Some Differences between Experts and Novices

As mentioned in Chapter 4, domains may differ from each other in many ways. Some have well-defined concepts, others have ill-defined ones. Some, such as physics, contain an enormous amount of expert knowledge, while others have much less. In some domains, applying knowledge to solve problems is easy and almost automatic; domain knowledge gives standard solutions. In others, problem-solving is difficult. In some domains, such as medical diagnosis, someone is trying to help the expert perform. In others, such as bridge and chess, someone is actively trying to hinder the expert. Different domains require different component skills; tennis requires quite different ones from chess. Despite these and other differences, experts in many quite different domains share some remarkable commonalities, which this section will briefly outline.

Experts Have More Well-Organized Domain-Specific Knowledge. Experts perform well because they have a lot of well-organized domain-specific knowledge that they are adept at using. The major evidence for this principle is that expertise is typically domain-specific, showing little transfer to other domains, and that low scorers on IQ tests can become experts and outperform much higher-scoring nonexperts. The most striking illustration is the *idiot savant* syndrome (e.g., Treffert, 1988), whereby a mentally retarded person develops uncanny expertise in a single domain (see Chapter 6). A major factor underlying such a person's performance is a lot of domain-specific knowledge.

One can speculate from principles given in Chapter 4 about how novice and expert knowledge structures might differ. Since knowledge is largely organized around interconnected concepts, one would expect experts' concepts to hold more information and be more adequate for dealing with the domain's referents. Experts should lack the misconceptions that novices often have; that gravity derives from air, for example. Expert concepts should be interrelated into the domain's taxonomies and other structures. For example, expert psychiatrists should know the taxonomy of psychiatric disorders and how to use it to classify patients, and particle physicists should know the taxonomies of particles and their relations to forces. Experts would be expected to know the deep theories and metatheories of the domain. Examples are the physical disease metaphor underlying psychiatry, views of the nature of physical reality suggested by relativity theory and quantum mechanics, and the information processing metatheory. Experts should know many principles of their domain and how to use them, and in some domains to know standard problem-solving schemas. One would expect them to have well-organized chunks of knowledge and a lot of procedural knowledge in some domains, such as how to do scientific research and report it to colleagues.

Much experimental evidence supports these speculations. For instance, Murphy and Wright (1984) compared knowledge organizations of three categories of psychological disturbance held by persons ranging from novice to expert in this domain. With increasing expertise, the number of features that a subject listed about each category rose; experts listed many more. Interestingly, however, there was increasing overlap in features listed for categories with expertise; experts saw the categories as sharing more features. Further evidence is the ubiquitous finding that experts have organized their knowledge into large chunks, which allow better recall of information in the domain. The archetypal example is that of chess experts and two chessboards mentioned in Chapter 1. This recall superiority of experts for domain material occurs with stimuli from many domains; dance routines, computer program code, electronic circuitry, and musical notation, for instance (Ericsson and Smith, 1991). However, a few studies have not found it in some domains, which may reflect peculiarities of those domains. For instance, expert and weaker volleyball players do not differ in perception of offensive volleyball position patterns, but experts detect the ball faster in slides showing game positions (Holyoak, 1991). Further evidence of knowledge differences comes from free-sort studies. Here, subjects sort a set of stimuli into whatever categories they wish. The researcher infers about underlying knowledge and propensities from their bases of categorization. When expert and novice free-sorts are compared, experts typically use different bases, ones which reflect a deep knowledge of the principles and theories of the domain. A good example is a study by Chi et al. (1981). Expert and novice physicists sorted physics problems quite differently. Novices used surface features (such as the presence of wheels in the problem), while experts typically sorted by the principle needed to solve each problem. Thus, problems X and Y on the surface might seem quite different, but experts saw them as similar because both could be solved by, say, Newton's second law. Lacking such deep knowledge and ability to apply it, novices sorted by superficial surface features. Weiser and Shertz (1983) showed this expert-novice difference with computer programming problems. Novices sorted the problems by the programs' goals (e.g., to compute take-home pay), while experts did by the algorithms that could solve them.

Some work has even examined how knowledge organization changes over long periods. Charness (1991) followed a chess player over nine years from about average skill level (rated 1,600) to expert level (rated 2,400). He showed great improvement in ability to recall piece placements, chunking, and ability to evaluate positions. Interestingly, however, he showed little change in strategies used, such as depth and extent of search of possible move sequences.

Experts in some domains know and use more schemas to solve problems. In many domains, standard schemas give a standard solution to a problem class (e.g., van Lehn, 1989). Experts then scan the problem stimuli and try to find a schema to fit it, which then suggests the solution. In chess, for example, there are many standard solutions to problems, standard ways to conduct, say, a kingside attack or a rook-and-pawn endgame. The player may just have to adjust the schema slightly to the situation. X-ray diagnosis by radiologists largely involves finding and applying the right schema to a given case (Lesgold et al., 1988).

Other Expert-Novice Differences. Chi et al. (1988) list some other major differences, which mostly reflect differences along the lines of characteristics of highly skilled performance, mentioned in this chapter's first section. First, experts are typically much faster at performing tasks or dealing with problems in their domain. Expert typists type much faster. Most chess experts can play reasonably well very rapidly, sometimes averaging one or two seconds per move. Much expert knowledge is proceduralized, and experts can readily recognize standard patterns that suggest standard actions. However, in some cases experts may not be faster. It may depend on the domain and the circumstances. Experts may take longer to solve a problem because they form a very detailed representation of it. For instance, Scardamalia and Bereiter (1991) found that expert writers on average take more time to start writing and agonize more over a writing task. However, there are doubtless individual differences here. Isaac Asimov reportedly could turn out a respectable book in a month or so, usually without needing a second draft. Wolfgang Mozart could compose a fine work very quickly, writing symphonies no. 40 and 41 in two weeks each. On the other hand, Ludwig van Beethoven reportedly took much longer to compose, agonizing over every note and continually rewriting drafts.

Second, experts typically are more accurate. Skilled typists, chessplayers, and ballet dancers make fewer errors. However, in some complex domains, expert performance may be only marginally more accurate than performance by relative novices. Such domains include economic forecasting, mental disorder diagnosis, and predicting performance of college entrance applicants (Camerer and Johnson, 1991). Camerer and Johnson list some possible reasons why. Experts often use "broken leg" cues, which are highly diagnostic but occur rarely. They weight cues inconsistently and make errors combining them. They use configural choice cues (whereby the impact of one variable depends on the values of others). Indeed, some complex categorization tasks require juggling many pieces of information, which may exceed the expert's processing limitations.

Third, experts often use forward-reasoning problem-solving strategies while novices use backward reasoning. These two strategies are sometimes called "knowledge-based" and "goal-based" reasoning. Forward reasoning is working directly from the givens of a problem forward to its solution, and backward reasoning is working from the solution back to the problem givens. Forward reasoning is usually more efficient but is riskier. Sweller et al. (1983) were able to observe the shift from use of backward to forward reasoning during the acquisition of a minor sort of expertise. Subjects were trained in a narrow kinematics domain. They were taught to solve kinematics problems by applying various equations. They initially used backward reasoning but switched to forward reasoning after solving some problems. The strategy was first used in one problem category and was later applied to others. The strategy switch reduced the number of steps needed to solve each problem. However, the forward-backward reasoning difference may not occur in every domain. In computer programming, for instance, experts and novices typically start with the goal of a program and divide it up into subgoals (Anderson, 1990).

Fourth, experts and novices typically differ in metacognitive skills (Chi et al., 1988). Experts have good self-monitoring skills; they are better at detecting their own errors, are better at knowing when they need to check their performance for errors, and they have a better idea of how difficult a given problem is and how long it will take to solve it. They also ask more questions about a given problem before starting to solve it again, evidently reflecting their better knowledge of what they need to find out about it.

These differences suggest that it is always better to be an expert at some domain. However, Sternberg and Frensch (1992) suggest that expertise sometimes may have disadvantages, too. Knowledge processing can become automatic, and the expert may become much less flexible in a domain. An interesting demonstration comes from chess experts given a problem with two solutions. One solution is a highly salient, very familiar combination; the other is less salient, but it wins in fewer moves. Experts often choose the first variation and miss the more efficient second one. Second, experts may have difficulties when the knowledge in a domain is drastically reorganized, as in a paradigm shift such as that from Newtonian physics to relativity. The experts' knowledge may be so automatized that they cannot readily adapt it and learn to look at phenomena in a different way. The physicist Max Planck once said that a new scientific idea only becomes established when the older generation has died off and the current generation has grown up with it and is comfortable with it.

Knowledge and Processing in Some Sample Domains of Expertise

This section outlines some findings about expertise in a few representative domains. This section's material will further illustrate some of the above principles and also note some differences in task requirements and performance across different domains.

Chess. Expertise in this complex domain was one of the first types extensively studied, research dating back to Alfred Binet in 1893. It is a complex game that relies little on luck. Each player needs to keep track of many pieces on sixty-four squares and sometimes must calculate possible variations for many moves ahead. Chess has been called the archetypal domain of expertise. Studies of chess expertise have heavily influenced studies of expertise in other domains. It has been dubbed an ideal domain for the study of expertise, a drosophila for the field, because skill level varies widely and quantifiably and expertise depends heavily on an extensive knowledge base (Charness, 1991).

Charness (1991) and Holding (1985) summarize some characteristics of chess experts in addition to the general ones listed above. First, they have a very large amount of knowledge—of sequences of opening moves, which may run up to thirty moves long; of standard endgame patterns; of classes and heuristics of endgame strategies and tactics; of general principles and strategies; and of an estimated fifty-thousand chunks of piece groupings. They know many standard tactical devices that repeatedly occur (the fork, pin, and skewer, for example), standard combinations, and the standard strategic plans that derive from a given opening. For example, in the French defence, black closes up the position and aims to reach an endgame where the pawn structure is favorable, while white counters by launching a direct kingside attack. There are many openings and plans and counterplans. Chess experts also have to keep up with expanding knowledge—of openings and opponents and so on—for which they increasingly use computer databases.

Holding (1985) suggests that a key aspect of chess skill is search. Players must look at the possible variations and aim for the most favorable one. Holding suggests that searching becomes relatively automatic with practice. Experts and novices evidently do not differ in extent of search, but experts are better at evaluating positions that may arise and perhaps in heading toward a desirable one. Holding also says that there is little evidence that chess skill relies heavily on visual imagery ability, though this issue needs more research. Holding says that players often report using verbal means to look ahead.

Restaurant Orders. Ericsson and Polson (1988) studied a head waiter who was an expert at remembering orders. He could accurately recall complete dinner orders from as many as twenty diners at different tables. The researchers examined what knowledge was involved in this skill. First, this expert had a good knowledge of how his own memory operated. He had worked out the short/long-term memory distinction and that multiple retrieval paths improve recall, for instance. He knew various strategies for encoding orders and evaluating the quality of the encodings. For instance, he encoded items into groups of four. He used a specialized encoding schema for each category of item in a dinner order. Interestingly, these memory skills could transfer to material other than meal orders.

Medical Diagnosis from X-Ray Photographs. Radiologists diagnose all sorts of ailments from X-ray photographs. Interpreting theses photos is a complex skill that develops over many years of training, which largely involves scanning many instances. Lesgold et al. (1988) examined the nature of expertise in this domain, looking at individuals with from 10,000 to an estimated 200,000 training trials. A trial was defined as an episode of examining photos associated with one case. They reported that the skill is partly perceptual, that expertise involves knowing many principles and schemas for various disorders, and that much of this knowledge can only be gleaned from clinical experience.

They also looked at how such knowledge is used to diagnose. When an expert is given a case, he or she tries to build up a representation. He or she scans the photos for clues that suggest a schema. Each generated schema that might apply has several tests to be satisfied before it is accepted as covering the case. Once an appropriate schema is elicited and these tests are satisfied, several processes linked to the schema allow the expert to reach and then confirm the diagnosis. Relative novices at this domain typically diagnosed worse than experts for such reasons as not finding an appropriate schema, not applying the requisite tests for a given elicited schema, or because details of the associated processes were incomplete. The experts also seemed to see things in the domain differently, their perceptions being guided by different representations.

Lesgold et al. gave a detailed illustrative example of expert problem-solving in this domain. The case concerned a patient who had had part of a lung removed and whose internal organs had shifted to fill the space. When shown X-rays, the expert looked closely at them, decided that they revealed a chronic rather than an acute problem, and then hunted for a covering schema. The first schema considered was that the patient had not faced the camera directly. Tests soon excluded this possibility. Then the collapsed lung schema was elicited and tested. The expert noticed that some ribs had been broken to get at the lung and then solved the case: a previous operation had been done.

Lesgold et al. also examined how this expertise was acquired. They argued that acquisition involved learning many schemas and refining them through discrimination and generalization. Over time, the learner's perception of human anatomy also changes, and this increasing deep knowledge allows better reasoning about what the photos show. Lesgold et al. also found that acquisition of expertise was not monotonic. On some photos, experts and first-and second-year residents diagnosed better than third-and fourth-year residents, evidently because knowledge was being reorganized in the intermediate phase.

Physics. Physics is a difficult domain that contains an enormous amount of knowledge. Students must study for many years to reach the boundaries of expert knowledge. Experts have a large store of knowledge of theories, principles, and mathematics, which they use to understand and predict new phenomena, conduct research to reveal new facts, and solve standard physics problems (Anzai, 1991). Anzai lists some characteristics of physics experts. They know and use more abstract concepts than relative novices and use forward reasoning and different sorts of spatial representations to solve problems. For example, experts use diagrams (such as Feynman diagrams depicting subatomic particle interactions) more than novices do, and they are more proficient at drawing diagrams and making inferences from them.

Acquiring Expertise

This section looks in more detail at some generalizations about how expertise is actually acquired. One can ask what processes are involved, what commonalities there are in acquisition across domains, and whether there are distinct stages in acquisition.

In most domains a great deal must be learned, and this learning may continue over many years as knowledge structures are refined. Some things that may need to be learned are schemas, rules for applying them, ways to use them and to fine-tune them, theories, skills, concepts, specific exemplars, principles, and ways to use such knowledge. In some domains, such as physics, misconceptions may need to be eliminated.

The knowledge underlying expertise may be acquired from many different sources, depending on the domain. In physics, for example, most knowledge probably comes from textbooks and formal courses, but some would come from popular books, magazines, and other students. For domains such as chess, knowledge may be gleaned from textbooks, magazines, other players, and also from analyzing old and new games by experts, which may illustrate methods of solving certain kinds of problems. Top players also extensively analyze their own games and those of possible opponents. After a defeat, a player may learn much from a bout of explanation-based learning, abstracting out errors and how to avoid them. Chunks of pieces may be gleaned from books or from playing countless games.

An interesting study by Rubin et al. (1993) looked at the beginning stages of the acquisition of expertise for poetic ballads. The ballad is a highly structured domain with constraints that allow experts to learn and remember new exemplars easily. For instance, a ballad's rhythm gives clues about the number of syllables in each line, and the end rhyme links the lines in a stanza. The story told gives the ballad an overall organization, which aids recall. As well, rhyme and rhythm can further aid chunking and recall. In the study, subjects learned one ballad a week for five weeks and recalled each one several times. Recall performance improved greatly with time. Subjects remembered about 50 percent more of the fifth ballad than the first. After five weeks, the subjects also detected and could state more of the regular features of ballads, such as those constraints mentioned above. Beginning expertise in this domain may be a matter of noticing and using the regularities in the stimuli, the constraints under which ballad writers operate.

Shuell (1990) suggested that learners on the path from being a novice to becoming an expert may go through stages. There may be no abrupt shift from one stage to another, however, just a more or less steady change. At different points along this path, the learning processes may differ; the learner may learn in different ways and perceive stimuli in the domain quite differently. Different variables may have differing effects in each stage. How long each phase lasts may depend on the nature of the domain, the learner's existing knowledge, and other factors.

The first phase is one of confusion. It is familiar to anyone who studies a very new field. The learner encounters many facts and ideas that seem unconnected. The learner does not know the key concepts, schemas, principles, and theories of the field and tries to learn by rote-memorizing facts and by projecting existing knowledge by analogy. Shuell argues that the initial knowledge acquired in this stage is concrete and tied to the context in which it is learned. The learner also tries to identify key landmarks, much as one might do in trying to build up a mental map of a new city. The learner may also determine that terms in the domain have somewhat different meanings than in everyday life (such as *neurosis* in psychiatry) and acquire these meanings. Shuell argues that learners use very primitive learning processes in this phase, such as operant conditioning and rote learning, and concepts may be acquired at only a surface level. (But not all necessarily are. Analogical reasoning is not at all primitive.) Eventually the learner starts to build up an overview of the domain. Analogies that initially helped may be abandoned or altered as increasing knowledge suggests their inadequacy.

The second phase is the intermediate one. The learner starts to link previously isolated facts and concepts into principles and various conceptual structures. Knowledge becomes more abstract and divorced from the context in which it was learned. The field starts to make some sense to the learner, but he or she still does not function like a speedy, automatized expert. The learner uses more sophisticated learning processes in this phase. Use of mnemonic devices and rote memorization diminishes in favor of meaningful propositional learning and procedural learning. Shuell argues that the learner also tries to extend knowledge by applying it, thus learning by doing. Actions are tried out, and feedback (from instructors or the environment) is used to refine knowledge gained.

In the terminal phase, knowledge structures are well developed and function autonomously. Performance is typically automatic, effortless, and speedy, at least when dealing with routine problems. The learner largely relies on domain-specific strategies and knowledge to solve problems in the domain. Learning does continue in this phase, however. Information may be added to existing concepts, and structures may be reorganized. Experts must update.

Finally, knowledge acquisition in a domain may be spiral. A learner may repeatedly go over aspects of the domain, adding new knowledge each time and seeing more connections. Indeed, most persons have experienced reading a textbook several times, each time getting more out of it as existing knowledge grows and allows more of the book to be understood and elaborated on.

--------------------------------— 6 —--------------------------------

Effects of Age, Intelligence, and Styles on Learning and Memory

Many variables affect learning and memory. Some examples are motivation, certain drugs, amount of knowledge, and training regime. This chapter looks at some effects of three particularly important variables: age, intelligence, and cognitive and learning styles. Each has been extensively researched but, with the exception of age in some cases, is rarely mentioned in most mainstream books on learning and memory. Much is known about each. Indeed, the relation between intelligence and learning has been well researched in the last decade. The journal *Intelligence* has many articles on the topic as does the new journal *Learning and Individual Differences*. This chapter will briefly survey some major issues, ideas, and principles. Discussion of each topic could easily fill a large volume, and this survey must necessarily be brief.

AGE

Many species have a long growth phase, a peak age or ages for many physical and mental abilities, and a senescence phase in which these decline. Functions may peak at different ages. For instance, in human males endurance peaks around age fifteen while physical strength peaks in the early thirties. The senescence phase may last many years, as in humans, or just a few hours, as in the salmon and some marsupial mouse species. It is still controversial exactly why a senescence phase occurs. Theories include wear and tear, planned obsolescence, and accumulation of cell damage from chemicals called free radicals combined with lack of selection pressures for maintaining repair mechanisms much past reproductive age. Many human mental abilities peak around age twenty, according to psychometric testing (Howard, 1991). Reaction time is fastest and people are best able to solve novel problems then.

Many questions arise about age and learning and memory. For instance, at various ages, what learning and memory capacities do people have, and how adept are they at using knowledge? When do such memory structures as the visuospatial sketchpad become functional, and how well do they operate at various ages? What are the major trends and milestones in development? For instance, how does domain knowledge grow with age? Do children represent categories in the same ways adults do, and if not, how do they, and what changes occur as they age? When do children begin to use strategies, and how does that use change with age? There also are questions about readiness, a concept sometimes criticized (Halford, 1993). What are children capable of learning at various ages; when are they ready to learn such topics as algebra? There are many questions about the senescence phase. Can new skills be acquired at any age? What aspects of memory deteriorate, and what causes the decline? Can deteriorating abilities be improved by exercise?

Such questions are worth asking for several reasons. One is their intrinsic interest. Second is their practical applications. For instance, educators would like to know typical learning and memory capabilities of children at various ages to design and sequence instruction. Employers need to know the likely course of age decline to guide decisions about compulsory retirement ages for occupations such as airline pilot and surgeon. Do skills and ability to keep up with a field's expanding knowledge diminish too much by a certain age, and are there ways to counter it? As well, many workers now can expect to retrain several times in their lifetimes, and trainers need to know about capabilities at various ages and whether the older should be taught in different ways. Another application is technological design. How can devices such as video recorders be designed so that the elderly can readily learn to use and operate them? An expanding research area is examining how machines, jobs, and houses can be redesigned to compensate for declining capabilities with age so that the elderly can stay in the workforce and live independently at home longer. Such designers need solid information about the age changes.

Much is known about this topic, though there are still gaps in knowledge and continuing controversies about some issues. Halford (1993) and Kausler (1990) discuss it in much more detail, but there is strong evidence for the following generalizations. First, implicit memory seems to emerge early and stay largely intact into late adulthood, while explicit memory may emerge later (or at least take longer to become fully functional) and decline earlier (Parkin, 1993). Second, there seems to be an age-related change in general processing capacity, an index of mental speed and available attentional resources for task demands. It evidently increases to a peak and then declines (Halford, 1993; Parkin, 1993), though some authors argue that the capacity does not change in the growth phase (Anderson, 1992). However, there are wide individual differences in aging patterns and rates, and perhaps even several different aging syndromes (Rabbitt, 1993). Third, children are overoptimistic about their memory abilities, are more susceptible to interference from distractions, and are less flexible at using encoding strategies, as are the elderly (Parkin, 1993).

Let us now examine each broad phase in more detail.

The Growth Phase

Knowledge Development. When do humans first begin to acquire knowledge, what concepts can (or do) they learn at various ages, when do they start to organize concepts into conceptual structures, and when can they make various sorts of inference? The answers have been elusive because children are notoriously difficult to study. Siegal (1991) points out that it is often hard to determine exactly what children know and when they know it. Siegal cites many underestimates of what children know due to experimental tasks confusing them or not allowing them to show all they know and can do, or because children know more than they can say.

Theorists have held that humans first start to acquire knowledge some time after birth. Jean Piaget held that a newborn infant perceives the world as a series of unconnected sensory impressions and cannot form stable representations until near the end of its first year. The empiricists held that the mind is blank at birth. William James described the neonate's world as a "blooming, buzzing confusion." But these ideas are wrong. Research shows that neonates are quite capable and can readily learn. In fact, knowledge acquisition starts well before birth, though just how much is acquired then is unclear. New methods have made prenatal learning easier to study. Some examples are ultrasound imaging of fetus motion, better surgical techniques, and electrodes for animal studies (Hepper, 1992).

Research using such methods suggests the following generalizations. First, various capacities needed to support learning are up and running months before birth. For example, the olfactory apparatus is present three months after conception, and the fetus can detect sound and vibration at twenty-six weeks (Kisilevsky et al., 1992). The fetus also may have a sleep-wake cycle in the last few months before birth (Parkes, 1992).

There is much evidence for prenatal learning. An early study by Ray (1932) tried to classically condition fetal movement. The CS was a vibration applied to the mother's abdomen and the UCS was a loud bang. The fetus reacted to the UCS, but the report is vague about whether conditioning to the CS occurred. However, DeCasper and Fifer (1980) found that neonates prefer their mother's voice, which they could have heard only before birth, to others. DeCasper and Spence (1986) had mothers-to-be repeatedly read out a passage in their last six weeks of pregnancy and found that the read passage was a more powerful reinforcer than another passage. Several studies have shown fetal habituation to auditory or vibratory stimuli, usually measured as a decrease in movement or in heart rate (Hepper and Shahidullah, 1992).

Prenatal animals are much easier to study. Studies show prenatal learning in mammals, birds, amphibians, and invertebrates (Hepper and Shahidullah, 1992). This early learning can powerfully affect later development. For instance, Hepper and Waldman (1992) injected frog eggs with orange juice or citral and found that tadpoles preferred the substance that they had been injected with. Lickliter and Stoumbos (1992) found that embryonic bobwhite quails exposed to a maternal call with a faster repetition rate than usual preferred that rate when they hatched. Caubet et al. (1992) found evidence that orientation of social behavior (particularly altruism) in ants is imprinted before hatching. For example, nestmate recognition may depend on knowledge of odors acquired before hatching.

What use is such early learning? There may be big selective advantages in having knowledge that cannot be readily genetically programmed (such as nestmate recognition) available as soon as the organism comes into the world. Frogs can learn specific odors of their external pond before hatching, which allows them to home. A mammal may recognize its mother right from birth, useful if many mothers and offspring share one site. One implication is that knowledge previously thought innate may be acquired during gestation. Perhaps the behavior of such creatures as insects is more plastic than thought (Caubet et al., 1992). However, the importance and limits of such early learning in humans is still unclear.

Much is known about infant knowledge and learning. Indeed, the topic is of such general interest that most issues of child development journals have one or more articles on infant capabilities, and it is a popular press staple. Most studies use one of two methods. One is the habituation technique, which involves repeatedly presenting one or more stimuli and measuring changes in a response such as looking. For example, if one wanted to know if a neonate could distinguish between a circle and an ellipse, one could repeatedly show a circle until the child hardly looked at it and then show an ellipse. The child's looking more at the ellipse is evidence that it discriminated. Another method is operant conditioning. A response such as foot movement or nipple sucking may be reinforced and the child then trained to discriminate between stimuli.

Studies with such methods show that infants have an impressive amount of knowledge and array of capabilities. For example, Swain et al. (1993) found that neonates could acquire representations of speech sounds and recognize them twenty-four hours later. Neonates also can recall a contingency between kicking and a reinforcer for at least a week (Parkin, 1993). They can distinguish between lines, curves, and patterns, between red, blue, and yellow, between long and short sound durations, between different pitches and speech variations, between the tastes of salt and lemon, and between the smells of licorice and alcohol (Farnham-Diggory, 1992). Children can relate sounds to sights at birth; can imitate actions and represent knowledge of differences in a set of syllables at 12–20 days; can match across sensory modalities at 26 days; can discriminate between displays containing two, three, four, and six dots at 22 weeks; can know that an object exists even when it is hidden at five months; and may be able to perceive cause-and-effect relations (Siegal, 1991) and remember pictures for at least two weeks at six months (Fagan, 1973).

There is a big puzzle about early learning, however. Adults evidently recall little or nothing acquired in the first three years of life, an intriguing phenomenon known as infantile amnesia (Nelson, 1992). A person's earliest memory generally dates back to age three (with an average of three and one-half) and is usually of an emotionally significant event. For example, Howes et al. (1993) asked subjects their earliest memory and checked their accuracy with their parents. Most were accurate. Almost all were of events (799 out of 800), usually linked to negative emotion, such as falling off a bicycle or playground equipment. The one exception was an accurate memory of a green stool. The gist of the memory traces was correct; alterations typically were of details. Usher and Neisser (1993) present some evidence that the lower limit may be the second birthday and that the likelihood of recall depends on the type of event. Very unusual or frightening events that form part of a narrative such as hospitalization or the birth of a sibling may be better recalled. However, there is the interpretation problem of reality monitoring. Do subjects actually recall these events or just hear about them later and forget the source? A famous story goes that Jean Piaget vividly recalled being saved by his nurse at a very early age, but the nurse later confessed having fabricated the entire tale.

Another puzzling fact about infantile amnesia is that very young children can recall early events. For example, Hamond and Fivush (1991) found that four-year-olds could recall much about trips to Disneyworld taken when they were just two. This knowledge afterward is forgotten or becomes inaccessible.

Why infantile amnesia occurs is still unclear. Sigmund Freud implausibly held that children actively repress recall because this period is a disturbing time of Oedipal and Electra conflict. Other hypotheses are that the neural mechanisms for episodic memory are still maturing or that recall is poor because youngsters cannot fit events readily to schematic outlines (Usher and Neisser, 1993). Yet another view is that the cues that elicit such memories (such as a crib, etc.) are not reinstated in adult recall, but this also is not very plausible. The issue still is not decided.

Children begin to acquire various concepts quite early. Children can readily group objects into categories by age one year and acquire the notion of class inclusion (that one class can be included within another, such as boys being people) by age five (Halford, 1993). Chi (1981) found that children aged five years could form conceptual structures that interrelated their classmates. Halford (1993) lists some additional milestones. Children can make transitive inferences at three or four years old, can make simple logical and deductive inferences by five, and can hold the notion of logical necessity by age eleven. Children can make inferences about category members by age three or four years. For example, Gelman and Markman (1987) found that children could generalize features of one category member to another and could distinguish between features common to all instances (such as all cats having tails) and features of individuals (that if an individual rabbit is cold, not all necessarily are).

Children's early concepts may be somewhat different from adults', however. For instance, one child used *moon* to refer to any semi-circular object or a child may use *car* to refer only to moving cars (Howard, 1987). Their early concepts may contain knowledge of fewer attributes and have more perceptual features than other kinds of feature (Chi and Ceci, 1987). They also may be based on knowledge of exemplars and characteristic features rather than defining features. For example, Krascum and Andrews (1993) had children aged around four learn about some categories. Few children evidently abstracted out defining features, instead typically remembering exemplars. They categorized new stimuli by overall similarity to their exemplar representations, but only did so successfully if exposed to more than one training exemplar. Keil and Batterman (1984) showed that children may shift to use of defining features with increased knowledge and age. Younger children typically represented such categories as islands and lies with characteristic features while older children used defining ones. (Of course, adults also may use exemplar representations.) Children's concepts may also represent categories with narrower boundaries than adults', but the boundaries may expand with age. For example, young children may not include insects, plants, and seeds as exemplars of *lifeform*, or tomatoes and dates as exemplars of *fruit*.

Wellman and Gelman (1992) argue that children's early learning is constrained by metatheories that they acquire early. These function like Kuhnian paradigms, constraining what a child can learn about and infer from various domain concepts. These theories consist of principles (see also Chapter 4). The researchers examined metatheories for such domains as lifeforms, artifacts, and minds, which they argue children quickly learn and use to constrain further acquisition. They argue that by age three or four months children have concepts of object and physical causality and by age three or four years have a good knowledge of how the physical world works (for instance, they know that objects have insides). By age three to five years, they have a concept of mental state and can reason about mental states in others. By age seven, they have a good knowledge of lifeforms and such characteristics as growth, reproduction, and inheritance. An example of how these metatheories constrain inferences is that children will agree that painting a dog to look like a tiger would not make it one. These theories tell children that lifeforms and artifacts are quite different sorts of things.

Constrained by such frameworks, children acquire knowledge of a variety of domains. Much evidence suggests that their growth in knowledge is domain-specific. A child can learn a lot about one domain and use this knowledge adeptly at an early age to outperform much older but less knowledgeable persons. For instance, some very young chess players can beat most adult players. Chi and Koeske (1983) studied a four-year-old with a good knowledge of dinosaurs. He knew the names of forty dinosaurs and was good at learning new facts about them.

Carey (1985) and Chi and Ceci (1987) propose that children's acquisition of further domain-specific knowledge is analogous to a novice-to-expert shift. A child is a universal novice and learns just as an adult novice (in, say, bridge or chess) does to become an expert. Carey's work provides evidence for the following acquisition pattern. Children learn concepts, then new relations between concepts, and new schemas, and then their core concepts may alter (just as they may in science, in which the concept of *temperature* replaced *heat*). Indeed, there are many parallels between the growth of a science's knowledge and children's conceptual development (Howard, 1987). Chi and Ceci also proposed that children add more features to their concepts. One view is that a novice-to-expert shift is all there is to cognitive development. Children differ from adults only in the amount and organization of knowledge. However, as will be described, there is much evidence against this view.

Growth of Knowledge of and Use of Strategies. A strategy is an approach to a task. A simple example is rehearsal to learn a list of words or chunking to improve recall of digits. Strategies can greatly improve performance. Using imagery, for example, trebled the number of paired associates recalled in Bower (1970). Children become more strategic as they get older. They acquire more strategies and become more adept at choosing the best one for a given task; six-year-olds use multiple strategies to solve addition problems, for example (Siegler, 1989). Children continually learn new strategies and change the rate of use of ones that they know. Even three-year-olds can use an analogical reasoning strategy; they solve problems better if they have previously solved analogous ones (Holyoak et al., 1984). With age, they need fewer hints to draw analogies, make better ones, and improve component processes such as encoding, mapping, and inference making (Siegler, 1989). Older children and adults also are more likely to generalize strategies beyond training stimuli and try out additional ones when their initial strategy does not work well. For example, Moely et al. (1969) found that category clustering in recall (which reflects use of a categorization strategy) only occurred at age eleven. Children also become more metacognitive with age; they learn more about how their memory works and improve at estimating how difficult a given task is likely to be.

They also get better at encoding; they take in more attributes at a time and become more selective about what they acquire (Siegler, 1989).

Changes in Memory Structures. When do various memory structures emerge, and does their capacity alter during development? Evidence suggests that the implicit memory system is operating well by age three and thereafter changes little (Parkin, 1993). For example, three-year-olds show priming (Parkin, 1993). However, relatively little work has been done here.

Farnham-Diggory (1992) reviewed much of the evidence on development of various memory structures and suggested the following generalizations. The registers, working memory, and LTM are operating at birth (and probably before, else prenatal learning would not occur). Evidence suggests that the structures develop further with age, however. The icon and echo both seem to last longer in early life, about 2.0 seconds for neonates versus the adult 0.5 seconds. Working memory capacity also improves. The measured digit span increases in the following classic sequence: age two, two digits; age three, three digits; age seven, five digits; age ten, six digits; and then to the adult seven. (However, one view now is that the adult span really is about four. Span is fixed at birth at four units, but measured span improves because articulation rate increases and people get better at using such strategies as chunking. However, others argue that capacity increases from two digits at age three or four, to three at age five, to four at age eleven. See Halford, 1993). Evidence suggests that neonates can form images but cannot readily manipulate them. For instance, Dean et al. (1983) found that 80 percent of six-year-olds could not rotate an image, but 40 percent of eight-year-olds and 80 percent of ten-year-olds could. Whether general processing capacity improves with age is still controversial and will be considered later. Working memory processes in general become faster and more efficient with age (Halford, 1993).

Language and the Theory of Mind. Eventually children acquire two capabilities that turn them into more capable learners. One greatly improves their overall capacity to learn and widens information sources, while the other may allow them to learn additional things. One, of course, is the acquisition of language ability, whose development follows a predictable pattern across all cultures and languages. The first word usually appears around 10 months, the first two-word sentences (such as "Me eat") at around 18 months, and telegraphic speech (whereby the child speaks in short sentences stripped of adjectives and adverbs) at 20–24 months. By age five or six, the typical child is speaking much like an adult. Being able to speak allows much verbal transmission of information, opens up more sources of information (such as books), and allows verbal reasoning.

The second is a metatheory of mind. Perner (e.g., 1991; 1992) has argued that children around age four develop the concept of representation and can see that others have mental representations that may differ for the same object. They develop a metatheory of the mental world, which allows them to learn and reason about others' mental states. A good illustration of this theory of mind comes from the paradigmatic false-belief study. Children watch a man enter a room, put a toy in a certain place, and leave. Then another man enters and shifts the toy to another place. The children are asked where the first man will look for the toy when he returns. Most children by age four say that he will look where he left it, but younger ones typically say he will look where it was moved to. To make the former inference, one needs a concept of mind and needs to know how a false belief can affect behavior. The argument goes that children have this knowledge and related notions such as deception by age four. Perner argues that this capability affects children's power to remember things and to distinguish between appearance and reality. He explains infantile amnesia as occurring because children need a concept of mind to be aware that they have experienced a situation or event before (though the Hamond and Fivush study above appears to contradict this idea). Their early memory traces may still be present but are not recognized as memories of past experience.

A theory of mind is needed to learn to deal well with others. A key aspect of social skill is being able to put oneself in someone else's place to predict the other's actions. One intriguing idea is that autistic children lack a concept of mind, which results in their enormous difficulties in dealing with other people (Perner, 1991).

What Causes Cognitive Development? The general phenomenon is clear. Children become more capable at learning, remembering, and using their knowledge with age. Researchers still dispute what mechanisms cause these changes. What pushes cognitive development along?

There are two general views (Canfield and Ceci, 1992). One broad view is that learning is the only mechanism of change. An instance of this general view is the behaviorist notion that development is the increasing complexity of behavior. Another instance is the more modern view mentioned earlier that children are universal novices and only differ from adults in extent and organization of knowledge and strategies they know for manipulating it. Evidence for this view is that some clearcut novice-expert differences parallel those between children and adults. Children, like novices, have less knowledge, know fewer strategies, and process information more slowly and with greater effort. The general view is that age is irrelevant. Development is due to the number and sequencing of learning experiences.

The second broad view is that learning plays a major role but that maturation does, too. An instance is Jean Piaget's theory that children go through invariant stages of cognitive development and at various stages have limited capacities and can only learn certain things. The sequence of stages is fixed and universal across cultures. This approach dominated the study of cognitive development for decades, and many parts of it are useful; however, much is now seen as wrong. For instance, Piaget underestimated the abilities of children at various ages. They can perform such tasks as class inclusion long before Piaget said they could (Siegal, 1991). However, a neo-Piagetian view retains much of Piaget's approach (see Labouvie-Vief, 1992, for details). Many researchers now reject the idea of fixed stages. Halford (1993) argues that data supporting their existence can be reinterpreted, and other changes in other things may seem like stage-like development.

The best guess is that several different mechanisms interact to induce cognitive development, learning being just one (Siegler, 1989). Learning may play a greater or lesser role at different ages, perhaps the greatest one in times of relative biological stability. There is indeed evidence for the effects of maturational changes. Changes in the nervous system after birth have been linked to cognitive changes. Siegler (1989) lists several instances. For example, in many parts of the brain, synapses are initially overproduced and then pruned. In the third layer of the middle frontal gyrus, synapse numbers rise from 10,000 to 100,000 from birth to age one, keep rising until age two, and then fall to adult levels by age seven. Ability to perform well on such tasks as delayed response and object permanence follows soon after the age at which synaptic density first exceeds adult levels (six months). Indeed, fully mature cognitive capacity may depend on eliminating excess synapses, a process that occurs during adolescence and young adulthood (Goldman-Rakic, 1987). Dempster (1992) gives another instance. The frontal lobes grow rapidly from birth to age one or two, slowly until ages four to seven (when they show another growth spurt), and then slowly until young adulthood. The cells change in size and complexity, and myelination, which allows impulses to propagate faster with less energy and less liability to abnormal transmission, is only complete around age thirteen or so. Myelination is nearly complete in sensory and motor areas by age two. The frontal lobes also shrink in late adulthood. They are concerned with planning and resisting interference from distractors, and Dempster suggests that cognitive ability improves with age because children's ability to resist interference and inhibit actions increases with maturation.

The age improvement in *general processing resources* also may be due to maturational factors. The term has several different meanings but generally refers to a kind of mental energy that affects performance and is in limited supply. For example, Kail (1988; 1992) argues for a central attentional mechanism with a limited amount of resources that is needed to perform cognitive tasks. The amount of resources available varies in people of the same age (see Just and Carpenter, 1992) and increases systematically with age. Kail tested subjects aged between eight and twenty-two years on various cognitive tasks and found evidence for a single estimate of processing resources tied to mental speed.

The Senescence Phase

Aspects of the ability to learn and remember worsen as the brain ages. The elderly complain much more about memory problems than the young do, and studies suggest that they have poorer memory for prose, medicine labels, maps, activities that they have recently performed, and names and faces, for example (Light, 1991).

However, gauging the effects of aging is very difficult. Several major methodological problems are as follows (Kausler, 1990). The first is the performance-competence complication. An apparent age difference may be due only to differences in motivation, health, or confidence to perform a task. A second is the cohort effect. A cohort is a group of people born about the same time (say, in 1955 or in 1920–25). People in a cohort differ from those in other cohorts in many ways due to historical events experienced, differences in mores, childrearing and educational practices, and so on. Cohort and age are confounded in a typical cross-sectional study that compares people of different ages. A classic illustration is from studies of IQ test performance. Once researchers believed that IQ score declined precipitously after age thirty, based on cross-sectional studies. But longitudinal studies, which follow the same group over many years, show a far less severe decline (Schaie and Strother, 1968). Cohorts differ in years of education, diet, amount of stimulation received, and so on, which may affect IQ score (Howard, 1991). Unfortunately, longitudinal studies have problems, too, such as attrition of subjects and attrition of particular types of subject. Another methodological difficulty is that many studies rely on group averages, which can be misleading. Rabbitt (1993) suggests that there may be several aging syndromes, and there are wide individual differences in what functions decline and at what rate. Aging may produce more variation in certain cognitive abilities. Grouped data may obscure what is really going on.

However, there is much evidence for some generalizations about the effects of aging.

Changes in Mental Abilities. A lot of psychometric work has examined score changes on various tests of general intelligence and more specific abilities over the lifespan. There is still some controversy over peak ages for various abilities, and there are wide individual differences in rate of decline (Morse, 1993). The conventional wisdom is that many abilities peak in the twenties, plateau until the late fifties or early sixties, and then decline, slowly at first but at a faster rate by the late seventies. Schaie and Willis (1993) report a cross-sectional study of 1,628 community-dwelling persons aged up to the late eighties. The researchers tested their verbal ability, perceptual speed, spatial ability, inductive reasoning, and other factors. Verbal reasoning scores declined less than inductive reasoning and spatial ability.

General processing capacity typically declines with age. The elderly have less attentional capacity and less ability to divide attention, though not all studies have found this (Light, 1991). There is a general mental slowdown with age. Salthouse (1985) estimates that people lose between five and 15 percent of their mental speed per decade after age thirty, and this global change induces changes in many other abilities.

One way to summarize the ability changes is as the classic WAIS (Wechsler Adult Intelligence Scale) aging pattern. The WAIS has six verbal and five performance scales (the latter tap speed and spatial ability, among other things). Verbal scale scores decline little with age, and scores on the vocabulary scale may actually increase. However, performance scale scores decline after a peak at ages twenty to twenty-four (Howard, 1991). These are much affected by diminishing mental speed. The verbal scales are sometimes said to measure crystallized intelligence and the performance scales fluid intelligence, a distinction made by Raymond Cattell (e.g., 1987). Fluid intelligence is an innate general ability, and crystallized intelligence is an ability largely based on knowledge. The two interact, however; one's crystallized intelligence level will partly depend on one's fluid intelligence level. Kausler (1990) argues that the decline in fluid intelligence may be due to such factors as less confidence, poorer health, and disuse of abilities rather than competence factors. However, there is only moderate evidence that the elderly can learn to improve performance on fluid intelligence tests, and such improvement is usually specific to training stimuli (Kausler, 1990).

Several studies have looked at performance level in various domains with age. Studies of bridge experts (Charness, 1983) and chess experts (Holding, 1985) show a typical performance decline with age. Chess players' peak rating usually occurs around thirty years old, though some stay near the top into their sixties. The decline partly may be due to less motivation. Conventional wisdom about performance in various academic fields goes as follows. Physicists and mathematicians are supposed to do their most original work before age thirty. Albert Einstein did his best before thirty, for example. These fields are thought to require a lot of fluid intelligence, which diminishes after thirty. Historians and novelists generally perform best in their forties. These fields require a lot of knowledge and more crystallized ability. Very few people write great novels before their thirties or forties because they have not acquired enough knowledge of the world.

Changes in the Ability to Learn and Remember. Much research has examined this topic and is summarized by Kausler (1990). This section will cover a few major points.

First, the elderly seem to be slower at maze learning and classical conditioning (Kausler, 1990). Finkbiner and Woodruff-Pak (1991) compared young, middle-aged, and elderly adults (ranging from seventeen to eighty-one years old) in eyeblink conditioning and found no differences between the first two groups but found that the elderly conditioned more slowly. They also found large age differences in rate of eyeblink conditioning in rabbits. Studies suggest little effect of age on prototype formation (Hess, 1982). Implicit memory seems to be little affected by age. The elderly perform worse at stem completion tasks but not at perceptual identification tasks (Kausler, 1990). Motor skills stay largely intact with age, though the elderly may perform them more slowly and may perform proportionately more slowly at complex tasks (Kausler, 1990). However, the elderly may develop strategies that overcome their increasing limitations. An excellent example comes from a study by Salthouse (1984) of typing. Subjects aged between twenty and seventy years typed at the same speed, but the older subjects performed much more slowly on a choice reaction-time task. The older compensated for slower reaction time when typing by looking further ahead, which raised their speed. However, very complex skills, such as chess-playing and driving, may become increasingly difficult to perform with age. The automobile accident rate climbs dramatically after age fifty-five. The mental slowdown, increased difficulty in paying attention to moving objects, and deteriorating eyesight are some reasons. However, some cognitive skills may be less affected by age (Rabbitt, 1993).

The elderly also can readily learn new skills but may take longer to do so than the younger. Elias et al. (1987) found little difference in time to learn to use a word processor for young and middle-aged subjects, but elderly ones took longer. However, Moscovitch et al. (1986) found that elderly and younger subjects learned to read upside-down text at the same rate, but the elderly performed this skill more slowly. Perhaps complex skills like using a word processor are harder for the elderly to learn than simpler ones such as reading upside down text.

There is no age decline in the capacity of the sensory registers or the duration of icon and echo (Kausler, 1990). Working memory capacity may diminish but only slightly until late adulthood. Digit span lessens slightly with age (about 8 percent), and the elderly perform worse at chunking and may have problems with imagery (Kausler, 1990). There is little decline in short-term memory forgetting rate. Older adults are more distractible, however. For instance, they are more susceptible to the Stroop effect (Light, 1991). Dempster (1992) links this finding to the early decline with age of the frontal lobes, making the elderly less able to gate out interference.

The declarative knowledge base stays quite intact with age, but people become less adept at using it (Light, 1991). Timothy Salthouse summarized the trend with the vivid metaphor of memory being like a reference library whose stock does not deteriorate with time but that has a frail librarian in charge, who gets progressively slower and inefficient. However, some disorders, such as Alzheimer's disease, evidently do destroy parts of the knowledge base.

Spatial memory and memory for faces worsens with age, however (Kausler, 1990). The elderly are as good as the young at recognizing old, familiar faces but make more errors (in the form of false alarms) with new faces (Bartlett and Fulton, 1991). Recognition memory in general declines only modestly with age, but recall declines significantly (Craik and McDowd, 1987). Recognition performance may be even worse if subjects must retrieve the context in which knowledge was acquired (Parkin, 1993). There is little evident decline in forgetting rate in LTM, but the elderly have more tip-of-the-tongue states, have more amnesia for sources of information, and perform worse at frequency encoding (Kausler, 1990). The elderly can learn to improve memory by using mnemonic devices but, like most people, tend not to use them in everyday life (Light, 1991).

Though the elderly complain of increasing memory problems, intriguingly they often are overoptimistic about their own memory abilities. For instance, Lovelack and Marsh (1985) had young and old subjects rate the ease of learning a set of word pairs and then actually learn and recall the pairs. There was no difference in rated ease of learning, but the elderly recalled many fewer pairs.

Kausler (1990) reviews the evidence for several other ideas about aging. One is that the elderly undergo a sort of reverse Piagetian stage development, moving backwards from the formal operations stage. There is little evidence for this idea. Second, the evidence is mixed that the elderly can improve their performance by physical and mental exercise. Some studies examining persons active over their whole lifetime have found less deterioration in memory functions, while other studies have found that they do not differ from inactive controls. Studies that have trained inactive persons show little clear evidence for memory improvement.

INTELLIGENCE AND LEARNING AND MEMORY

Everyday observation suggests very wide individual differences in the ability to learn and remember. Some individuals often complain about their poor memories, while others say that they never forget a face and apparently have a huge knowledge base. Studies confirm such differences (Conners, 1992). For instance, various authors describe cases of phenomenal memorizers. Hunter (1982) described Alexander Aitken, with an auditory short-term memory span of ten letters and thirteen digits. He could learn word lists very rapidly. He was a teacher and could recall all thirty-five names of his students in a class after reading the list just once. S.V. Shereskevski, described by Luria (1968) and mentioned in Chapter 4, had no measurable memory capacity limits. Tests showed that he could recall at least seventy items (letters or words) backwards or forwards at once or months later. The Nineteenth Century explorer Richard Burton reportedly spoke forty languages fluently. Wilding and Valentine (1994) report evidence for overall superior memory in some "memory champions." Studies of children learning in school show large differences in learning rates. Some children may learn nine times faster than others (Gettinger and White, 1980;

Gettinger, 1984). (Such differences pose enormous problems for educators who cope with them by such means as dividing children into separate classes and accelerating fast learners through the system.) Carroll (1993) cites much evidence for large individual differences in memory functions and for a general memory ability that affects performance on many memory tasks. He also argues that there are differences in some specific memory abilities: short-term memory span, associative memory (the ability to form arbitrary associations), free recall memory (the ability to recall arbitrarily related, or unrelated material), meaningful memory, and a visual memory ability (in recalling or recognizing images).

Such observations occur across cultures. Indeed, Reuning (1988) found that Kalahari Bushmen of southern Africa believe that some people learn faster and remember more than others, and their actual assessments of various individuals' abilities matched scores on standard psychometric tests. Faster learners also are thought to behave more intelligently. These observations prompt people to form a concept of general intelligence (Howard, 1993). This term refers to a capacity that people have in varying degrees that underlies the learning rate and memory performance differences.

How are intelligence and learning related? The question at first seems poor, because intelligence often is seen as synonymous with learning ability (Jensen, 1989). Bright people by definition learn quickly and remember much, while the retarded learn slowly or not at all, recall little, and are not adept at using what they do know. Indeed, the original intelligence test was devised by Alfred Binet in 1905 to distinguish between unable and lazy students and predict what students could learn (though Binet himself denied that it was measuring intelligence). Very intelligent persons should learn more material and learn it faster because they can easily grasp essentials. The kind of understanding needed to perform well on IQ tests seems much like that needed to grasp essentials of fine points of algebra, foreign affairs, and quantum mechanics.

However, the question is sensible because the issue is more complicated than it seems. First, IQ test scores (a measure of general intelligence) correlate in complex ways with measures of learning. Second, researchers disagree as to whether general intelligence exists at all, or whether intelligence is just a cluster of unrelated specific abilities. The latter issue needs examination before looking at data on IQ-learning relations.

General Intelligence or Many Unrelated Abilities?

The notion of general intelligence goes back a long way. Charles Spearman (1904; 1927) proposed that there is a largely innate general ability (called g) that is distributed unequally in humans. It aids performance of virtually every mental task, from playing bridge and carrying out scientific

Figure 6.1
Items Like Those on the Raven's Advanced Progressive Matrices Test. The Task Is to Complete Each Matrix.

1.	O/	/	O/
	/O	X	X/O
	O/O	X/	?
2.	X	XX	XXO
	XX	XXO	XXOO
	XXO	XXOO	?

research to doing crossword puzzles and playing the tambourine. G is the ability to reason and to educe (draw out) correlates. It is the ability to abstract, to see similarities and differences, and to extrapolate trends. The Ravens Advanced Progressive Matrices test is thought to be a good measure of g. To illustrate g further, Figure 6.1 shows some Ravens-type items. G would help perform almost any mental task because it is difficult to think of one that does not involve abstraction, for instance. However, some tasks are more g-loaded than others (e.g., doing the Ravens test versus doing crossword puzzles). G is analogous to a general athletic ability that aids performance of all track and field events, from sprinting and marathon running to javelin throwing.

Spearman's g has been an enormously influential concept. The major rationale of most traditional IQ tests is that they tap g by assembling a variety of mental tasks. G's existence is a major justification for streaming students. The rationale is that g level limits what knowledge and abilities a person can acquire. Outstanding achievers need a high g level. An extreme example is the British Eleven-plus system. All children were tested at age eleven, and the top 10–15 percent went to academically oriented grammar schools and the rest to lesser secondary schools, from which it was very difficult to enter university.

There is much evidence that g exists. First, one line of evidence comes from factor analysis studies. If a large group of people do many different mental tasks, performance on all of them typically correlates. On average, persons who do well on one task do well on all, and those who do badly on one do badly on all. A factor analysis of the data typically reveals a general factor that aids performance on all tasks. No one has yet devised a set of mental tasks in which a general factor does not emerge (Anderson, 1992). Scores on the British Abilities Scales test, which measure a wide variety of cognitive functions ranging from mental speed to spatial relations and moral reasoning, also reveal a general factor. Second, measures of g correlate better with job performance than scores on specific aptitude tests, and g is the best predictor of job training performance (Ree and Earles, 1991). Third, the mentally retarded do worst on tasks that best measure g (Larson and Alderton, 1992). Fourth, there is much physiological evidence (e.g., Vernon, 1991), though some argue that it is not conclusive (Andrist et al., 1992). Three sources of physiological evidence suggest that g is a kind of neural efficiency. One source is from studies with the evoked potential, a brain wave pattern that occurs in response to a stimulus. Its amplitude correlates up to 0.72 with IQ scores (Vernon, 1991). The second source is cerebral glucose metabolism, the rate at which the brain takes up glucose, measured by PET scans. A PET scan given to subjects performing some task can show brain areas then most active. Studies show negative correlations between IQ scores and glucose metabolic rates in various cortex areas. High IQ subjects use less glucose, suggesting that their brains work more efficiently. They need less energy and fewer brain areas to perform tasks (Vernon, 1991). The third source is nerve conduction speed, which correlates with IQ (Vernon, 1991).

If g is a kind of neural efficiency, where is its locus? Is it an excess of neurotransmitters, for example? The answer is still unclear. The question may be answered when the human genome project identifies the genes for intelligence differences and what they code for. Views differ as to what g represents at the cognitive level. One is that g is mental speed, the rate of executing elementary processes such as encoding, short-term memory scanning, and retrieval from LTM (Jensen, 1989; Anderson, 1992), which correlate from -0.2 to -0.4 with IQ (Kranzler and Jensen, 1991). IQ also correlates with inspection time, the time it takes to see if two lines are identical. Small speed differences over many years can produce large knowledge base differences (Hunt, 1976). A related view is that g corresponds to differences in general processing capacity (Larson and Alderton, 1992).

However, many researchers say that there is no g, no general intelligence. They point out that the brain is organized into modules, regions that perform particular functions. There are modules for various types of knowledge (e.g., words, visuospatial representations, and faces, and for size, color, and features of objects). Martin and Weingartner (1992) say that there are good evolutionary reasons for modular design. Parts of a brain with independent subsystems can change during evolution without affecting other parts. If every component were essential to operation, damage to one would stop the whole system from working, as would taking a component out of a television set (Marr, 1982). The argument goes that the brain has many relatively independent modules for handling different types of representation and that cannot perform other types of processing tasks. Since humans have a variety of different abilities localized in different modules, intelligence cannot be a unitary entity such as g, but is a collection of independent modules with specific processes by which they operate. An example is Gardner's (1983) theory of multiple intelligences. He argued that people have at least seven largely independent intelligences (e.g., linguistic, spatial, and musical), which are largely innate, are localized in different brain regions, and develop at different rates. A person may be high in one and low on all the others, or average on some and low on others.

Several lines of evidence are cited for this general view. First, many patients suffer brain damage that impairs one ability and leaves others intact. Second is the *idiot savant* syndrome, mentioned earlier. In this case a mentally retarded person develops one super ability. About 0.06 percent of retardates are savants. Their superabilities usually are in art, musical performance, verbatim memorization, spatial ability, or calendar calculation. The last ability is an intriguing one. Give one a date such as September 15, 1935, and they quickly and accurately say what day of the week it fell on. Howe (1989) gives some more examples. Some savants are fine artists. Kiyoshi Yamashita scored just 68 on an IQ test, but the critics consider his artwork exceptional. Treffert (1988) describes a child called Leslie who never spoke voluntarily but if asked could repeat verbatim the conversations of an entire day with the correct intonations. Exactly how *idiot savants* do it and why the savant syndrome occurs is still unclear, but one factor may be a lot of practice. Such strong performances are inconsistent with the view that g limits achievement.

The third line of evidence is that some persons with average or above-average IQ scores have very poor ability in one or two domains. These problems are called learning disabilities or learning problems (e.g., Kirby and Williams, 1991). Common ones are in language, reading, and arithmetic. Kirk and Gallagher (1986) describe a university student with fine grades and high scores in spatial and quantitative tests but with very poor verbal ability.

The controversy continues. However, one interpretation of the data is that people may differ in many specific abilities and much practice can lead to impressive ability in a single domain, but that there is also a g that aids performance in virtually all tasks. High-g individuals will have a big advantage in learning. The physiological evidence is particularly strong. A useful working assumption is that g exists and traditional IQ tests measure it to some degree. In this book, intelligence will be defined as g.

Effects of IQ on Learning

How is g related to learning? Do high-g individuals learn faster, remember more, and make better use of what they acquire? Does g affect all types of learning and exert the same effect at all stages of learning?

A lot of research has investigated the IQ-learning link, but the overall underlying principles are still not completely clear. Many early studies suffer from methodological problems, such as using poor measures of learning like gain scores (Ackerman, 1990; Jensen, 1989). However, there is evidence for some principles. Jensen (1989) suggests the following. IQ has little or no effect on relatively simple types of learning, such as classical conditioning and rote learning, except in very low scorers. IQ effects are strong when learning is intentional, the task is of moderate difficulty and complexity, the task is of meaningful information, and learning is helped by transfer from related past learning. Jensen therefore argues that some types of learning are more g-loaded than others and the link between g and learning ability is time. High-g individuals have faster elementary cognitive processes, which has cumulative effects on learning and performance. Faster mental speeds mean more operations per unit time, more information that can be stored, and faster forgetting of unneeded traces in the registers and working memory. As mentioned earlier, over many years this can result in a much larger knowledge base which itself will aid learning and performance. Another principle is that with skill learning, IQ effects are greatest in the early stages of learning, but after much practice performance converges.

Here are some studies.

Associative Learning. Much early research suggested that IQ had little effect on measures of habituation and classical conditioning, such as rate at which they occur (Zeaman and House, 1967). Estes (1982, 176), reviewing many such studies, concluded that "gross properties of conditioning such as rate of acquisition of a conditioned response have not been proven to vary greatly . . . from moderate retardation to normal adult levels." However, Estes pointed out that the retarded may show slower trace conditioning (whereby the CS begins and ends before UCS onset), perhaps because they have a shorter short-term memory span. Estes said that there is some evidence that high IQ scorers may habituate faster, but many studies that found this result have interpretation problems. Schafer (1985) found that IQ scores correlated about 0.5 with rate of habituation of the evoked potential to a click. The situation with operant conditioning is not clear. Estes argued that IQ has little effect on conditioning rate when learners are unaware of the contingency but that one might expect IQ effects when they are. Evidently, the brighter would grasp the response-reinforcer relation faster, especially a complex one, but no studies have been done. However, it is problematical whether humans show operant conditioning when unaware of the contingency (see Chapter 2).

Skill Learning. Here the picture is still a bit murky. First, let us consider relatively simple skills such as typing and playing a musical instrument. Early work found little effect of IQ on learning simple motor skills (Ferretti and Butterfield, 1992). However, later studies suggest that IQ has a big impact in the early stages of skill learning and progressively less as task performance becomes more automated. Ackerman (1987; 1988) presented supporting data and the following theory to explain this finding, based on Fitts and Posner's model of the stages of skill learning. Initially, IQ and abilities specific to the task (such as spatial and verbal abilities) are important because higher scorers can better devise new procedures to do the task and may better and more rapidly work out novel task requirements. (Indeed, Sternberg, 1985, suggested that brighter persons can better cope with such novelty and perhaps automate their performance faster.) High IQ scorers may have more attentional resources to bring to bear. In the second phase of skill learning, as performance becomes more automatic, the effect of IQ decreases and that of perceptual speed increases. In the third phase, when performance is largely automated, psychomotor ability differences then have most impact. Even so, individuals eventually converge on the same performance level, given enough practice. This implies that almost anyone may become an expert with enough practice. Ackerman (1988; 1990) presents evidence for this model with category word search, spatial figure, and choice reaction time tasks. There also is some evidence for it from the applied area; IQ tests correlate better with initial than long-term job performance (Ree and Earles, 1991).

However, with quite complex skills, the IQ-learning relation may be different and may vary with the task and other, still unknown factors. For example, Rabbitt et al. (1989) had subjects learn to play the computer game "Space Fortress" over five days. IQ did not correlate significantly with initial performance but correlated strongly with learning rate and maximum performance. Perhaps more training may have led to performance convergence. Haier et al. (1992) had eight subjects varying in IQ score from 101 to 137 learn the complex computer game "Tetris," which involves fitting geometrical shapes together. IQ score did not significantly correlate with initial or terminal performance, though these correlations were generally positive. (Perhaps they were not significant because of the restricted IQ range or small sample.) However, IQ score did correlate with the magnitude of glucose metabolic rate change in many brain areas concerned with learning. This finding supports the idea that IQ measures a kind of neural efficiency.

Complex Learning. Several studies have shown strong effects of IQ on learning tasks that require using strategies. High scorers typically learn faster, though the differences do not always hold across all parts of the IQ scale. For example, Ferrara et al. (1986) had children of average and above-average IQ score learn to solve letter series problems. The problems could be solved by applying two rules. If initially unable to solve a problem, each child was given the next of a series of graded hints. The average-IQ children needed more hints to learn the task and more to transfer the knowledge acquired to other tasks. Ferretti and Butterfield (1992) compared above-average, average, and mentally retarded children's learning of how to do a balance scale task. There was no learning difference between the first two groups, but the retarded children needed more training to learn and to transfer knowledge to other tasks. They also were less likely to keep on using the strategies. Indeed, much research on the retarded shows that they have great problems acquiring, using, and transferring strategies, at which the intellectually gifted excel (Howard, 1991). For instance, Campione et al. (1985) found that the more intellectually able could more readily transfer strategies to do a novel task. Studies also suggest that the retarded take longer to encode semantic information but do not differ in recognition memory performance or in rate of long-term forgetting (McCartney, 1987; Woodley-Zanthos, 1993).

How Important Is G? Here are two principles supported by some evidence. First, *g* can affect initial skill learning, but after much practice all performance may converge. Second, a person with a lot of domain-specific knowledge may outperform persons with much higher IQ scores but much less domain-specific knowledge. For example, Schneider et al. (1989) had children read a passage about a soccer game. Children with low verbal aptitude scores but who knew a lot about soccer understood and recalled more of the passage than high-aptitude but low–domain knowledge children. This finding parallels Chi's (1978) observation that child chess experts have better memory for chess positions than adult novices. Knowledge can outweigh age and *g*.

How important is *g* in everyday life, then? Does *g* level really limit what a person can acquire, how far along the path to expertise in a domain he or she can go, or is the really important factor a lot of practice? One view is that *g* is not all that important, but motivation to practice is. For instance, Howe (1988) asked, "Can anyone become a genius?" and answered that he is no longer sure that the answer is an unequivocal no. Lines of evidence he cites are the *idiot savant* syndrome and studies of genius. For instance, Simonton (1988) found that common background factors of scientific geniuses are high motivation and much time spent dealing with their domain. Almost all geniuses are domain-specific. Some researchers also claim that many experts in certain domains have only average or modestly above-average IQ scores. For instance, James Watson, co-discoverer of the structure of DNA, says that he has an IQ score of 115. Some chess experts have only average IQ scores (Holding, 1985). (However, not all studies have found this. Frydman and Lynn, 1992, surveyed thirty-three young Belgian players at a chess tournament and found an average IQ score of 121.) An informal, uncontrolled, but supporting experiment on the role of practice in creating high performance has been conducted with the Polgar sisters, Zsuzsa, Sofia, and Judit. Their father said that he wanted to see what a lot of training could do and chose chess as a test domain. All three sisters were schooled only at home and received much instruction in chess.

They performed astonishingly well in the game at an early age. All three have international chess titles and are high in the female rankings, and Judit was for a time the greatest chess prodigy ever, gaining the grandmaster title at the youngest-ever age of fifteen. They may well have much innate talent, but practice has had a very powerful effect. Ceci and Liker (1986) present some evidence that IQ is not important in performing another complex task, picking winners at the racetrack. They found that the performance of race handicappers did not correlate with IQ scores, though the task involved juggling much data to pick a winner. One handicapper scored just 80 on an IQ test but still handicapped well. Ceci and Ruiz (1992) found that two persons with IQ scores of 81 and 121 both transferred well from race handicapping to stock market predictions.

Such findings led Ericsson et al. (1993) to propose a strong view: Motivation and practice are crucial to high performance in a domain. Innate talent may not exist or, if it does, may be unimportant. Performance differences just reflect differences in amount of practice. They cite supporting studies. Novice and expert pianists showed huge differences in amount of practice. The experts on average started playing four years earlier and spent close to 60 hours a week on music. High-performing violin students had practiced a great deal. Even the treasured ability of absolute pitch (the power to identify any note) may derive from practice. Anyone may acquire it if trained early enough. What appears to reflect innate talent really may reflect a lot of practice.

However, on plausibility grounds, g (or innate talent) would surely be important. Much work has shown effects of g on learning, and everyday observations suggest its great importance. At the very highest levels of expertise, there are still great performance differences. Judit Polgar greatly outperforms her sisters, though she is younger than both and has had fewer years to practice. Another big problem is that studies cited in support have self-selected samples. Detterman and Spry (1988) point out that experts in a domain (such as race handicapping) select themselves and that performance of persons in that domain may not correlate with IQ because the sample is very atypical. The issue could be resolved by controlled experiments in which random samples from the population get equal amounts of practice at a complex task such as chess playing over many years.

However, several points are clear. Expertise can outweigh IQ, and much practice can lead to high performance. G probably affects initial learning, perhaps rate of learning, and perhaps terminal performance in complex domains. G is important, but not all-important.

STYLES AND LEARNING

Research has repeatedly shown that using such strategies as imagery, rehearsal, organization, and elaboration can improve learning. Various factors may determine whether a person actually uses one strategy or another, an obvious one being that he or she knows it and knows how to use it. Then there are personality and motivational factors. Some individuals may not use various strategies through fear of failure, perceived lack of self-efficacy in their use (Cole and Chan, 1990), and laziness. Indeed, the rationale of some educational programs is to improve learning by trying to remove such blocks.

Another well-known class of factors is cognitive and learning styles. People differ in their general preferences for using certain types of strategy, which hold over many different tasks (Schmeck, 1988). These preferences are called cognitive and learning styles. Cognitive style is a somewhat ill-defined notion but is usually seen as a general, habitual way of processing information, cognitive in the sense that it involves attending, perceiving, remembering, and thinking (Baron et al., 1986). It is a preference but is somewhat vaguely defined as being between a personality trait and an ability (Baron et al., 1986). An ability is a capacity to perform at maximum effort, and a personality trait is an index of a person's tendencies to behave in particular ways. A learning style is a preferred way of acquiring knowledge. The two types of style are closely related. Indeed, Das (1988) defined a learning style as a cognitive style applied to learning. A style is generally considered to be a continuum, with an individual being somewhere along it between two extremes.

These styles are important in the study of learning for several reasons. First, they affect what is learned and how it is learned. Persons with a certain style learn better in certain sorts of situations. Second, perhaps people can improve their ability to learn by switching between styles according to the situation. Indeed, an important question is whether and how readily persons can learn to be more flexible. Styles have mainly been studied by educational psychologists, and there is more evidence for some styles than others.

Cognitive Styles

The concept of cognitive style has been criticized as fuzzy and indeed is periodically questioned. Some researchers argue that they are really more like abilities than preferences (Zelniker, 1989) since scores on various tests of cognitive styles (such as the Embedded Figures Test) correlate with ability measures (such as the Ravens). Like abilities, style levels also may change with age, persons notably becoming more field-independent and reflective (Globerson, 1989). Other researchers have suggested that a style may not represent a continuum (Zelniker, 1989). Though the value of the notion is still uncertain, it is clear that styles affect performance. Another issue is their origins. Why do people differ in styles? There is no consensus (Waber, 1989).

One can also ask how many styles exist and how they interrelate. Biggs and Telfer (1987) counted at least twenty, though only few have been extensively studied. Schmeck (1988) suggests that all styles may derive from one broad dimension, which has various names but which can be classified on a global-versus-analytic scale. Persons with an extreme analytic style have strongly focused attention, notice and remember details well, divorce their feelings from facts, and are good at critical and logical thinking. Persons with a strong global style form overall impressions readily, are more intuitive, and mix feelings and facts. Riding and Douglas (1993) suggest that there are two major style dimensions, global-versus-analytic and a verbal-versus-imagery style (described later). However, it is still unclear how many styles there are and if they indeed derive from such general dimensions.

Here are some major styles and some research on how they affect learning.

Field Independence vs. Field Dependence (FI vs. FD). This style was the first discovered and has been extensively investigated. Its story dates back to World War II, when an observer noticed that some aviators flew into a cloud and came out at an odd angle, while others always entered and exited bolt upright. The usual interpretation is that the former are FD, and the latter FI. FIs make judgments internally rather than relying on external cues. They are adept at disembedding stimuli from their context and at breaking stimuli into parts. FDs tend to perceive stimuli as a whole and rely on external stimuli (such as the ground and sky) to make judgments. A good illustration of the difference is performance on a measure of FI, the Embedded Figures Test. Its items are figures with one of several simple figures embedded within, which testees trace out. FDs have much more trouble because they perceive each figure as a whole, while FIs can readily break it into parts. Indeed, some FIs say that they are unable not to see the simple figure.

FIs and FDs differ in many ways. FIs are supposed to be more intrinsically motivated and less sociable. FIs perform better at school and on a wide range of cognitive tasks (Globerson, 1989). They also are more likely to use analogies and metaphors and to try to build up a broad framework to understand a new domain. FDs are more likely to learn by rote. O'Donnell et al. (1991) illustrate this difference. They examined FI-FD differences in learning to administer intravenous therapy. Subjects read a 1,200-word description of the procedure and later were tested for recall of the passage and ability to perform the task. FI subjects recalled more and performed better. However, FDs performed better under some instruction methods than others; when they received more direction, for instance (e.g., by consulting with partners and by being referred back to the study passage). O'Donnell et al. suggest that FDs are worse at integrating material, less capable of using known schemas, and less adept at switching strategies to do the task.

Reflection vs. Impulsivity. This style relates to differences in the way people trade off speed and accuracy (Baron et al., 1986). The reflective prefer accuracy; they respond more slowly to task demands and make fewer performance errors. The impulsive go for speed; they react quickly, with little evident thought, and make many more errors.

The different styles affect performance. Reflectives on average do better on IQ tests and on a wide range of cognitive tasks (Globerson, 1989). Even when IQ score is held constant, the impulsive do worse at school and tend to be poorer readers (Messick, 1976). Impulsivity in the early stages of learning may have cumulative negative effects (Baron et al., 1986). However, being impulsive is not always bad, because some tasks demand speed more than accuracy. For instance, Zelniker (1989) presents some evidence that reflective children analyze stimuli into parts while impulsive children focus more on the stimulus as a whole in a wide range of tasks. When the task requires detailed analysis, the reflective perform better, but when it involves treating the stimulus as a whole, the impulsive do better.

People typically get more reflective with age, which Baron et al. suggest produces the developmental trend from similarity-based to dimensionally based classification in free classification tasks. With age, children may devote more time to the task and see less superficial bases of classification.

Verbal vs. Imagery. People prefer to use different formats to represent information. Some favor using verbal representations, while others prefer mental images. Research suggests that image preferrers learn best from pictorial material and verbalizers from verbal presentation. Image preferrers recall highly descriptive text better than acoustically complex and unfamiliar text, and the reverse is true for verbal format preferrers. Riding and Douglas (1993) looked at the effects of this style on learning material about car brake systems. Imagers recalled more than verbalizers when they had a picture of the braking system, while the verbalizers recalled more than imagers when neither saw a picture. Imagers also were more likely to use drawings in recall.

Hemisphericality. This style has been less researched than the above two, and its existence is more problematical. It relates to the well-known partial division of functions between the two cerebral hemispheres. The left hemisphere (in right-handed people) is concerned with language and logical thinking and the right hemisphere with intuition and imagery. In fact, these functions overlap to some degree in the hemispheres. The notion is that people differ in their preferred mode of thinking; analytics favor left hemisphere–style thinking and holists favor right hemisphere thinking. The latter are more intuitive and take things in as a whole (Dunn and Reddix, 1991). Dunn and Reddix found some evidence that the style may affect learning. Subjects were classified as holists or analytics by a physiological measure (EEG activity) and then learned different types of texts. In one experiment, analytics recalled more of the gist of a passage. In another experiment, male holists recalled more metaphors from a text containing highly metaphorical descriptive poetry, but females did not differ.

Learning Styles

Learning styles are very important in education, and several tests measure them. For instance, Schmeck's (1983) Inventory of Learning Processes has four scales: deep processing, elaborative processing, fact retention, and methodical study. Entwistle's (1988) Approaches to Study Inventory has scales called active learning processes and organized study methods. Many styles have been postulated (Schmeck, 1988; Dunn and Dunn, 1978), but this section will briefly describe some major ones. The styles postulated overlap to some degree. No one has yet devised a universally accepted list or taxonomy.

Surface versus Deep Processing. Surface processors are pragmatically motivated. They prefer to learn only what is needed to solve a practical problem, such as passing an exam, with minimal effort (Biggs, 1988). They focus on what seems important and try to memorize it verbatim. They do not try to understand material, to consider its implications, or to pose questions about it. They prefer to learn by rote. Deep processors prefer to organize material, to critically evaluate it, to compare and contrast its parts, and to connect it with their existing knowledge. They are more likely to learn meaningfully and learn from intrinsic interest (Schmeck, 1983).

Much research has shown effects of this style on learning. Deep learners usually acquire more knowledge and perform better in school (Kozminsky and Kaufman, 1992). Marton (1988) argues that deep learners are more likely to profit from formal schooling because they can acquire more concepts and are better able to use them. Learning with a surface style is more likely to lead to misconceptions about important concepts and a lot of rote-learned facts but little understanding of a topic.

Various factors may create a learner with either style. One, of course, is poor motivation, a lack of interest in learning school or other material. Another is a particular concept of what learning actually is. Saljo (1982) says that people may hold these notions:

1. A quantitative increase in knowledge.
2. Memorizing facts.
3. Acquiring facts, methods, and so on.
4. Abstracting meaning.
5. An interpretive process aimed at understanding reality.

A person who defines learning as items 1 or 2 above is more likely to adopt a surface style, while someone who sees it as item 5 is more likely to adopt a deep style (Marton, 1988). A learning style may only be changed by altering a person's concept of learning. Gow and Kember (1990) found that the concept of learning held may affect both how a person learns and how he or she teaches others.

Biggs and Moore (1993) list some other factors. Higher IQ scoring students tend to be deep learners, as are students who have a least one college-educated parent. Another factor is the teaching methods that a person is exposed to. Selmes (1985) found that formal and repetitive teaching methods and limited time to cover material helped induce students to adopt a surface style, perhaps just to cope with many assignments and exams. Biggs (1982) found that many beginning Australian university students rapidly switched from deep to surface styles, evidently to survive their courses. Science students are more likely to be surface learners than humanities students (Ramsden, 1983), possibly because science teaching often stresses learning of facts and equations, so students poorly understand basic concepts (White, 1993). For instance, Dahlgren (1978) found that university students in economics and physics have many misconceptions about basic concepts that are not altered by formal courses. As he put it,

only a minority of students had apprehended basic concepts.... Complex problems seem to be solved by application of memorized algorithmic procedures.... In order to cope with overwhelming curricula, the students probably have to abandon their ambitions to understand what they read about and instead direct effort toward passing examinations . . . which reflect the view that knowledge is a quantity. (Dahlgren, 1978)

Holist versus Serialist. These styles are closely related to the above one. Holists take a broad approach to a topic, trying to gain an overall picture of it and how its parts are related. Serialists learn step by step, part by part, and do not form an overall picture unless forced to. They are not concerned with how the parts are interrelated (Pask, 1988). Pask and Scott (1972) demonstrated these styles when subjects learned about two hypothetical Martian animal species that had various traits, habitats, and subspecies. Some subjects learned about them in a global fashion, others just accumulated information serially.

What factors induce persons to adopt either style? One is the nature of the discipline that a person studies and how its course grades are assigned. Science students are mostly serialists, while art and architecture students are mostly holists (Pask, 1988). However, this may partly reflect self-selection; perhaps holists choose art because of their general preferences, for example.

Training Cognitive and Learning Styles

Adopting a certain style for a particular task may produce better learning and/or performance. For instance, it may be better to be impulsive when speed is more important than accuracy and field-independent when a learner needs to acquire an overall framework. There probably is an optimum level on each style dimension for any task (Zelniker, 1989). So an important practical and theoretical question arises: How modifiable are styles? Can people learn to switch between levels on each style continuum?

Perhaps they can. Some studies described above suggest that styles are modifiable. Australian students rapidly became surface learners under a new educational regime, for example. But a lot of training studies have found little evidence of style change (Globerson, 1989; Zelniker, 1989). The problem may be finding the right training methods, motivators, and training periods, however. For instance, Baron et al. (1986) trained subjects to be less impulsive after eight months of sessions. The regime emphasized taking time to think, sticking with a problem, and considering all the alternatives. Subjects also learned and practiced use of mnemonic devices. They indeed became less impulsive, perhaps less rigid in using strategies, and more persistent. Globerson (1989) successfully trained field-dependent eight-year-olds to modify their style, and at the end of training they understood as much and performed various cognitive tasks as well as FI subjects. Weinstein (1988) reported a one-semester university course that alters learning styles. Subjects were taught various learning strategies and got much feedback and practice on their use. Quality of work in their course assignments improved, as did their grades and reading test scores.

Machine Learning: Symbolic and Connectionist

By one definition, a computer system that learns is one that improves its performance with experience. A simple example is Samuel's (1959) checker-playing program, which increased its skill by competing against itself and humans and eventually reached expert level. A more formal definition of computer learning is "a process in which a learner produces a representation of a target mapping working from training information derived from some environment" (Thornton, 1992). A target mapping is a mapping between two sets of objects, such as input and output stimuli. For instance, given sets of symptoms as input, the machine would produce a mapping of a given set and a disease diagnosis (e.g., "This set signifies measles").

Computer learning has been mentioned several times in this book, notably where efforts to program computers to learn have shed light on human learning and performance. Some examples are the nonviability of empiricist learners, the importance of commonsense knowledge to everyday performance, and the domain-specificity of expertise. Psychologists now often use computer simulations to test models.

Computer learning also is an active subfield of AI, in which researchers have several major aims. Some, like psychologists, are interested in better understanding human learning and memory. Others want to create an ultra-intelligent machine with an intelligence superior to human intelligence, which of course must be able to learn. Many are mainly interested in engineering and hope to build systems that can acquire their own knowledge, a long-term holy grail of the field (Firebaugh, 1989). Life then would be much easier for programmers. For instance, in creating an expert system, the major bottleneck is getting knowledge from human experts and putting it into a machine. Human experts often cannot readily specify what they know, and it may take hundreds of hours of interviews to draw it out and then many hundreds more to codify it into rules. If only the system could gather this knowledge itself. As well, performing some complex tasks needs knowledge that is very difficult to codify, examples being running a chemical factory and performing various sorts of complex pattern recognition. In addition, some researchers hope to design machines that abstract out rules and regularities better than humans do, and actually contribute to human knowledge. Some research projects produce huge masses of data far beyond human ability to deal with them. The classic successful example of this wish is the system INDUCE (Michalsky and Chilausky, 1980). From many descriptors about soybean diseases (such as leaf spots and seed shriveling), it generated a set of rules for classifying them. The system then used these rules to correctly classify 99.5 percent of 376 seeds, doing much better than a human expert, who managed 83 percent correct using his own rules. The local university's plant pathologists now use the machine's rules.

Research to meet the last two aims may not cast light on human learning. Indeed, some AI techniques, such as genetic algorithms (described later), bear little or no resemblance to human ways of doing things, and the rules from systems like INDUCE can look very strange. However, the field often uses human learning as a source of ideas.

Machine learning AI uses two major approaches, with different techniques and somewhat different histories. The first is the symbolic approach, which involves designing systems that learn and manipulate symbols. The second approach uses connectionist modeling and is called connectionism or neurocomputing. Some psychologists argue that the symbolic approach in AI has little to say about human learning and memory because many systems use methods unlike those used by people. However, I do not agree. This subfield can shed light on human learning and the complexities of learning in general and is well worth knowing something about.

This chapter briefly surveys the two approaches; first the symbolic one and then the connectionist one.

THE SYMBOLIC APPROACH

Research in the symbolic tradition goes back to the late 1940s at least, when Samuel started work on his checker-playing program. Research effort gathered pace in the 1970s. One landmark was Lenat's automated mathematician, mentioned in Chapter 4, which acquired mathematical concepts by manipulating its knowledge base. Another was Winston's (1976) concept-learning program. It represented knowledge in a semantic network and acquired the concept of *arch* from experience in a simple two-dimensional world. The field really took off and became respectable in the 1980s (Carbonell, 1992). The first machine learning conference had just twenty-four participants, but in the 1980s attendance spiraled and now is in the hundreds. The field has major journals (e.g., *Machine Learning*) and is an undergraduate AI course staple.

Building symbolic learning systems has proved very difficult. It soon became clear how complex learning is and that many steps are needed in even simple tasks. However, Carbonell (1992) lists some of the field's accomplishments and the following six major challenges for its future:

1. To discover a new scientific law and report it in a refereed journal.
2. To build a system that improves its chess playing strength by 500 points, from average to expert level.
3. To improve planning performance a hundred fold in two domains, such as medicine and manufacturing.
4. To build a system that learns in an aspect of investment and produces an investment strategy that earns over a million dollars in a year.
5. To build a system that outperforms the best hand-built natural language processing program.
6. To build a system that produces a diagnostic or treatment system in medicine that outperforms hand-built systems.

How Symbolic Learning Systems Work

A machine learning system typically has several parts (e.g., Firebaugh, 1989). It has a knowledge representation component, a task module that solves the problem at hand, a critic to evaluate results, and a learning module that uses error signals to alter the symbolic representations. Several different representation formats are used; semantic networks, production system rules, and frames (which are like schemas), for instance (Alty, 1989). Learning involves modifying representations. For instance, the ACT* system mentioned in Chapter 5 learns by adding, deleting, and combining production system rules and extending or narrowing the conditions that trigger a given rule. In symbolic systems, the rules also may be changed by adding metarules and uncertainty factors as a control structure. With a frame-based representation, the system can generate hypotheses to explain data and modify instantiations. Some systems use feature-based formats whereby stimuli are represented as sets of features. The system may learn a concept, for instance, by deriving a list of defining features that categorize a set of stimuli. Machine learning researchers generally assume that concepts consist of defining features. A system may use several of these formats at the same time.

Machine learning systems gather knowledge in several ways, mostly modeled on ways that humans use. Michalski (1987) lists several methods, the first two not really being instances of learning as defined in this book. First is direct implanting of knowledge, the system making no inferences from it. Second is learning from instruction, whereby the machine is given information that it applies to different tasks. This is the major method of educating expert systems. Third is learning by deduction, whereby a system deduces new knowledge by inference from what it already knows. Fourth is learning by analogy, which is applying knowledge from one domain to another. Fifth is learning from examples, which is inducing a concept description from examples alone. Sixth is learning by observation and discovery. This occurs without a teacher. The system examines a set of data (such as astronomical observations) and hunts for general laws that describe regularities in it.

Researchers in the field use a variety of paradigms (Winston, 1992), mostly based on concept learning. Three major paradigms are used in addition to the connectionist one. These are inductive (similarity-based) learning, analytic (knowledge-based) learning, and learning with genetic algorithms. Let us look at each in more detail.

Inductive Learning

Induction is generalizing from data; for example, that all swans are white from seeing several white swans. Much work in machine learning involves building systems that induce generalizations such as concepts or even scientific laws from data. Most research involves concept learning.

The basic task that systems are designed to do is partition a set of stimuli into categories and then describe the defining features of the concept representing each category. An archetypal example is Winston's (1976) program. It learned the concept of *arch* by encountering a series of examples and nonexamples in turn and being told which was which. When it encountered the first exemplar, it assumed that an arch was something with all of the exemplar's features, thus constructing a featural description represented in a semantic net. With each new stimulus encountered, it refined its concept description by comparing the current description with one of the new stimulus's features. Eventually it concluded that an arch was a brick or wedge supported by two bricks that did not touch.

Winston's program had a teacher, and stimuli were clearly examples or nonexamples. The real world is much more messy, however (Carbonell, 1989). Stimuli may be unlabeled or mislabeled, features may vary in relevance, and attribute values may be measured inaccurately. As mentioned in Chapter 4, humans cope with such problems by forming different sorts of representations than defining features sets. Some computer systems cope by using statistical techniques with their learning algorithms. Some systems also seek their own instances and some produce a best-guess concept description.

An interesting illustrative program is CLASSIT (Gennari et al., 1989). It represents physical objects by using numerical attributes, and it can construct a taxonomy itself. In one study, the researchers used a small domain whose stimuli were four-legged animals. Each animal was describable as a set of eight cylinders (e.g., each leg was a cylinder, the head was one, etc).

Each cylinder had such features as values for height, radius, and location, with seventy-two attribute values pairs per instance. When the system was shown various examples of horses, giraffes, cats, and dogs, it constructed the latter four categories itself. In another study, the system was exposed to stimuli from the domain of cardiac disease. Instances were real patients, each being described with thirteen numerical attributes and either heart-diseased or non-heart-diseased. After encountering ten instances, the system constructed three categories. One was of patients without heart disease and two were of patients with heart disease. Its classification of new instances was fairly good.

Another famous classification system is ID3 (e.g., Quinlan, 1986). It is exposed to a set of stimuli and tries to find the most discriminatory feature among them. Then it places instances into categories according to this feature and splits each category up according to the most discriminatory feature its instances have. It repeats this process until each subclass has just one instance. ID3 has induced rules for commercial expert systems, and it abstracted out a set of rules for chess endgames involving king and rook versus king (Firebaugh, 1989). This is a simple endgame, which the side with the rook should win quickly. ID3 abstracted six rules for conducting the endgame that were claimed to be more complete, concise, and understandable than those given in chess textbooks.

Langley and Zytkow (1989) describe some accomplishments of scientific discovery by machine learning programs (also see Nordhausen and Langley, 1993). Versions of a system called BACON were fed masses of data of observations of the physical world and looked for general laws to summarize it. It is an analog of a human scientist who looks at data and tries to find an equation to fit it. BACON uses heuristics that may propose hypotheses, define terms, and alter the scope of a hypothesized law. BACON formulated several fundamental physical laws from data: Kepler's, Ohm's, and the ideal gas law. However, systems such as BACON have many limitations, and their strong performance often derives from clever choice of initial parameters (Schaffer, 1993).

Another illustrative example is EURISKO (Firebaugh, 1989). It derived rules for playing a complex war game called "Traveller." Each player starts with a budget, which he or she uses to finance the building of a fleet of less than one hundred ships. The player decides on their attributes, such as type and size of weapons. EURISKO began with a knowledge base of 146 concepts (such as *weapon*), fought ten thousand Traveller battles, and from the results derived an optimal fleet size of ninety-six small ships. Using its rules it won the U.S. Traveller championship two years in a row and then retired undefeated because the directors threatened to cancel the tournament otherwise. EURISKO also designed a three-dimensional AND-gate, which won a patent.

Some recent work has tried to build systems that design experiments to discriminate between scientific theories (Rajamoney, 1993).

Analytic Learning

Analytic learning contrasts with inductive learning. In the latter, learners acquire generalizations from many instances. Analytic learning involves acquiring concepts or rules from just one instance (or a few) and a rich domain theory (Carbonell, 1989). The system uses its knowledge base and ability to deduce to form rules. This sort of learning is quite common in humans (see Chapter 3). An archetypal example is the apocryphal tale of Isaac Newton observing an apple falling and using his domain knowledge of physics to abstract out the notion of gravity. A travelogue on South America featured a local resident who accidentally dropped an object and uttered a common expression: "It fell from me." From this incident, the narrator inferred that locals tend to ascribe responsibility for events elsewhere and that a manifestation is their tendency to place all responsibility for the welfare of a state in the hands of a dictator. A third example is from chess. A novice may watch two experts play and see one deliver a "fork," which is a simultaneous attack by one piece (say, a knight) on at least two others (say, a king and a queen). The novice may note that the device won the game, infer that players should avoid being forked, work out that the tactic is ubiquitous and can be done by any piece, and then work out ways to set up forks. Many years ago I was trying to learn to program electro-mechanical equipment to run experiments. A technician explained to me how a relay worked, and from this I worked out how relays could be used to program many contingencies.

There are several types of analytic learning (e.g., Minton et al., 1989). This section will just describe one very important one, explanation-based learning. As mentioned in Chapter 3, this involves learning from a single example by manipulating a knowledge base. A system using it constructs causal explanations for things it encounters and uses the explanations to abstract out a concept or improve its performance. For instance, the GENESIS system processes natural language input and learns new schemas (Minton et al., 1989). Given a story about a kidnapping, it used low-level schemas to build up a causal structure that relates the goals of participants to their actions. It eliminated details irrelevant to the kidnap schema and used the schema it constructed to understand a second story. Minton et al. also describe a game-playing program that learns by analyzing how an opponent forced it into a trap, as in the chess example above. It analyzes why the trap worked and abstracts out a rule to avoid the trap in the future or to spring it on others.

Analytic programs also may use experience to refine their existing substantial knowledge base. For instance, the ODYSSEUS apprenticeship program described by Wilkins (1987) improves an expert system's knowledge base by observing another expert perform. It watches the expert work (e.g., at diagnosing diseases) and tries to construct explanations for each action. For instance, if the expert asks if a patient has vision problems, the system tries to work out why he or she asked that. If it finds no explanation, it signals, "Explanation failure," and tries to identify what knowledge is missing. Mahadevan et al. (1993) describe an apprenticeship program called LEAP that assists a human user to design digital circuits from scratch. It suggests ways to decompose circuit modules into submodules and to choose among different decompositions. It learns by observing and generalizing from the actions of its users. Experimentation with it showed that it could learn part of a manually created knowledge base of operators for Boolean circuit design and learn new control rules from its users' decisions.

For explanation-based learning to work well, the system needs a rich and versatile knowledge base. Instilling one is still the most difficult aspect of building these systems.

Genetic Algorithms

Holland (1975) came up with the idea of the genetic algorithm, which is based on an analogy to Darwinian selection. A system using a genetic algorithm produces a variety of "individuals," selects the fittest according to criteria, alters the individuals, and repeats the process on the next generation. Individuals are possible solutions to a problem, an example being different concept descriptions that categorize a set of stimuli. The building blocks of individuals may be features or rules (Booker et al., 1989). If the system is trying to learn concepts, it generates variants of a concept description (which may consist of various combinations of features), evaluates how well each one categorizes the stimuli, and then changes them. There are two major methods of change. One is mutation, which involves randomly changing a small part of each individual (say, one feature). The second is crossover. Individuals are paired off and bits are swapped between members of each pair to make new individuals. The new individuals are then evaluated and the best selected for the next stage of the process. The process goes on for many generations until the system decides it has a good solution.

An illustrative example is a concept learning program called GABIL, from De Jong et al. (1993). It induces descriptions of concepts from a set of exemplars and nonexemplars. It generates rule sets and looks for ones that perform well at categorizing a given set of exemplars and nonexemplars, using both mutation and crossover. The researchers exposed it to a data base of 286 real breast cancer patients, each being described as a set of nine features. It performed quite well compared to a variety of other machine learning systems in acquiring useful diagnostic concepts.

Systems using genetic algorithms have been applied to various problems. They are particularly useful for solving optimization problems, which involve finding an optimal set of parameters for tasks such as wire routing and scheduling, transportation, and control (Janikow, 1993). They even have been used to find the optimal set of weights for links in a connectionist network (Whitley et al., 1993). The subsequent net performed quite well. However, this approach is still developing. To date, it has not worked very well for machine learning in very complex domains (Janikow, 1993). Humans could not learn this way, so it is not a model of human learning.

CONNECTIONISM

Computer systems that learn by connectionist algorithms are called neural nets. The field that studies neural nets and their properties and examines their uses as psychological models is called connectionism, neurocomputing, or parallel distributed processing (PDP). A neural net has units that very roughly correspond to neurons and that have links varying in strength. The system can "learn" by adjusting the strength of connections according to a preset rule.

There is much excitement about the potential of neurocomputing. Neural net techniques have big engineering possibilities. Nets can perform functions that symbolic programs find difficult, such as very complex pattern recognition and other tasks for which the needed rules are too complex to be readily specified. Connectionism has had an enormous impact on psychology in the last decade or so. There are connectionist models of language acquisition, working memory, semantic memory, and various other functions. Some hail connectionism as a paradigm shift, like that from behaviorism to cognitivism, that will bring together many disparate areas, sweep away old problems (Tryon, 1993), and overcome the limitations of symbolic processing as a model of cognition (e.g., Dorffner, 1993). Some believe that the approach may help solve perennial issues such as the mind-body problem by showing how "mind" emerges naturally from numerous interacting simple units (Phillips, 1988). An introductory cognitive psychology textbook appeared in 1991 written from a connectionist viewpoint (Martindale, 1991). Other researchers are less enthusiastic, seeing the approach as a useful modeling tool for cognitively impenetrable functions, those inaccessible to consciousness. The symbolic approach may be needed for higher-order functions. The problems and prospects of the approach are considered at this chapter's end.

The field is moving very fast, and much of what is presented here may date rapidly. However, this section will outline some essential aspects of the approach.

History of Connectionism

The roots of connectionism go back to Aristotle's work on association formation and to James's (1890) notion of summing activation and the importance of the rate of co-occurrence of two events in forming an association (e.g., Quinlan, 1991). Hebb (1949) wrote at length on ways in which such functions as memory could arise from interacting neurons. He proposed the Hebb rule of learning: If two neurons are active at the same time, the link between them will be strengthened. (Interestingly, early computer simulations showed that the Hebb rule alone could not explain much of human learning.) Quinlan (1991) noted that Hebb laid down much of connectionism's early groundwork, and some nets still use his rule.

In 1943, Warren McCulloch and Walter Pitts described a model net consisting of artificial neurons that either fired or did not fire. The net's properties were explored, but research eventually showed that it had too many shortcomings as a model of the brain. For instance, real neurons are analog rather than digital like the model's.

The next landmark was Frank Rosenblatt's work on the perceptron (Rosenblatt, 1958; 1962). A perceptron is an artificial pattern recognition device loosely modeled on the brain. Rosenblatt actually built a large machine that received input through an artificial retina. The machine had a single input layer of simulated neurons and a single output layer. Experiments showed that it could learn various discriminations and could learn to classify patterns. This work generated much interest, which almost vanished completely after a now-famous incident. Minsky and Papert (1969) showed mathematically that the perceptron had many limitations; it could not compute certain kinds of function, for instance. They also briefly considered properties of nets with hidden units intervening between input and output units, but argued that the likelihood of developing an algorithm to overcome the perceptron's limitations was slim. (However, the back-propagation algorithm, described later, is often put forward as an answer.) They suggested adopting the symbolic approach to AI instead of the connectionist one. Their book was so persuasive that work on neural nets ground to a halt, except with a few hardy researchers such as Steven Grossberg, James Anderson, and Teuvo Kohonen.

However, in the mid-1980s, the field suddenly took off. The physicist John Hopfield (1982) had presented work on a Hopfield net, which was based on an analogy to a magnetic material called spin glass. The net had some impressive capabilities. It could solve practical problems such as finding an optimal path for a traveling salesman through a set of cities, and had interesting emergent properties. Then the bible of the field, *Parallel Distributed Processing* (Rumelhart and McClelland) was published in 1986, and the bulky two-volume work became an instant academic bestseller. Since then, the field has expanded enormously. Several specialist journals (such as *Connection Science* and *Neural Computation*) and a professional society (The International Neural Network Society) have started up. The approach has made great inroads into psychology. Researchers in learning and memory have had to learn new terms and mathematics and look at their field in a different way. The influence has been so great that Hintzman (1990, 110) remarked, "Many researchers are privately wondering if it would be easier to take tensor calculus or early retirement."

Why did connectionism suddenly take off, and why is it so popular now? Doubtless there are several reasons. One major one is that more powerful hardware and better algorithms allowed nets to do much more than previously. Second is their engineering potential. Nets may do some wonderful things and even learn to do them. Third, there was some dissatisfaction with the traditional information processing approach and the apparent intractability of some of its problems. Connectionism promised a quite different and possibly more successful approach that might resolve (or sidestep) difficult problems. Fourth, neural nets seem neurally plausible. They indeed mimic some impressive properties of the human brain, such as content addressability, whereby input from one part of a stimulus can reinstate a whole memory trace of it. Fifth, the behavior of nets is easily studied and is amenable to a rigorous mathematical analysis. Nets are much easier to study than actual organisms. Crick (1989) expands on this point, arguing that some researchers believe that the brain is too horrendously complicated to study but also arguing that it is necessary to do so rather than work with model nets. Sixth, the field has a lot of clearcut and answerable questions. McClelland (1988) adds these further and related attractions: to give unified accounts of apparently contradictory phenomena and to give new accounts of phenomena that may explain otherwise puzzling anomalies. (An oft-cited example of the latter is Hinton and Shallice's 1991 model of deep dyslexia that mimicked an otherwise puzzling language error of humans.)

Here is a brief description of how nets work.

Parts of a Neural Net

Detailed descriptions of the technical aspects of neural nets are given in Quinlan (1991), Hinton (1989), and Churchland and Sejnowski (1992).

Nets are typically simulated in a serial computer, which can be readily programmed to mimic a set of interconnected units. The units have input links from other units and may have output links to other units. There are three major types of unit. Input units take data from the environment, output units make a response to the environment, and hidden units intervene between input and output units. They are termed "hidden" because they are not directly linked to the environment. Figure 7.1 gives some illustrations.

Figure 7.1
Two Types of Neural Net

1. A pattern-associator.

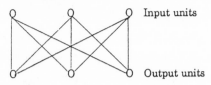

Input units

Output units

2. A net with hidden units.

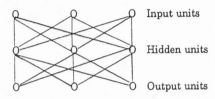

Input units

Hidden units

Output units

Nets come in several types. A net with no hidden units (with only a layer of input units and a layer of output units) is called a pattern associator. In such a setup, typically all units in one layer connect with all in the other. In nets with hidden units, units are arranged with one layer or more of hidden units between input and output units. Units in each layer connect only with those in the adjacent layers. In a Kohonen net, units in the same layer may be linked to each other. Impulses of activation from one layer to another usually propagate only in one direction, from input to output units. However, in a feed-forward net, impulses may go in either direction. A given net may have only a few units or many hundred.

A given unit may have one or more input and output links, called the fan-in and fan-out. A link may be excitatory (e.g., the output of one unit increases the activation of another) or inhibitory (it decreases it). In some nets, a given unit may have excitatory links to some units and inhibitory links to others (which never actually occurs in the brain). Each connection has an associated weight; the weight (or strength) of the link between any pair of linked units i and j is designated W_{ij}. It is a real number. In a given net, the many links may have a multiplicity of different weights. The weights of the links may be hand-set by the designer, or the net may adjust them itself (e.g., learn).

A given unit takes its input on a particular cycle of operation and decides whether to fire according to a function called the activation rule (e.g., Rumelhart, 1989). The function may include a threshold value that must be exceeded before the unit fires. For instance, say that the threshold value is four and the unit has five input links from five other units, each with a weight value of one. If three input units fire, the computed value would be

Figure 7.2
A Net That Tells When Either but not Both of Two Inputs Has Been Presented

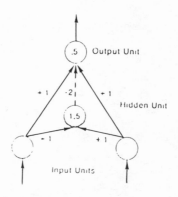

From Rumelhart and McClelland (1986). Copyright © (1986) by MIT Press. Used by Permission.

three, so the unit would not fire. On another cycle, if four input units fire, the value is four, so the unit itself fires. Unit firing may be all or none or according to some real number.

The activation state of a net at a given time refers to what units are then firing. It can be represented by a vector. (A vector is a set of numbers, such as 3, 5, 11.) For instance, say that in a five-unit net units 1, 2, and 5 are active at a given time. Its activation state is 1, 1, 0, 0, 1—1 meaning that the unit is active and 0 meaning it is not.

Nets deal with an environment, which consists of the set of patterns that might be presented. Usually the environment is simulated. The net is fed vectors that represent stimuli in the environment. For example, a stimulus might be an object in the environment with values for five features, each ranging from 1 to 10. The input stimulus would be the vector 4, 6, 3, 4, 8.

Nets work in runs. A run of a net might proceed as follows. Say that a net is no longer learning (e.g., unit weights are no longer being changed). A stimulus is presented to the input units. Some fire and in turn fire other units, which themselves fire an output unit or units, which might in essence say, "This is an *a*," or "This blip represents a submarine."

Figure 7.2 further illustrates some of the above ideas. The net depicted recognizes when either but not both of two input patterns has been shown. If pattern *A* alone is shown, the first input unit fires and activates the output unit. The hidden unit does not fire because its threshold is 1.5 and the input is only 1. If pattern *B* alone is shown, the output unit fires but again the hidden unit does not. However, if both *A* and *B* occur simultaneously, the hidden unit fires and decreases the output unit's activation level below threshold. The activation of the output unit is 2, but the hidden unit reduces it to 0, so the output unit does not fire. These weights could be set by hand, or the net could learn these or another set to perform the task.

Knowledge is represented in the weights of the links. There is no executive, no homunculus. Knowledge may be local or distributed. In the former, a single unit may represent a particular concept. The well-known grandmother cell notion is that a particular neuron fires when a person sees his or her grandmother. A distributed representation has no such units; knowledge is widely spread throughout the links. A particular stimulus (such as a grandmother) is represented by the activity of many units across the net. Interestingly, some studies have tried to determine what particular units in a well-trained net actually do. The system NETtalk takes written English as input and gives spoken English as output (Sejnowski and Rosenberg, 1987). Some units evidently recognize particular vowels, while other knowledge is widely distributed across many units.

Learning in Neural Nets

Some nets do not learn; their weights are hand-set. But setting by hand is tedious, and the resulting performance often is uninteresting. Most net research examines nets that learn. Some questions asked are what a given net can learn and simulate and what the effects are of different numbers of units, interconnection patterns, and learning algorithms.

Training usually proceeds in trials. A stimulus is presented, the net processes it, and the net makes an output response. The net may or may not have a teacher (called supervised versus unsupervised learning). In supervised learning, after each trial a teacher tells the net if its output response was right or wrong and may give a measure of the extent of error. The net then adjusts the weights on some or all links according to a rule. Then another stimulus is presented, and the process continues until some learning criterion is met, the net settles into a stable state, or all training stimuli are shown. Unsupervised nets self-organize their weights to mirror the stimuli presented.

Often a learning problem has no unique solution; a net finds a "good enough" one. A different net might come up with a different set of weights. As well, setting up a net with a good number of units and layers to solve a learning problem is an art (Quinlan, 1991).

Various rules are used to change weights. Here is a brief description of major ones.

The Hebb Rule. The Hebb rule is used with unsupervised learning. At its simplest, the rule is:

$$\Delta W_{ij} = \varepsilon\, Y_i Y_j$$

The equation simply means that ΔW_{ij}, the change in the weight of the link between units i and j (any pair of units), is equal to a preset constant ε

(called the learning rate) times the states (Y_i and Y_j) of units i and j on a given trial. Units i and j are either on (represented by a value of 1) or off (represented by 0). So unless both units were on in that trial, the weight will not change. If both were on, the weight changes by the value of the learning rate parameter. Thus the weights of all links between units active on the last trial increase by the learning rate parameter, which can be preset to determine how quickly weights will change. The net applies the rule to each pair of units and repeats this process in each subsequent trial until the whole set of stimuli is shown. Nets using this rule do not need a teacher but have many limitations (Rumelhart and McClelland, 1986).

A variant of the Hebb rule is the competitive learning rule (Rosenblatt, 1962). Consider a pattern associator in which each input unit is connected to each output unit. Initially, the link weights are randomized. Then an input is given (a vector). The net then looks for the weight vector that was closest to the input vector. (Say that a unit has three links, with weights of 2.0, 3.1, and 3.4. Its weight vector is 2.0, 3.1, 3.4.) After each stimulus is shown, the weight vector in the net that is closest to the input vector is found, and that unit becomes the "winner." The weights of the winner are then altered to move closer to the input vector, and this process continues until all stimuli have been shown. This rule is useful for finding regularities in input data, which may not be apparent to humans. Nets using it may learn prototypes of categories.

Competitive learning itself has variants. For instance, in a Kohonen net, all units in the winner's neighborhood change, neighborhood being defined as within a predefined distance.

The Delta Rule. The delta rule is a variant of the Hebb rule that is used in supervised learning. It is sometimes called the Widrow-Hoff rule. The net is given inputs in trials. After each trial, it makes an output response and then is given the desired output pattern. It then adjusts weights to try to reduce the difference between the desired output and its actual output on the last trial. Weights are changed according to the following equation:

$$\Delta W_{ij} = \varepsilon \, (t_j - Y_j) \, Y_i$$

Here t_j is the desired output pattern, so ($t_j - Y_j$) is a measure of the net's error on the previous trial. It is called the delta rule because the net reduces the difference (the delta) between actual and desired output. It also is related to the Rescorla-Wagner rule for classical conditioning (see Chapter 2).

Back-Propagation. The versatile back-propagation rule is used in a hidden unit net, and much connectionist work uses it. The basic principle is simple. A net is run and after each trial is given a desired output, which it compares with its actual output on that trial. Then the net randomly modifies connection weights between the output units and the adjacent layer of hidden units to minimize the error. When this process is complete, that set of weights is fixed, and the next layer of connections is modified in the same way. Weight modification thus is propagated backwards from the output units through the net. The formal rule, from Quinlan (1991), is as follows:

$$\Delta W_{ij} (n + 1) = \eta (\delta_{pj} O_{pi}) + \alpha \Delta W_{ji} (n)$$

Where $\Delta W_{ij} (n + 1)$ is the weight change at time $n + 1$ on the link between the ith hidden unit and jth output unit, η is the learning rate parameter, δ_{pj} is the error of the jth output unit, O_{pi} is the state of the ith hidden unit, α is the momentum term, and $\Delta W_{ij} (n)$ is the previous weight change at time n. The momentum term is a constant that scales previous weight changes. Without it, the net may oscillate wildly (Quinlan, 1991).

Back-propagation can be seen as analogous to gradient descent. One can see the ideal solution to the net's learning problem as lying at the foot of a hill. When adjusting weights and evaluating their adequacy, the net is metaphorically traveling down a rugged gradient. The problem is sometimes getting stuck in a local minimum: The slope may rise briefly and then continue downward, but the net may believe it has hit the global minimum (the bottom), which represents the best solution.

Back-propagation has limits, however. First, getting it to work for a given problem partly is an art. The designer must select a good number of units, a good net architecture, and a good learning rate value. A net may learn very slowly with it, sometimes needing many thousands of trials. It also only works well on small problems involving a few hundred units at most. Finally, it is not biologically plausible. The algorithm is too slow and complicated for the brain to use.

Some Connectionist Research Areas and Achievements

Some research issues are what the capabilities of various net architectures and learning algorithms are, how well various setups solve certain kinds of practical problems, and how various psychological functions can be modeled. First let us consider the engineering aspects and then the approach's application to the study of learning and memory.

Neural Nets and Engineering. Much research has applied neural net techniques to practical problems that traditional programs find difficult. Now, for many problems traditional computers work faster and more efficiently than nets. Nets may be useful when rules are difficult to discover and codify or far too many are needed to deal with even simple problems. Examples are face and speech recognition. Making a useful reading machine for the blind is an extraordinarily difficult task with traditional computers because there are so many rules of spelling and pronunciation and exceptions to them to implement. Evidently engineers declared that one could not be built (Robinson, 1992). However, the system NETtalk mentioned earlier has just a few hundred units and does just this with about 90 percent accuracy. It takes strings of letters as input and in thousands of trials has learned to pronounce them passably well. It uses hidden units, some representing vowels and some representing consonants. Another difficult problem is correctly reading handwritten text, a task still beyond traditional systems. However, Le Cun et al. (1992) described a net that could read handwritten zip code digits with about a 15 percent error rate and a 9 percent rejection rate. Computer nets that learn to read the user's handwriting are now commercially available.

Nets have proven useful for resource allocation problems. These basically involve finding optimal solutions to the allocation of resources in an unstable environment. Examples are the traveling salesman's problem of finding an optimal route between a set of cities, setting airline capacities and fares on various routes, and scheduling crew training. Nets can find good solutions to these problems (Bell et al., 1992). Nets also are useful for solving some problems in computer vision (Lisboa, 1992). Nets can run a chemical factory better than symbolic programs (Robinson, 1992). A successful net built by Gorman and Sejnowski (1988) takes sonar echo spectrograms as input and discriminates between echoes from rocks and metal objects as well as or better than humans do. Carbonell (1989) gave this assessment of the engineering uses of nets compared to symbolic AI programs: Nets are best for single-step pattern recognition in unstructured complex domains if many training examples are available. However, analytic methods are best for well-structured knowledge-rich domains that require deep reasoning and multistep inference, even if only a few training examples are available. Inductive and genetic algorithms are useful for problems between these extremes.

Applications to Psychology. Nets have much appeal as psychological models for several reasons. One is that nets are neurally plausible, though this is downplayed nowadays because real neurons are so much more complex. Nets seem to work much like the brain does, with complex behaviors and capabilities emerging from simple units working together. The units self-organize to produce some interesting emergent properties, just as, to use a popular analogy, simple units such as ants work together to produce a complex society. Examples of emergent properties are as follows. As mentioned, nets show content-addressable memory, an impressive but otherwise puzzling aspect of human memory. A severely degraded stimulus or just part of a stimulus resembling a memory trace in the net may elicit the whole trace. Nets also may show graceful degradation; like the brain they are fault-tolerant. If parts of a net are lesioned, performance worsens gradually and in proportion to the amount of damage. Lesioning any part of a traditional program usually leads to catastrophic failure, as would taking out almost any part of a television set. Nets also are good at things that people are good at, such as complex pattern recognition. Nets also can make a best guess. They can settle for a good enough solution, as do people. Nets also may automatically generalize from training stimuli to new instances and may form prototypes from instances.

Computer neural nets have been used to illustrate and discover more about real ones. For example, Robinson (1992) describes some work on the brain's vestibulo-ocular reflex, which keeps the eyes pointing in the same direction when the head moves. Robinson trained a simulation of the real circuit and found that every unit in the model net carried a combination of position and velocity signals and no others, as do real neurons. One proposal had been that the real net's signal integration might be step-by-step, but this did not occur in either real or model net. The simulation also developed some rogue cells, which had velocity and position signals going in opposite directions and which had no special function. Interestingly, real nets also have these rogue cells. However, Robinson is generally pessimistic about the long-term value of this kind of simulation work.

Nets also have been used to test out ideas about various neural disorders. For example, Seidenberg and McClelland (1991) developed a connectionist model of word recognition and naming that mimicked aspects of surface dyslexia. Hoffman and Dobscha (1989) tested an idea about the neural basis of schizophrenia. Brain imaging data suggest a hypothesis that schizophrenia may occur if axonal pruning goes on past its normal end in early adolescence. Their net's connections were excessively pruned and it developed "schizophrenic" symptoms—of a sort, anyway.

Nets have been used with some success to model many psychological functions and phenomena, such as classical conditioning and many associated phenomena (Kehoe, 1988), *idiots savants* (Norris, 1990), aspects of language acquisition (Bechtel and Abrahamsen, 1991), concept learning (Kruschke, 1993), LTM (Humphreys et al., 1989), and even humor (Katz, 1993).

Such relative successes have led to much enthusiasm. Tryon (1993) lists several recurrent issues that he says the connectionist framework may resolve or turn into nonissues. One mentioned above is the mind-body problem. Mind is an emergent property of simple interacting units. Nets do not need executive processes, so terms such as *psychosomatic* are unnecessary. A second is the perennial nature-nurture problem. One could say that initial synaptic weights are genetically set and may be modified by experience. Learning and development thus are two sides of the same coin; development is changes in synaptic weights over time. A third is whether animal and human learning differ. They can be seen as basically the same. Though human nets are much bigger and more complex, the same principles apply.

These ways to sidestep issues seem reminiscent of behaviorism. Several authors have noted the similarities. Behaviorists sidestep complex issues such as the relation between mind and behavior by saying they cannot be investigated and need not be anyway. Behaviorists see animal and human learning as describable by the same principles. They also see a few elementary types of learning as the building blocks for the complexity of human behavior, just as some simple units and a learning rule do in nets. Another commonality is the great emphasis on learning.

Some Problems and Major Criticisms of Connectionism

The general approach has met with various criticisms, some technical and some philosophical. Several works give detailed analysis of the latter criticisms (e.g., Bechtel and Abrahamsen, 1991; Horgan and Tienson, 1991), and this section will just look at some major arguments.

Technical Problems. Nets built to date have some major technical limitations. First, nets may work well with small problems requiring relatively few units but typically flounder with large problems. This is called the scale-up problem; nets with more than a few hundred units perform poorly. An analogous problem occurs in symbolic AI; an expert system may work well in a small domain with a limited set of rules but may go to pieces when the domain is widened and too many rules are required. This may be a fundamental limit of neural modeling, or it may be eventually solved. Second, nets often need vast amounts of training to perform some task, which is a practical constraint on their use and which makes them less neurally plausible. Third, nets often perform poorly unless they get a lot of help. As mentioned, the designer has to carefully select parameters, and these may take a lot of adjusting before the net performs adequately. Most need teachers, too. Even the input stimuli are specially prepared—vectors rather than the huge range of environmental stimuli processed by humans (e.g., Churchland and Sejnowski, 1992).

Problems as Psychological Models. Various researchers have criticized the value of nets as models of the mind. The brain is indeed a huge, massively parallel neural network, but do model neural nets really cast much light on how it works? First, some critics argue that model nets are not really neurally plausible despite a few surface similarities. Crick (1989) points out that real neurons are far more complex, are far from being completely understood, are never both inhibitory and excitatory, and have many connection patterns. For instance, a real neuron can have a hundred thousand links, and neurons are never connected to every other neuron in an adjacent layer, as in model nets. Real neurons could not use such algorithms as back-propagation. As Crick put it, model nets are "unrealistic in almost every respect." Second, model net learning is often not much like human learning. Nets sometimes make similar mistakes as humans but also may make very unhuman ones. Nets cannot readily learn in one trial, as humans often do. Nets cannot readily learn by adding to or extending existing knowledge as people do; a net overrides what it already knows (Levelt,

1990). Fodor and Pylyshyn (1988) make a number of criticisms. For instance, they point out that the brain is highly modular with many special-purpose components tacked on during evolution. Its parts are not as interconnected as in model nets. (However, some nets are more modular nowadays.) They also argue that some high-level aspects of cognition cannot be modeled by nets and must be modeled by a rule-based approach. A recent study by Ling and Marinov (1993) provides some support for this idea by comparing some well-known language-learning nets with a program that uses symbols. They analyzed performance of one net and argued that it did not actually perform the assigned task of learning the past tenses of English verbs, and connectionist nets may not be able to. A program using a rule-based approach performed the task much better.

Another major criticism is that nets often just provide demonstrations (Crick, 1989). Say that a connectionist net that models some cognitive function performs very well and apparently like humans. This does not necessarily show that the brain carries out the function in that way. It just shows how the brain could perform it. Crick says that the difference is between science and engineering. Engineers try to build a system that works, while scientists try to find out how an existing system actually does work, not how it could work. Indeed, a net does not find a unique solution to a given problem, and many connectionist studies do not even contrast a net's performance with that of actual organisms. Massaro (1988) experimentally illustrated that this is a serious problem by showing that nets with hidden units were too powerful. They could simulate results generated by quite different process models and results made either with highly unrealistic assumptions or that imply mutually incompatible processes. Nets with hidden units may be too unconstrained to be useful models of human performance.

Smolensky (1988) gave a detailed analysis of the connectionist framework, arguing that it is unclear whether model nets can perform high-level cognitive tasks and if they are a sound way to model the brain. He suggested that the nets may be useful on a subsymbolic level of analysis, between the neural and the cognitive, and examines some of its uses.

The controversy about connectionism will continue for some time. It is probably too soon to say how it will be resolved and whether connectionism will become the new paradigm and displace others. My view is that it will not, that some real limits of the approach will become very apparent, but that connectionist techniques will be useful for modeling low-level functions and as heuristics to test out ideas and account for anomalies (such as error patterns in dyslexia). The symbolic level of analysis will be needed to study high-level functions and also for applications to practical concerns such as education and industrial design.

8

Applications

Psychology has been applied to practical problems for many decades. For instance, back in 1905 Alfred Binet devised the first IQ test to try to distinguish between lazy and unable pupils. J.B. Watson, the founder of behaviorism, had a profound impact on the application of psychology when he lost his university post in 1920 after a divorce scandal. He ventured into advertising and used his knowledge of psychology to pioneer many practices still common: expert endorsements of products, market research, tests to measure and alter employee performance, and products arranged around the cash register (Goldstein and Krasner, 1987). Psychology is applied in many areas, such as industry, health, the law, education, and the armed forces. It can be applied at various levels; to an individual (e.g., one receiving psychotherapy), to a large organization, and even to whole communities. For example, Lavelle et al. (1992) applied behavioral principles to encourage drivers to use child safety seats in two Colorado towns. The local police evidently gave enforcement of the relevant law a low priority. The researchers gave officers a talk on the law's importance and described how issuing citations would increase safety seat use and decrease mortality. They also arranged rewards for issuing citations. Citation rate rose dramatically: Officers were 44 times more likely to issue a citation, which increased drivers' use of safety seats.

Applying a good theory can help understand a problem and suggest direct solutions, just as understanding how a virus works suggests approaches to developing a vaccine. As Kurt Lewin's famous quote goes, "There is nothing so practical as a good theory." Often, however, a theory just gives guidelines. There may be several relevant principles that conflict or that are not obviously applied. Theory can suggest possible solutions or even questions to ask that then are answered by experiments. One can try out various possible solutions suggested by the principles. For example, some years ago the British post office wanted to introduce an alphanumeric code for addressing letters (eventually settling on codes such as SW1P 1PT). Theory would suggest grouping items in threes, keeping the number less than the short-term memory span of seven, and mixing letters and numbers for maximum discriminability. But various experiments were needed to find the system that sorters could read most rapidly and efficiently. Such experiments can even be carried out on a whole community. For example, Warren and Walker (1991) wanted to find the best pitch for a printed appeal for charity funds. Social psychology principles suggested that readers would be more likely to donate if they could empathize with recipients and if the recipients' need was short-term. They sent out different types of appeal to a sample of 2,648 persons in a city of a million: Perth, Australia. Appeals that emphasized empathy and stressed that normally self-reliant recipients just needed to be helped back on their feet drew the most donations. This general theme comes up again and again: Theory suggests solutions, but further research is needed to determine the best one.

Applying psychology can have problems, however. A major one is actually getting a solution used, sometimes even by those who requested one. People often resist change and may need persuasion to adopt a certain solution. For instance, some teacher educators say that student teachers are often loath to apply new work on learning. The new ideas may not fit their own views on learning and instruction or may take too much effort to understand and learn to apply. Levy-Leboyer (1988) suggests that applications are much less likely to be used if their adoption requires attitude change or a reformulation of the initial problem. He cites a telling example. The French post office asked his research group to help reduce phone vandalism. The post office believed that the damage was being done by thieves or young social delinquents, but research showed the damage was mostly done by angry customers frustrated by equipment malfunctions. The researchers designed a poster that told such a customer where the nearest alternate phone was. Studies showed that customers read the poster and did not hit the phone. However, the posters were not used because this solution did not fit the post office's analysis of the problem. Levy-Leboyer says that application is likely to occur when it gives a quick and easy solution that fits existing ideas.

There are many areas to apply the study of learning and memory to. The topic is at the heart of many domains and is central to questions of behavior change. Education has, of course, always been a major area of application. Behaviorism has been much applied and indeed has had an enormous impact on American society (Goldstein and Krasner, 1987). Despite its poor reputation in mainstream psychology, its principles have proved useful in education, psychotherapy, industry, the armed forces, and community life. The U.S. education system is still largely based on behavioristic principles (Farnham-Diggory, 1992). To use behavioral principles one need not subscribe to the radical behaviorist view of people as automatons. Indeed, sometimes behavioral and cognitive principles are applied together. For instance, one might use a cognitive analysis of an amnesiac's deficits to suggest what treatment is needed and use behavioral training principles to teach new skills and behavior modification principles to induce relaxation. However, behaviorism is of little use in some areas, such as industrial design.

This chapter describes six major areas of application: the law; dealing with animals; education; psychotherapy and health promotion; electro-convulsive therapy, drugs and neurology; and machine design.

THE LAW

Research on memory has had several useful applications in the legal arena, and psychologists are sometimes called as expert witnesses to testify on the capabilities and frailties of human memory. One major concern is the accuracy of eyewitness testimony. Eyewitness testimony is of enormous importance in court, and juries assign it great weight. Indeed, sometimes it may be the only evidence. A positive identification in a line-up by one witness or an uncorroborated report of a crime by an evidently truthful witness may be enough to convict. However, false identifications are common. Another major concern is whether various alleged memory phenomena actually do occur. For instance, in 1990 George Franklin of California was convicted of murder after his daughter testified that a repressed memory of her father killing her friend in 1969 had recently come to consciousness. Do such phenomena actually occur? Loftus (1993) describes many similar cases coming up and causing concern. A common one is a claim of recovery of memory of childhood sexual abuse. Loftus analyzes several such cases and suggests that therapists often may be implanting these memories.

Methods and theory from the study of learning and memory can help answer these and other questions. First, how reliable is eyewitness testimony, and what conditions may foster reliable or unreliable testimony? Theory holds that human memory is approximate, schematic, and often prone to errors, distortions, and forgetting. A variety of experiments (mentioned below) have investigated how it works in eyewitness cases. Another type of question is about memory capabilities. For instance, how reliable are child witnesses, how accurate can memory for faces be over many years, and how accurate are memories recovered through hypnosis (e.g., Wells, 1993)? Many laboratory experiments give some answers, though some researchers question their generalizability to real-life cases (Bekerian, 1993). This section will sketch out some important findings.

First, much research by Elizabeth Loftus and her colleagues (e.g., Loftus, 1984) suggests that eyewitnesses often are unreliable and that memory traces may be malleable, distorted by schemas, and altered by information given after the event. A classic illustration, mentioned earlier, is the study by Loftus and Palmer (1974) that showed subjects a film of a car crash and asked how fast the cars were going when they "hit" or "smashed into" each other. Those given the "smash" wording gave higher speed estimates and were more likely to recall having seen broken glass, which was not present in the film. This phenomenon is quite general; memory traces can be readily altered by subsequent information. Even three-month-old infants show it (Rovee-Collier et al., 1993). Postevent information seems to create a new updated memory trace of the event. It is still controversial whether a new memory trace replaces the old one, but the practical point is that clever questioning by a lawyer or the police (or just time passing) may distort a memory trace. Research also shows how readily a schema can affect recall and make testimony less reliable. List (1986) showed subjects a film depicting instances of shoplifting and tested their recall of details a week later. Subjects falsely recalled events not in the film but that are common in shoplifting situations. Another concern is accuracy of face recognition in line-ups. Wells (1993) summarizes research on optimum conditions: Sequential lineups (in which each suspect is shown singly in succession) lead to fewer false identifications when the culprit is absent. Lineups work best when the witness is not told how many suspects will be shown. Finally, the single-suspect line-up (in which only one person is ever shown) can produce low rates of misidentification of innocent persons.

Fisher and Geiselman (1988) used such findings to suggest several guidelines for careful witness interviewing. For instance, to get more accurate recall, interviews should try to reinstate cues present at the time of the crime, use open-ended questions, encourage recall of every detail, and try to get the witness to recount the event in various ways. A study showed that these factors improve recall.

Another question is how accurate recognition memory for faces is under extreme emotion. A crime victim or a bystander witnessing a violent crime is likely to be highly aroused. One might expect good recognition because the event is distinctive or poor recognition because of repression or attention being taken up by extreme arousal. Baddeley (1990) reviews much evidence and suggests that low arousal may enhance recognition memory while very high arousal may lessen it. For instance, Loftus and Burns (1982) showed subjects versions of a bank robbery film. In one version, the robber escaped peacefully, while in the other a young boy was shot in the face. Subjects shown the violent version recalled and recognized less detail. The authors likened the phenomenon to retrograde amnesia after head injury; the violent shock of the film may disrupt consolidation. Another example is from Peters (1988). Subjects were given a stressful inoculation and were later asked to pick out the injecting nurse or someone they had spoken to after the shot. The nurse was more poorly recognized, evidently because of heightened arousal at the time of the shot.

Another capacity question is how accurate memory can be over very long intervals. Sometimes a witness may have to recall a face or details of an event from many years before. A good example is the case of John Demjanjuk, a Ukrainian resident in Chicago who was accused of being Ivan the Terrible, a sadistic guard at the Treblinka concentration camp during World War II. He was extradited to Israel, convicted and sentenced to death in 1988. But there was little hard evidence against him. The major evidence was from five former Treblinka inmates who identified him in court and a 1951 photo of Demjanjuk as Ivan. A face changes a lot over so many years and memories fade, and subsequent developments suggested that their testimony was unreliable. In 1993, Demjanjuk was released because of doubt that he was Ivan. Another such case is the famed Nineteenth-Century Tichborne claimant, who returned to England and claimed to be the heir that had disappeared thirteen years before. Though taken to be the heir initially, he was eventually called an imposter. Bruch et al. (1991) performed an elegant study that gives some idea of the accuracy of face memory over long intervals. Subjects were asked to match photos of classmates (taken twenty-four to twenty-six years before) from their high school yearbook to current photos. They had not seen their classmates in this time. They matched photos much better than controls unfamiliar with the faces. Some subjects were much more accurate than others, however. In addition, some faces changed much more than others in the quarter-century and were harder to match. The implications are that some witnesses may reliably recognize persons after a long interval and that some witnesses are likely to be inaccurate.

Another ability question concerns child witnesses. Children are sometimes called upon by courts after being victims or bystanders. Theory suggests that young children's memories are less reliable than adults' and that children are more likely to confuse fantasy and reality. They may also forget more and may be more suggestible to leading questions. Can their testimony be trusted, and in what circumstances? Dent (1992) summarizes results of studies using a paradigm in which adults and children watch an event and are later asked to recall details. Adults usually do as well as or better than children, typically recalling more, and children are more susceptible to suggestive questions. However, children as young as three may still give accurate information about events. Goodman and Schwartz-Kenney (1992) examined the effects of repeated questioning about an event on children's recall. (In an actual case, the authorities may quiz a child again and again and may praise him or her for giving certain answers.) Children aged between three and seven were asked either once or twice about an inoculation they had received. Repeated interviewing did not lessen accuracy and may have actually improved it. However, it is not clear what many more interviews might do.

A final issue is the accuracy of recall under hypnosis. Police may hypnotize a witness to try to enhance recall. How accurate are such memories? Should they be admissible in court? Much research suggests not. Orne et al. (1984) review many studies that show that hypnotically recovered traces may be distorted by questioning and that interviewers cannot readily distinguish between real and confabulated traces. Indeed, Dinges et al. (1992) found that hypnosis could increase incorrect recall of items in readily hypnotizable subjects. Orne et al. suggested that "hypnotically refreshed memories" should only be used if they could be verified by physical evidence.

DEALING WITH ANIMALS

Humans interact with animals in several situations; with pets at home, in zoos, at circuses, on farms, and in laboratories, for example. Behavioral principles have been usefully applied to animals in a variety of ways. Training them, of course, is one. Breland and Breland (1961) successfully used behavioral principles to train animals for circuses and television shows. Here are some other applications to animals.

A famous suggested application was to control coyote predation. Lamb losses from coyotes are high in the western United States, and the usual remedy is to kill the coyotes. Gustavson et al. (1974) proposed an idea that would spare both prey and predator: to apply work on taste aversion learning. The plan was to condition coyotes to associate mutton with nausea so they would avoid sheep in the wild. They experimented with seven adult coyotes and used lamb and rabbit flesh. Each animal ate one type of meat, was given lithium chloride to induce nausea, and then was later exposed to rabbits and lambs. Just one or two aversion trials stopped attacks on the prey species linked to nausea, but not on the other. The researchers suggested scattering poisoned baits that smelled and tasted like sheep and poisoned sheep carcasses over a wide area for the wild coyotes. In addition, mother coyotes may socially pass on the aversion to their pups, as do rats. The method may also work with large cats. Gustavson et al. also suggested using a reverse procedure with endangered species reliant on a diminishing food source; perhaps they could be taught to favor other foods.

Zoos have become more naturalistic in recent decades. Some animals now roam large areas rather than tiny concrete cages, although no zoo can ever provide a completely natural environment. Keepers would like to induce captive animals to exercise more of their natural behavior repertoire. Markowitz (1982) used behavioral techniques to induce servals at the San Francisco zoo to perform their natural hunting and pouncing actions. They were exposed to a small, hairy rodent substitute propelled through a tube.

The serval got food if it chased and pounced. Conditioning also can help ease animal handling in zoos and laboratories. Operant conditioning is used to train animals to enter smaller cages while their large one is being cleaned or to present themselves for an injection (Priest, 1991; Forthman and Ogden, 1992).

Another application is for pets and agricultural animals. For example, overly aggressive dogs may be trained by operant methods not to attack children. One cause of such attacks is a dominance contest. Dogs are social animals and may treat familiar humans as part of their pack, seeking to place them in the pack's hierarchy. One approach is to provide attention, affection, and even food only when children are present, so the child becomes a discriminative stimulus signaling food (Moran, 1987). The owner can also try to establish dominance. Treatment of agricultural animals such as battery pigs and chickens often is controversial. Some work has tried to improve their conditions by finding out the animals' own preferences for conditions, so that limited resources can be optimized from the animals' viewpoint. For example, would a pig prefer more space or more bedding? Dawkins (1977) pioneered operant choice tests to answer such questions. Other work has shown that pigs' early learning based on initial contact with humans has a big impact on their reactions to humans and their stress level and reproduction (Moran, 1987). Making early encounters positive may reduce their stress levels.

EDUCATION

Education and training are fundamental concerns of every society and are particularly important in a complex technological one. Youngsters need to be socialized, to learn about their culture and the world, to acquire basic skills (from the three Rs to computer programming), and to be prepared to join the workforce. A nation's education budget is usually huge. In industry, training is very important. U.S. industry spends an estimated $30 billion on formal training and $190 billion on informal training (Howell, 1993). Employees with widely differing abilities, preferences, and knowledge bases need to be trained and retrained for increasingly complex jobs. Many workers can now expect to retrain several times in a lifetime. An aging workforce poses more problems, such as how best to tailor training programs to their changing capacities and propensities. The major issues in education and training at all levels are what and how to teach, when to teach it, and how to adapt instruction to individual differences. Or, as Tannebaum and Yuki (1992) put it, "Why, when, and for whom does a particular method work?"

Educators and trainers often borrow heavily from basic research on learning and memory. The field has had many educational applications. However, it is not always clear how theory should be applied, and Egan

(1984) has even argued that psychology has nothing to contribute to education. Most application is by educational psychologists. However, some at least is by pure researchers. As mentioned, the behavioral conceptualization of learning has had an enormous impact on U.S. education and industry. U.S. schools are still largely behavioristically oriented, though educators may have forgotten the origin of their current practices (Farnham-Diggory, 1992). Some illustrative practices are setting behavioral objectives for instruction, emphasis on counting of responses, and primitive testing for factual knowledge. In the last decade or two, educational psychology has largely gone cognitive, and this work is percolating through to the schools.

The first section below surveys some behavioral applications and the second some cognitive applications.

Behavioral Applications

A behavioristic learner is a passive behaving organism that reacts to environmental stimuli. Learning is a change in behavior, and operant conditioning is the major type of school learning. (Classical conditioning might be used to change attitudes, however.) Apply this quite limited model to school learners and some prescriptions follow. First, the educator's goal is to change behavior. Educational aims therefore should be couched as objective, measurable changes in behavior (behavioral objectives) rather than changes in thinking and the like. When a course is finished, the students' behavior can be measured to see if the behavioral objectives have been met. Indeed, many course syllabuses still give behavioral objectives such as "By the end of the course the student will be able to type 40 words a minute with less than two errors per 500 words" or " . . . solve differential equations . . . " or " . . . replace fillings . . . " or " . . . be able to disassemble and reassemble an engine." In some courses, aims may be usefully couched this way (such as typing or even pilot training), but in others, such as philosophy and art appreciation, may not be. Another prescription is to use lots of reinforcers. A third is to build up a terminal behavioral performance by starting right at a topic's beginning and progressing through it, and to use such trusty behavioral techniques as shaping and fading (Farnham-Diggory, 1992). Despite its limitations for schools and universities, the behavioral approach is widely applied and is very useful for training the mentally retarded.

An application that incorporates the above and other behavioral principles is programmed learning. The method gets around B.F. Skinner's criticisms of the typical school classroom setup as not optimizing the conditions of learning according to behavioral principles (e.g., Skinner, 1968). Skinner argued that schools provide too little reinforcement, too long a delay between students' responses and what few reinforcers there are, and too much punishment (which Skinner argued is not effective for changing behavior) and rarely have a progressive build-up to the terminal behavioral performance. Skinner proposed use of programmed learning, initially implemented in a teaching machine but later in booklets or even a computer. A course is divided into self-contained units. Each unit consists of a series of easy questions about the topic that start with one that the learner can already answer and move in very small steps to the topic's end. The learner reads each question, answers it, and then sees if he or she is right. He or she almost always is, because the gaps between questions are so slight. The behavioral principles at work are clear. The aim is a behavior change (to answer all questions correctly). The learner is responding (by answering questions), and learners are responders. Responses are immediately reinforced (usually) by the learner being told he or she is correct, and there is a progressive build-up to the terminal performance.

Programmed learning took off in the early 1960s, when it was hailed as a major educational advance. Many programs were written, and whole textbooks were written in programmed learning code. Companies were set up to write and market new programs. By the early 1970s enthusiasm waned, however, and the method is not often seen today. Why? The programs take a lot of time and effort to write, and students may find them boring. They work well for some types of material but in general work no better than other teaching methods (Holding, 1987).

Another behavioral application is the Keller method of running a course, which usually operates as follows. A course is divided up into a progressive sequence of units, with behavioral objectives and a test with a criterion pass score of, say, 80 percent correct. There may or may not be formal classes. Each learner works through the units at his or her own pace and takes a test on a unit when desired. If he or she passes, he or she goes onto the next unit, but if not can retake the test later. Usually learners must complete a minimum of units to pass the course, and more units completed after that earn progressively higher grades. The behavioral principles at work are clear. The learner is responding (reading and taking tests), responses are reinforced (by passing the units and with higher grades for more responses), and material is sequenced progressively. The method works well. Kulik et al. (1979) reviewed seventy-five evaluation studies with university students and found that, in general, students in courses using it scored higher in final exams.

Another very useful educational application is in classroom management. Classroom teachers generally want to keep children reasonably attentive, quiet, settled, and working on assigned tasks. The problem can be seen as one of increasing the rate of desired behaviors such as working and decreasing the rate of disruptive ones such as fighting. The teacher can use reinforcers (such as praise, gold stars, and the chance to go on a field trip) and punishers (such as reprimands and spells in the detention room). These can be applied according to behavioral principles (e.g., Woolfolk,

1993). Reinforcers and punishers can be given immediately after responses and for every response. Some classrooms even use token economies, which also have been used in psychiatric hospitals and prisons. Students earn tokens (exchangeable for tangible rewards) for desired behaviors and good academic work. Token economy principles can work very well (Woolfolk, 1993).

Cognitive Applications

The cognitive conceptualization of a learner is much more complex and has a wider range of applications. A lot of work is being done on it, and educational psychology journals typically feature many papers using it. The journal *Cognition and Instruction* is devoted entirely to the topic. Glaser (1990) gives a good overview of some application areas. Here are some examples.

What and How to Teach. The question "What should be taught?" can be answered on two levels. One level involves a societal and not a psychological issue. What topics from the vast number available should be taught: physics, algebra, philosophy, comparative religion? The second level concerns what aspects of a topic should be taught. For instance, what aspects of introductory physics ought to be taught: facts and equations, key concepts, principles? Should one just use physics as a vehicle for teaching abstract thinking skills, such as analysis and use of the scientific method? A debate over the last few decades goes along these lines, which is usually called process versus content, or teaching thinking skills versus teaching factual knowledge. Hirsch (1987), reviewing the controversy, argued that schools have focused too much on thinking skills and that students finish high school knowing too little about their culture and the world. They are not culturally literate, are not conversant with key concepts of their culture. Hirsch notes that cognitive psychology research has shown that useful knowledge is domain-specific and is organized around key concepts. He proposed that the high school curriculum be organized around about fifteen hundred key concepts, so that students know them when they graduate. Examples of the concepts are *absolute zero, Cubism, El Dorado, ICBM, quark, radar, roman à clef,* and *zeitgeist.*

Indeed, cognitive research on learning and memory suggests some general instructional guidelines. For instance, consider the following findings. The knowledge base is of fundamental importance to learning and performance; what one can learn depends on what one already knows. Knowledge is organized in domains. Individuals can know a lot about a few domains and little about others. Domain-general processing strategies often are little use, so the suggestion is to organize instruction around specific domains and teach domain-specific knowledge and skills. Procedural and declarative knowledge are acquired differently, and declarative knowledge is much more readily forgotten. However, this forgetting can be resisted by organizing it well and periodically reviewing it. Declarative knowledge is often approximate and is largely organized around concepts, which are used to understand and predict. Some obvious implications are that it may be better to teach skills, which are more likely to be retained than facts, and that teaching of declarative knowledge should be organized around concepts and principles, which themselves are retained better than unrelated facts.

One general approach to applying the above guidelines is to analyze expert knowledge in a domain and use it as a goal of instruction (e.g., Snow and Swanson, 1992). One studies some experts and sees how their knowledge is organized, what domain-specific skills they have, and how these are used. Instruction then is designed to guide learners along the path to developing these same knowledge structures. (It is not always clear how to devise such instruction, however.) Here are two examples. Anderson (e.g., 1990) looked at expertise at using the computer language Lisp and devised a model of a Lisp expert, which embodies knowledge of about five-hundred production rules. The goal of instruction is to teach students these rules and how to apply them. Anderson devised a computer "intelligent tutor" that teaches the rules, monitors whether the students have learned them, and provides practice in applying them. (It also can diagnose "bugs" in students' knowledge and performance and take steps to overcome them.) Students learned Lisp faster with this tutor than in an ordinary classroom, but not as well as with a personal human tutor. The tutor is now used in various universities and in government and industry. Another example is from Koedinger and Anderson (1990). They studied expert geometry problem-solving, finding that experts know certain schemas and parse problems into chunks that then cue schemas that can solve them. They suggest that instructors should teach such schemas and rules of solving problems in relation to them.

Research on skills suggests many instructional guidelines, some general and some specific to certain skills. (Those involved in computer use are described later in this chapter.) Kyllonen and Alluisi (1987) summarize many practical teaching principles. First, complex skills such as reading and writing can be analyzed into components and trained separately. Many skills are best learned in parts. The components can be practiced until they are automatic, then the whole skill can be practiced. Elementary components also can be practiced for review to retard forgetting. Even experts do so, practicing parts of golf swings, for example. Second, a lot of practice is generally needed. Lots of practice may overcome a low g level, as mentioned in Chapter 6. Third, practice should be spaced out and should take place in a variety of different contexts, at least for some skills. Fourth, novices should model themselves after experts, watching experts perform when possible. Fifth, giving feedback is essential and should be immediate and frequent. Sixth, instructors should try to keep learning tasks interesting to maintain attention and promote active learning. Video game designers use many interesting tricks to keep people playing, which can be adapted to skill teaching: graphics, sounds, increasing levels of difficulty, competitions, and so on. Mental practice also can be useful. Anderson's ACT* model also can help guide instruction. Its application to computer use is described later. There is also a wide literature on teaching thinking skills (see Howard, 1991).

Declarative knowledge should be taught as it is largely organized in memory: as concepts, principles, conceptual structures, and domains. Instruction in a given domain should teach its important concepts and show how they are interconnected and how to use them. Learners can use the concepts to understand a domain's phenomena. Thus, history teaching should aim to teach concepts such as *revolution, balance of power, totalitarian society*, and *ruling class*. Art instruction should teach such concepts as *impressionist style* and *light and shade*. Science teaching should teach such concepts as *gravity, force, radiation*, and *quark* and how they are interrelated in principles and taxonomies. Literature students can understand, appreciate, and write literature better if they know such concepts as *archetype, satire*, and *poetic metre* and concepts of various literary styles and devices. Several authors have made this point (Skemp, 1979; Hirsch, 1987); many educators pay lip service to it, too, but infrequently organize instruction around concepts (Stones, 1984). Another implication is to teach the metatheories behind a domain's concepts. Psychiatry students need a firm grounding in the mental disease metatheory behind the psychiatric taxonomy and its metaphorical basis, and psychology students in the information processing metatheory, for example.

Research on concepts also suggests some useful teaching methods. Concepts may consist of different types of information, and a given concept may best be taught as a mix of types (e.g., defining and characteristic features, metaphors, knowledge of exemplars, etc.). Howard (1987) suggested some general models of concept teaching to be used according to the nature of the represented category and the learner's ability, knowledge, and intended use of the concept. Some concepts can be usefully taught as defining feature sets. For instance, the concept of *satire* could be taught as the following set of features, illustrated with examples:

1. Is a literary work.
2. Has a definite target.
3. Is humorous.
4. Ridicules target by irony, exaggeration, and so on.

Some concepts may be best taught as sets of characteristic features, either because exemplars of the represented category have no unique common features or students cannot readily learn them. For instance, *totalitarian state* could be taught as the set of these (and other) features:

1. Has a single all-powerful leader.
2. Tolerates no political opposition.
3. Has a single party that permeates society.
4. Has government control of the economy.
5. Has an ideology with the aim of remaking the society into a utopia.
6. Has a secret police operating outside the law.

Students could be taught that a state is totalitarian if it has many of these features, and that an exemplar's typicality may depend on the number of features it has. Typical examples, such as North Korea, have many, and poor ones (such as the former Soviet Union under Gorbachev) have few. Some concepts might be taught as exemplar representations. Some oft-used concepts are based on a single well-known exemplar, which is used to categorize new exemplars by analogy. Examples are *a Pandora's box, a catch-22, Big Brother, the thought police,* and *a Svengali.* One can teach the original exemplar and give practice in using knowledge of it to categorize. Some concepts are so complex and ill-defined that they may best be taught as a set of exemplars given with perhaps a vague definition. Examples are *surrealist art* and *film noir.* One can also use atypical exemplars to show the boundaries of each represented category and also show how boundaries can vary.

Much recent work has looked for ways to alter students' misconceptions. As mentioned in Chapter 4, these may make much of the curriculum incomprehensible to students and prevent new learning. Nussbaum and Novick (1981) outlined a special method to change them, which partly borrows from work of Jean Piaget and of Thomas Kuhn (1970). The idea is to elicit students' misconceptions, present anomalies to make the students dissatisfied with them, and then present a new concept and show how it resolves the anomalies. Nussbaum and Novick illustrate the method with instruction on the particle model of matter. Students typically hold a variety of misconceptions about matter, which were elicited by showing a flask and asking what the flask would be like if some air were pumped out. Ideas were that a vacuum would be left at the top or bottom or both. Then some anomalies were presented by asking what makes air compressible and showing that students' existing ideas could not handle this phenomenon, followed by an exposition of the particle model and how it could. Another example is the concept of *statistical significance test,* which many students have trouble with. A common misconception that makes it hard to learn is that any difference between group means is due to the independent variable. This can be elicited and countered with anomalies (see Howard, 1987). In fact, getting students to see the anomalies and motivate them to change their concepts often is very difficult. Some concepts are deeply held. Pintrich et al. (1993) list some ways in which students can dodge the dissatisfaction that anomalies are supposed to elicit. They can ignore the anomalies, say that they represent a special case, or pay lip service to a conceptual change, for example. The new concept needs to be plausible, intelligible, and applicable to many things. Often these conditions are hard to satisfy. Some concepts, such as those in quantum mechanics, are very implausible and unintelligible. As Niels Bohr said of quantum mechanics, "Anyone who is not profoundly disturbed by it has not understood it." And as Richard Feynman put it, "No one really understands quantum mechanics." But for other concepts, the difficulty may be less severe.

Computers provide new and useful ways to teach concepts and principles. An impressive illustrative example is a computer package called ThinkerTools (White, 1993). Its aims are ambitious: to teach a mental model that embodies Newtonian principles of motion that students can apply to solve problems, make predictions, and explain phenomena. The program generates several manipulable microworlds in which the learner controls the motions of an object by applying forces. The learner can see the role of various forces by manipulating a microworld first without them and then with them. The microworld can be programmed with or without gravity or friction, for example. Students can design and carry out experiments to see the effects of forces such as gravity and test out the range of things that the forces apply to. Students can more readily abstract out the important concepts and principles. An additional benefit is that students can learn scientific inquiry skills; forming hypotheses, experimenting, abstracting out and generalizing conceptual frameworks and theories, and so on.

Teaching Abstract Ways to Process Information. Much research has looked at ways to improve learning and teaching abilities by using abstract knowledge structures. One way is to teach learners (or teachers) to use abstract schemas to fit information to. Ley (1978) gives a prototypical example, a schema for medical information. Studies show that patients often leave a doctor's office without completely understanding the information given and that they may forget much of it soon after. Ley suggested improving recall by fitting medical data to the following schema.

What is wrong with you.

What tests we are going to carry out.

What I think will happen to you.

What treatment you will need.

What you must do to help yourself.

Brooks and Dansereau (1983) provide an abstract schema for scientific theories, with slots for history of the theory, description of it, evidence for it, competing theories, and so on. In a study, students who used it to learn

Figure 8.1
A Semantic Map of Knowledge about Operant Psychology Useful for Instruction

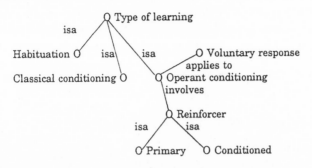

about plate tectonics recalled more details of the theory than those who did not use it. Another example is abstract schemas for reading instructional text (see Howard, 1987).

Another line of research involves teaching metacognitive strategies. Many persons are poor learners because they are unsure what they do and do not know and do not apply such learning strategies as elaboration and organization (and vary them according to the learning task). Remedial programs teach such skills and give practice in using them. For instance, to improve comprehension of text, students are taught to read summaries, underline key points, summarize the material read so far, and repeatedly test themselves for understanding and recall of that material. And, as mentioned, there are various programs to teach problem-solving skills.

A final example is teaching concept mapping (Nowak and Gowin, 1984). This is a method of acquiring knowledge of conceptual structures or a way to teach them. The general idea is to teach use of the notations of semantic memory models. Students or teachers can draw diagrams that show the key concepts in a domain and their interrelations. Figure 8.1 gives a simple example. An instructor can use it to identify key concepts, and students can draw a map to represent information presented in a text or lecture. Instructors can also ask students to draw a map to determine what they already know before instruction. If important concepts or links are missing, instilling them is a useful instructional goal.

Diagnosing Learning Problems. About 4 percent of school students have specific learning disabilities (sometimes called learning problems) (e.g., Kirby and Williams, 1991). Their IQ scores are average or above average, but in some area they perform very poorly. Some typical problem areas are reading and arithmetic.

The general cognitive framework has been used to devise tasks to diagnose their specific problems and to try to remedy them. For example, Hulme and Mackenzie (1992) examine the role of working memory in learning problems (such as failure to use the articulatory loop) and look at ways to counter them, such as designing instruction to minimize the load on working memory. Kirby and Williams (1991) look at some ways to try to remedy various problems, such as teaching strategies or much content knowledge in a domain. One very useful test to diagnose learning problems is the British Ability Scales (see Howard, 1991). It uses a variety of information processing concepts, theories, and tasks to get a cognitive profile of a student.

PSYCHOTHERAPY AND HEALTH PROMOTION

Behavior problems take a great personal and economic toll. Much psychological research involves trying to find ways to prevent and treat the myriad disorders to which people are prone. Until the 1950s, psychotherapy was largely dominated by the medical model, a metatheory based on a physical disease metaphor. Psychological disorders were conceptualized as analogous to physical ones such as measles. Thus a patient was placed into a specific disease category that had associated symptoms, signs, causes, time courses, prognoses, treatments, and so on. Behavior problems were seen as symptomatic of an underlying disorder, such as deep conflicts, repressed traumatic memories, and the like. The approach borrowed heavily from classical Freudian psychoanalysis. Treatment involved finding and treating the underlying causes, which could take years of therapy. Some psychiatrists believed (and some still do) that virtually all disorders have physical causes. Indeed, new techniques such as brain imaging have turned up evidence of brain abnormalities in some disorders, such as obsessive-compulsive disorder and schizophrenia, but their interpretation is still problematic.

In the 1950s, psychologists began in earnest to apply principles of learning to behavior disorders. Their metatheory of disorders conceptualized abnormal behavior as due not to deep underlying conflicts or physical ailments but to faulty or inadequate learning. The troubled individual had acquired some faulty behaviors, which could be altered by using standard learning principles such as classical and operant conditioning. A maladaptive behavior, such as an autistic child's headbanging, could be treated by removing its reinforcers (such as attention), punishing it with electric shock, and reinforcing adaptive incompatible behaviors. Some problems were seen as due to lack of skills (such as assertiveness or social skills) that could be trained. An inspiration for the general approach was the classic study of Little Albert by Watson and Rayner (1920). Little Albert was a hospitalized infant who was classically conditioned to fear a white rat with a loud noise UCS. Watson and Rayner put classical conditioning forward as an account of how phobias could develop, as due to a simple learning process rather than a complex Freudian etiology. The essence of the approach is in the statement of aims of the journal *Behavior Research and Therapy*, which began publication in 1963:

In recent years there has been an ever-growing interest in applying modern learning theories to the control of maladaptive behavior. . . . The main conception . . . has been the belief that behavioral disorders . . . are essentially learned responses and that modern learning theory . . . has much to teach us regarding the acquisition and extinction of such responses.

The approach ultimately became known as behavior therapy or behavior modification. Some argue that these represent somewhat different fields, but these terms are now often used synonymously. The field developed an impressive array of techniques, which are quite successful for many disorders, especially specific ones such as snake and height phobias. Initially, the field's practices were very controversial. Many therapists argued that behavior therapy treated only symptoms and not causes and that the latter would soon induce other symptoms. However, today the practices are widely accepted. As Peterson (1993) put it, "Behavior therapy is recognized as the intervention of choice for many disorders by public institutions as diverse as federal funding agencies, third-party payers, and the *Reader's Digest.*" Many contemporary behavior therapists do not subscribe to the behaviorist notion of people as automatons, however (e.g., Lowe et al., 1987). They are more concerned with what works than with why things work.

In the 1960s and 1970s, the cognitive framework also began to be applied. The key principle adopted is that an individual's ways of thinking and looking at the world may induce anxiety, depression, and maladaptive behavior. The two therapies have converged to a large extent in the 1990s, often under the banner of cognitive-behavioral modification. Clinicians use methods derived from both, again sticking with what works. A variety of journals now publish articles in this general area. Examples are *Behavior Therapy, Journal of Applied Behavior Analysis, Journal of Behavior Therapy and Experimental Psychiatry,* and *Cognitive Therapy and Research.*

Here is a brief description of some techniques in behavior therapy and in cognitive therapy. This section concludes with a brief look at the widespread application of behavioral principles to health promotion.

Behavior Therapy

Disorders are conceptualized as behavioral problems in various ways. Some are seen as problems in stimulus control. An inappropriate stimulus has acquired control over behavior, and its control can be vanquished by classical conditioning or other means. For example, a phobia is an intense, irrational fear response to a class of stimuli such as snakes, and a behavioral analysis may go as follows. Phobias may be acquired in various ways; for example, from a snake bite or observing the reactions of other phobics. The phobia may be maintained by avoidance, so that the individual never comes in contact with the feared stimulus and the response never has the chance to extinguish or be counterconditioned. Theory suggests treatment by habituating the fear response or by counterconditioning an incompatible one, such as relaxation. One useful method is flooding, which involves presenting feared stimuli at their worst in reality or imagination, so that the fear response habituates or inhibition builds up. A snake phobic might visualize being tossed into a snakepit or might actually have to handle several live but harmless snakes. Flooding has been used to treat Vietnam veterans with post-traumatic stress disorder, a symptom of which is fear responses to certain stimuli associated with the war. The therapist can set up a room with projectors and tape recorders to recreate the Vietnamese jungle and expose the client to it. Another oft-used method is systematic desensitization (Wolpe, 1958). The therapist first draws up a hierarchy of stimuli that get progressively closer to the feared object. Thus a hierarchy for a snake phobia might start with "in the same park as a snake" and go to "five hundred yards from a snake," "one hundred yards from a snake," and finally to "holding a live snake." The client is taught to relax deeply and then imagine being in the situation depicted in the first step. When he or she can stay relaxed at the thought of it, he or she imagines the next step, and so on. It is the treatment of choice for many specific phobias, though some (such as agoraphobia) may resist it.

Another technique based on classical conditioning is aversion therapy. It is sometimes used to make a problematic class of stimuli aversive and avoided, such as alcohol for an alcoholic. A fictional case of its use was in the film *A Clockwork Orange*, in which the violent anti-hero Alex viewed scenes of violence after being injected with an anxiety-inducing drug.

The technique works well in the therapist's office, but evidence that it generalizes well is scanty. With alcoholics, the aversion is typically specific to one type of drink (e.g., whiskey), and alcoholics may just switch to another.

Operant conditioning has been widely applied to alter many problem behaviors. The general principle is to try to reduce the rate of undesirable behaviors with extinction, reinforcement for incompatible ones, or punishment. Reinforcers can be used to increase the rate of desired behaviors. Here are some illustrative examples. Wong et al. (1991) treated a hospitalized autistic man who displayed aggressive and destructive behavior on which drugs had little effect. They periodically restrained him. For each fifteen-minute interval during which he was not restrained, he was rewarded with candy, a soft drink, or the like if no aggressive behavior occurred. The aggressive behavior rate diminished, and frequency of applying restraints dropped from an average once a day to less than once a month and a year later still was low. O'Donohue et al. (1992) treated a forty-two-year-old female who was housebound with agoraphobia and who reported panic attacks if she ventured out. They reasoned that she might have stayed at home partly because of the many reinforcers there (television, phone conversations, etc.), and she agreed to engage in such activities only elsewhere (e.g., to watch television only at a neighbor's house). So they arranged fewer reinforcers for staying home and more for going out. In an eighteen-day intervention period, she actually did venture out and engage in out-of-home activities for the first time in many months, attending parties in neighbors' houses, walking to other parts of her street, and so on. Operant conditioning also is useful in teaching social behaviors to such groups as autistic children (e.g., Kamps et al., 1992).

Some other examples of application are to relatively minor problems, such as sleep-onset insomnia, and to obesity due to overeating and lack of exercise. Insomnia can be seen as a problem in stimulus control. When unable to sleep, many insomniacs eat in bed, do crosswords, or toss and turn. All responses are incompatible with falling asleep, so the bedroom situation can become a discriminative stimulus for such behaviors and not for sleeping. Insomniacs are instructed only to try to sleep in bed and if unable to do so after thirty minutes, to rise and return only when feeling sleepy. They also are asked to avoid stimulants such as caffeine and any intellectual activity before bed, and to sleep fewer hours. This regime can work well. For example, Chambers and Alexander (1992) treated 103 insomniacs with stimulus control instructions and sleep restriction, and about 77 percent reported improvement. The mean reported sleep-onset latency dropped from 78.2 minutes to 48.4 minutes. Jacobs et al. (1993) used stimulus control instructions, sleep restriction, and relaxation training and obtained a mean latency drop from 66 to 35 minutes. Stimulus control treatment for overeating involves instruction in avoiding situations in which a person is likely to overeat. Subjects are instructed to eat in one room only, so that it alone becomes a discriminative stimulus for eating, and to avoid high-risk situations in which they are likely to overeat. They also are taught to set weight loss goals and provide non-food rewards for meeting them. The method can work quite well (Wadden and Stunkard, 1986).

Despite its successes and many applications, the current state of the behavior therapy field has been criticized. For example, Ross (1991) argues that the field has "grown but not progressed." It has moved into many areas, argues Ross, but has not applied new principles from experimental psychology for decades, instead sticking with the old ones. Indeed, a glance through current issues of behavior therapy journals supports this view. Many studies apply the same old methods to new cases. Ross also charges that the field has strayed from its conceptual underpinnings, which was the application of explicit findings in experimental psychology. Behavior therapists now apply whatever works; conceptual source and empirical evidence seem irrelevant. He suggests looking at theoretical work in perception, personality, and cognition for more ideas about principles to apply. (See Teasdale, 1993, for further details about this problem.)

Cognitive Therapy

Cognitive therapy partly derives from the cognitive conceptualization of learning. However, its early variants largely were taken directly from clinical experience, and even now its exact link to cognitive science is problematic. Cognitive therapists use terms such as *schema* and *semantic network*, but it is not clear if their meanings are all that similar to those in cognitive science (Teasdale, 1993). Cognitive therapy is often combined with skills training and various behavior therapy techniques.

The basic underlying principle is that people acquire and use schemas to make sense of the world. An individual's schemas may be organized into a theme (Eysenck, 1992), a large-scale conceptual structure. An example of a theme is the world as a hostile, dangerous place or as uncontrollable and that any individual's actions are futile. The view is that behavior disorders derive from maladaptive schemas and inferences from them. For example, anxious persons may see the world as very dangerous and thus are overattentive to signs of threat and become overanxious (e.g., Eysenck, 1992). Depression-prone persons may make many faulty inferences. Beck (1976) gives the example of a man who goes into a deep depression when his shoelace snaps. The event may seem trivial, but he may see it as the final proof that the world is hostile and uncontrollable. Cognitive therapists try to identify faulty schemas, themes, and inferences, show the client their inaccuracy and how they can lead to emotional problems, and teach better schemas and ways of thinking. Of course, this process can be very difficult. Schemas develop over many years and may greatly resist change (Williams, 1987).

There are several approaches within the framework. One is Albert Ellis's rational-emotive therapy (RET) (Ellis, 1977). He argues that most emotional problems arise from a person holding and acting on irrational beliefs. Ellis gives a long list of these. Some examples are as follows:

1. Conditions under which I live must be arranged so that I get practically everything I want quickly and easily and virtually nothing I don't want.
2. Things like justice and fairness clearly have to prevail, and when they don't I cannot stand it and life seems too unbearable to continue. (Ellis, 1977)

Therapy involves teaching persons these ideas, to look for instances of them in their own thinking, and to replace them with more realistic ones. RET has been widely applied. Indeed, some argue that normal children should be taught it in school to lessen their likelihood of later maladjustment. However, some surveys of such prevention programs show little or no apparent effect on emotional distress and little behavior change (Gossette and O'Brien, 1993).

Another extensively used approach is Aaron Beck's (e.g., Beck, 1976). His approach to depression holds that depression-prone persons have negative schemas about themselves, the world, and the future. The self is seen as negative, the world as a terrible place, and the future as a time of hardship and toil. These schemas direct attention to schema-consistent negative events, which may reinforce the schemas. Beck also holds that the depression-prone make several types of thinking error. Here are some examples:

1. *Thinking in black and white.* Something is either completely good or bad, someone is completely for them or against them.

2. *Overgeneralizing.* A single event may be generalized beyond all reasonable bounds, as in the shoelace example above.

3. *Arbitrary inference.* This is making an inference that does not follow from the premises or that is almost certainly false.

Treatment involves eliciting an individual's schemas, showing how using them and making such errors as those above can create emotional disturbances, and teaching better schemas and ways to avoid the thinking errors. The therapy works as well as antidepressant drugs, but exactly why is not always clear (Teasdale, 1993).

Eysenck (1992) reviews various cognitive approaches to treating anxiety. There is some empirical evidence that the anxiety-prone are hypervigilant to signs of threat. One therapy approach is to correct their misinterpretations. For example, Salkovskis et al. (1991) treated panic attack sufferers by changing their catastrophic inferences from physical symptoms (e.g., that a slight chest pain indicated a heart attack). They showed reduced rates of panic attacks.

Some recent research has used the cognitive framework as a general framework for understanding the thought patterns and actions of persons in various psychiatric categories. Hypotheses can be generated from theory and tested. For example, Williams and Broadbent (1986) found that depressives are slower to retrieve memory traces of positive events and may block their recall. Foa et al. (1993) looked at information processing in persons with obsessive-compulsive disorder (characterized by repeated unwanted thoughts and actions). A supported hypothesis is that they process threat-related stimuli differently from normals. They were slower to name words signifying contamination and threat in a modified Stroop task (which involves color-naming various words of different colors). This kind of research is still in its infancy but may lead to information-processing profiles for various disorders and suggested avenues of treatment.

A simple illustration of a cognitive approach to treating a relatively minor disorder is from Booth and Rachman (1992). They applied it to claustrophobics. Clients were told how important thoughts could be in invoking anxiety, learned how to identify automatic thoughts, and discussed their own automatic thoughts in relation to claustrophobia and anxiety. They were trained to identify and deal with logical errors in thinking and to counter automatic thoughts. Then they were actually tested in a tiny closet. Scores for reported fear and panic while in the closet declined significantly.

Zinbarg et al. (1992) review much research on cognitive-behavioral treatments for anxiety and conclude that they work well. At the core of the disorder, they say, is a negative emotion, a preparatory set for coping with threats, and a diminished sense of control over events. The anxiety-prone may continually scan for threats. Therapy that works well involves exposure to feared stimuli and restructuring thinking about anxiety.

Promoting Health

Behavioral principles have been used extensively to promote health (e.g., Rodin and Salovey, 1989). For instance, operant conditioning techniques are used to train persons to reduce blood pressure or muscle tension that causes headaches, to decrease smoking, to increase rate of physical exercise, and so on (Kaplan et al., 1993).

An illustrative example is a case report by Nelson and Hekmat (1991). A forty-one-year-old female had poor nutritional habits and often skipped meals. She ate too many sweet snacks and fewer fruits and vegetables than she had a year before. She was given nutritional information and applied a self-monitoring procedure to see what food she ate and when. Food consumption goals were set and meeting them was reinforced by positive self-statements (such as "I did very well then"). Over time her sugar intake decreased and her intake of fruits and vegetables rose. The changes were maintained five months later.

MORE HEALTH APPLICATIONS: ELECTRO-CONVULSIVE THERAPY, DRUGS AND NEUROLOGY

The information-processing framework has been applied extensively to the following additional health-related areas. One is to better gauge the effects of psychoactive drugs and electro-convulsive therapy (ECT) on learning and memory. (Operant techniques have been used extensively with animals to study drug effects.) For instance, ECT patients often complain of memory loss; sometimes the framework can help pinpoint what is affected, how much so, and for how long. ECT's benefits can then be weighed against its costs. The same questions can be asked about psychotropic drugs. Finally, the framework can guide inquiry about the precise cognitive deficits in such syndromes as schizophrenia, amnesia, and Alzheimer's disease. Understanding the deficits better may lead to better tests to assess new patients, better advice to patients on what their problems will be and their effects on daily functioning, and better advice to patients on their chances of recovery. It may also suggest better treatments (Goldstein and Harvey, 1992). This section will outline some work in this area to give its flavor.

Drugs and ECT

Psychoactive drugs such as antidepressants and tranquilizers are widely prescribed, and new ones often come on the market. How do they and nonprescription drugs such as alcohol and cannabis affect learning and memory and everyday functioning? Some say that long-term use of cannabis affects memory, and some may give this as a major argument against its legalization. Does it?

Much research has tried to answer such questions. Stephens et al. (1992) review work on a variety of different drugs, with the following conclusions. Benzodiazepines evidently do not affect short-term memory or retention in and retrieval from LTM but do impair new learning. The acute ingestion of alcohol can impair memory. Intoxicated persons evidently take longer to transfer information from the registers to working memory, for example. However, alcohol does not affect depth of processing. The infamous blackout (amnesia for events while very intoxicated) is real, permanent, and is for all events then experienced. Long-term heavy alcohol use can lead to various deficits; for instance, in dealing with visuospatial information and in frontal-lobe functions such as planning. The Korsakoff syndrome, which results from many years of heavy alcohol use, has effects parallel to severe amnesia. Short-term memory stays intact, and the patient can learn simple skills but is disoriented in time and space and has difficulty acquiring declarative information. Lithium evidently slows down information processing (and can make patients feel unalert and inefficient) and may disrupt retrieval. Golding (1992) presents evidence that cannabis impairs short-term memory encoding. This deficit may last at least six weeks, but it is not clear if it is permanent.

Sackheim (1992) reviews work on ECT's effects. ECT is widely used to treat severe depression because it works well, but it may induce complaints of memory loss for events before and after the treatment. Research shows that retrograde amnesia indeed occurs; loss is greatest for events closest to the treatment and is less severe for remote events. However, the loss typically lasts only a few days. For instance, Jackson (1978) compared patients receiving one of several forms of ECT with an untreated control group. Ten days after the treatment, there were no significant group differences in all memory measures examined. Sackheim suggests, however, that ECT effects in some cases may persist for months.

Clinical Syndromes

Several classic psychiatric syndromes may be linked to learning and memory deficits. For instance, various disassociative syndromes have memory loss as a key feature, examples being fugue and multiple personality. Research on cognitive processing of schizophrenics shows various deficits; in focusing attention, for example. The preceding section mentioned that highly anxious or depressed persons may process information in characteristic ways. Knowing what these are may help better understand and treat the disorder. For instance, depression impairs performance in some tasks but not others. One interpretation is that the depressed commit less effort or use fewer and less sophisticated strategies. Smith et al. (1993) provide some evidence for this view by showing that depressed persons show impaired learning about categories with defining features (which may need hypothesis-testing to learn about) but not about categories with instances linked by family resemblance (which require much less effort to learn about). Similarly, work on processing in the mentally retarded shows that they are mentally slow; know, use, and generalize few strategies; and have a poor knowledge base (Howard, 1991). One avenue of treatment to improve their functioning is to teach them strategies.

Much research has examined neurological syndromes resulting from head injury, brain disease, poisoning, aging, and other such factors. Study of such patients has improved understanding of memory, and the framework can be used to better understand the patients' problems. For example, the classic amnesiac syndrome produced by closed head injury involves greatly impaired episodic memory but intact working and semantic memory and procedural learning (e.g., Baddeley, 1990). A reasonable picture of the deficits produced by Alzheimer's disease has been gleaned from much research. The disorder is responsible for about 51–60 percent of cases of dementia, and its incidence rises with age. The exact cause is still unknown. The symptoms are early memory loss and a progressive decline in many cognitive functions. Morris and Kopelman (1986) review much research on it and conclude that most aspects of memory are affected. The disease cuts a wide swathe of destruction through the memory system. The registers are affected; patients report fewer letters in the Sperling brief-exposure task and only detect exposures lasting at least 100 milliseconds. Short-term memory span is reduced, possibly because rehearsal rate decreases (Hulme et al., 1993). The articulatory loop seems to stay intact, but the central executive's general processing resources may diminish. Semantic memory organization is impaired. The information that their concepts contain may diminish; they contain fewer features and associations (Nebes, 1989). Hodges et al. (1992) found deficits in verbal fluency and object naming and from the pattern of scores on a battery of neuropsychological tests argued that information is actually destroyed rather than access to it being blocked.

Episodic memory and recall from LTM are impaired (Morris and Kopelman, 1986).

Much work has looked at possible treatment for neuropsychological cases. Many deficits spontaneously improve over time, but treatments are often needed. There are various treatment approaches. Harrell et al. (1992) review some applications of the cognitive framework to clinical treatment. One widespread approach is direct retraining of an impaired memory function. The basic idea is that external stimulation induces the brain to reorganize and recover the deficit function. For instance, a patient with problems in manipulating visuospatial information can be given many visuospatial problems to solve. A patient with reduced short-term memory span can do much practice with digit span tasks and with using such strategies as chunking. Training nowadays is often computerized. The approach is popular, but there is little hard evidence that it works. Another broad approach is to teach compensatory strategies. A patient can learn alternative ways to do tasks that involve the impaired ability (possibly along with direct retraining). Examples are learning mnemonic devices, learning to take extensive notes, and learning to use a tape recorder on particularly important occasions. Patients with severe amnesia can reorganize their homes with signs and a layout to partly compensate for the deficit. There also are commercially available special devices such as alarm clocks, watches, computer diaries, and cognitive orthotic devices. The last-named are computers that carry out an artificial thinking skill. Harrell et al. list many. Some examples are automated telephones that record callers and messages and dial spoken numbers. It is problematical how well these devices work. They may take much effort to learn to use. The patient's motivation is a big factor in their efficacy.

MACHINE DESIGN

Members of a complex technological society must grapple daily with many machines. Some are simple and easy to use, such as toasters, while others are very complicated and often difficult to use, such as many computer systems. The pace of technological innovation nowadays is great; many new devices continually enter the home and workplace. The typical home now has machines undreamed of a few decades ago: video cassette recorders (VCRs), compact disc players, home computers, and so on.

Machines have abolished many jobs and have made others easier to do. Computers have made jet airliners much easier to fly, for example. However, machines have added a layer of technological expertise to performing, or at least learning, some tasks. (Howell, 1993). Secretaries have shifted from simple typewriters to multifunction word processors. Architects have moved from drafting boards to computer-aided design and virtual reality systems to visualize interiors. Many workers have to learn to use additional new technology every few years. The U.S. workforce itself is changing; it is aging and has lower average educational levels (Howell, 1993).

There is a big problem: All these new devices need to be designed so that people can quickly learn to use them and when skilled can operate them easily and efficiently with few errors. Many everyday devices clearly fall far short of this design ideal. The legendary example is the VCR, which surveys continually show many owners cannot program. It is easy to see why. Controls are not standardized across different makes and are very complex and poorly laid out. Manuals typically are inadequate. Users often must spend many hours experimenting to work out the controls. Norman (1988) describes the problem of poor design in great detail and gives many examples. For instance, water faucets are not standardized and operate in different ways. Some are pushed, others are pulled or rotated and often give no clue as to which. At an English residential college he stayed at, guests are issued written instructions on how to use the faucets. Doors also operate in different ways and often give no clue on approach as to what to do. Stove and light switch arrays sometimes do not correspond to the actual element or bulb layout. Digital watches, stereo systems, and automatic ticket dispensers often baffle users. Some computer systems require unnatural series of keystrokes to operate with no obvious clue as to how to proceed or what the program is up to at various times. Hitting the wrong key can stop the whole system working and give no indication as to how to restart it. Poor design can also lead to accidents. A major cause of the near-meltdown at the Three Mile Island nuclear power plant in 1979 was the poor layout of its controls.

Norman (1988) lists many reasons why devices are often poorly designed. Manufacturers assume that users will quickly learn whatever is required for operation. They design more for looks than usability. They try to get a few knobs to perform many functions. They promote "creeping featurism;" updated versions of such devices as word processors and VCRs come studded with new features, which are major selling points but which make the machine more complicated and which many users never touch. Another reason is the expense; testing for usability at every design step is costly. Finally, designers may get so familiar with a device they are developing that they cannot readily put themselves in the position of someone coming to it fresh.

The general problem is easy to state: Devices need to be designed for easy learnability and usability by taking account of human capabilities, limitations, and tendencies so that systems can be safer and more efficient (Howell, 1993). Solving the problem is the general province of engineering psychology or human factors research. The field borrows heavily from the information-processing framework. The behavioral approach is little use, aside from guiding skills training. Indeed, its poor applicability to practical design problems in World War II was one seed of the cognitive revolution.Thus there are two major briefs, designing devices that a novice can readily learn to use and that experienced users can operate quickly, easily, and efficiently. Some component issues are how information should be displayed on a device such as a computer screen, how actions should be linked to consequences, and what feedback should be given and when. Unfortunately, the requirements for easy learning and easy expert performance are not always perfectly correlated (Kyllonen and Alluisi, 1987). For example, a computer command involving a single keystroke might be fine for experts but poor for novices, and vice versa for an English word. One solution is to design various versions of a machine or a computer system to cater for different types of users. Some computer systems have different setups for novices and experts that can be chosen at the start. Another solution is to design the device to take account of the predominant users. If it will be occasionally used for short periods, design for maximum learnability. If it will be mostly used heavily by experts, design for ease of performance.

This section briefly outlines some key concerns in this area of application and illustrates some principles with a detailed example, the design of computer systems.

A very useful starting point for design is what the study of learning and memory tells about human capabilities, limitations, and tendencies. Norman (1988) summarizes many key human characteristics. First, working memory capacity is very limited (Hitch, 1987). Humans have a narrow focus of attention and a limited ability to attend to more than one stream of information at a time. Devices need to minimize the information demands, particularly in the early stages of learning. Necessary information should be displayed externally when possible. For instance, a computer system should allow the user to see where he or she is rather than having to keep that in memory. Second, humans readily learn and use natural contingencies but have trouble learning unnatural ones (and may revert to natural but wrong ones under stress), so systems need to be designed so that actions are natural. A light switch layout should correspond to the light bulb layout. A computer mouse manipulandum that allows more natural actions is one application of this principle. It is usually easier to use than a keyboard, particularly one with arbitrary symbols for commands. Third, people often learn to use a new machine by trying to form a functional mental model of the device and how it works, which then guides their actions. An erroneous mental model (such as a refrigerator thermostat having more than just an on-off state) can lead to later errors and problems in further learning. A device should be designed so that users can quickly form a functional mental model. One can also test for the erroneous models that people are likely to adopt and try to correct them, and determine what errors will occur and design a system that can rapidly recover from them (Marshall et al., 1987). Humans often try to learn about new devices by using metaphors and analogies, some of which are better than others. Trainers should give useful initial analogies. Fourth, there are huge individual differences in capabilities, learning preferences, and existing knowledge and skills. One way to cope is to design different versions of a device. Some computer systems actually build up a model of each user from his or her initial performances and adapt themselves to the peculiarities (van der Veek, 1991). Fifth, humans forget easily.

A very active area of application of such considerations is in human-computer interface design (e.g., Gardiner and Christie, 1987; Green, 1991; van der Veer, 1991). Many new computer systems come on line every year. The user population is huge and diverse, with different propensities and purposes, and the systems often are very complex. There are many guidelines for design (e.g., van der Veer, 1991). First, designers need to consider the range of users. Human memory limitations mean that input and output should be clear and actions and spatial arrangements should be compatible. Information on screen should be displayed so it can be readily chunked or otherwise organized. To deal with wide individual differences, the system can form a model of each user, or the same function can be accomplished in many ways. Norman (1988) suggests that systems should be designed to be explorable, so that users can experiment and learn various ways to do things and determine the system's capabilities. Commands should be clear and actions should be readily reversible so that an error does not lead into a mode with no clear escape route. Designers should use constraints; they should minimize the number of possible actions to make errors less frequent, for instance.

The three-stage model of skill learning outlined in Chapter 5 also has been used to guide design. Hamond (1987) gives some applications. First, the initial cognitive stage is very important. The manual's instructions may seem meaningless, its concepts unknown. The learner may be overwhelmed with information and may selectively ignore very important information needed to proceed. The learner may use inappropriate analogies that lead to certain kinds of errors and render some parts of the system hard to learn. Some remedies are to minimize the declarative information needed to be acquired at the start and to greatly restrict user choice of actions. Some systems have a training mode with few functions. If analogies are given, they should be made explicit and their limitations emphasized. Learners also are likely to forget much information between sessions, which may be remedied by initial review at the start of each session. Practice and feedback are essential; learners should learn by doing and should practice actions until they become automatic. Feedback should tell what effects actions have and where the user is in the system. As performance becomes more automatized, users may become prone to different sorts of errors, which the system can be designed to deal with. One way is by maximum discriminability of screen items. Another is for different models to come into operation with increasing expertise.

Norman (1988) gives the following good overall design principle: Design so that users can form a sound representation of the system, so that they can easily see where they are in it, what is going on in it and what to do, and can form and meet subgoals.

References

Ackerman, P. L. (1987). Individual differences in skill learning. *Psychological Bulletin* 102: 3–27.

———. (1988). Determinants of individual differences during skill acquisition. *Journal of Experimental Psychology: General* 117: 288–318.

———. (1990). A correlational analysis of skill specificity: Learning, abilities and individual differences. *Journal of Experimental Psychology: Learning, Memory and Cognition* 16: 883–901.

Adams, J. A. (1987). Historical review and appraisal of research on the learning, retention and transfer of human motor skills. *Psychological Bulletin* 101: 41–74.

Alexander, P. A., Schallert, D. L., and Hare, V. C. (1991). Coming to terms. *Review of Educational Research* 61: 315–43.

Allan, L. G. (1993). Human contingency judgments. *Psychological Bulletin* 114: 435–48.

Allan, L. G., and Siegel, S. (1993). McCollough effects as conditioned responses. *Psychological Review* 100: 342–46.

Alty, J. L. (1989). Machine learning. In *Human and machine problem solving*, ed. K. J. Gilhooly. New York: Plenum.

Anderson, J. R. (1978). Arguments concerning representations for mental imagery. *Psychological Review* 85: 249–77.

———. (1980). Concepts, propositions, and schemata: What are the cognitive units? In *Nebraska symposium on motivation*, ed. J. H. Flowers. Lincoln, NE: University of Nebraska Press.

———. (1982). Acquisition of cognitive skill. *Psychological Review* 89: 369–406.

———. (1983). *The architecture of cognition*. Cambridge, MA: Harvard University Press.

———. (1987). Skill acquisition: Compilation of weak-method problem solutions. *Psychological Review* 94: 192–210.

———. (1989). A theory of the origins of human knowledge. *Artificial Intelligence* 40: 313–51.

———. (1990). *Cognitive psychology and its implications*. New York: Freeman.

Anderson, J. R., and Bower, G.H. (1973). *Human associative memory*. Washington, D.C.: Winston.

Anderson, M. (1992). *Intelligence and development*. Oxford, U.K.: Blackwell.

Anderson, S. J., and Conway, M.A. (1993). Investigating the structure of autobiographical memories. *Journal of Experimental Psychology: Learning, Memory and Cognition* 19: 1178–96.

Andrist, K., Kahana, M. J., Spry, K. M., Knevel, C. R., Persanyi, M. W., Evans, S. W., Luo, D., and Detterman, D. K. (1992). Individual differences in the biological correlates of intelligence. In *Current topics in human intelligence*, ed. D. K. Detterman. Norwood, NJ: Ablex.

Anglin, J. M. (1977). *Word, object and conceptual development*. New York: Norton.

Anzai, Y. (1991). Learning and use of representations for physics experts. In *Toward a general theory of expertise*, ed. K. A. Ericsson and J. Smith. New York: Cambridge University Press.

Armstrong, S. E., Gleitman, L. R., and Gleitman, H. (1983). What some concepts might not be. *Cognition* 13: 263–308.

Atkinson, R. C., and Shiffrin, R. M. (1968). Human memory: A proposed system and its control processes. *Psychology of learning and motivation* 2: 89–195.

Atran, S. (1989). Basic conceptual domains. *Mind and Language* 4: 7–16.

Baddeley, A. (1983). *Your memory: A user's guide*. Harmondsworth, U.K.: Penguin.

———. (1986). *Working memory*. Oxford, U.K.: Oxford University Press.

———. (1990). *Human memory*. Hove, U.K.: Erlbaum.

———. (1993). Short-term phonological memory and long-term learning. *European Journal of Cognitive Psychology* 5: 129–48.

Bahrick, H. P. (1984). Semantic memory content in permastore: Fifty years of memory for Spanish learned in school. *Journal of Experimental Psychology: General* 113: 1–24.

Bahrick, H. P., and Hall, L. K. (1991). Lifetime maintenance of high school mathematics content. *Journal of Experimental Psychology: General* 120: 20–33.

Bahrick, H. P., Bahrick, P. O., and Wittlinger, R.P. (1975). Fifty years of memory for names and faces. *Journal of Experimental Psychology: General* 104: 54–75.

Baker, T. B., and Tiffany, S. T. (1985). Morphine tolerance as habituation. *Psychological Review* 92: 78–108.

Baron, J., Badgio, P. C., and Gaskins, I. W. (1986). Cognitive style and its improvement. In *Advances in the psychology of human intelligence*, ed. R. J. Sternberg. Hillsdale, NJ: Erlbaum.

Barsalou, L. W. (1987). The instability of graded structure. In *Concepts and conceptual development*, ed. U. Neisser. New York: Cambridge University Press.

Bartlett, F. C. (1932). *Remembering*. Cambridge, U.K.: Cambridge University Press.

Bartlett, J.C., and Fulton, A. (1991). Familiarity and recognition of faces in old age. *Memory and Cognition* 19: 229–38.

Bechtel, B., and Abrahamsen, A. (1991). *Connectionism and the mind*. Cambridge, MA.: MIT Press.

Beck, A. T. (1976). *Cognitive therapy and the emotional disorders*. New York: International Universities Press.

Bedford, E. (1993). Perceptual learning. *Psychology of learning and motivation* 30: 1–60.

Bekerian, D. A. (1993). In search of the typical eyewitness. *American Psychologist* 48: 574–76.

Bell, T. M., Hutchison, H. R., and Stephens, K. R. (1992). Using adaptive networks for resource allocation in changing environments. In *Neural networks: Current applications*, ed. P.G.J. Lisboa. London: Chapman and Hall.

Berry, D.C., and Dienes, Z. (1991). The relationship between implicit memory and implicit learning. *British Journal of Psychology* 82: 359–73.

Biggs, J. B. (1982). Student motivation and study strategies in university and CAE populations. *Higher Education Research and Development* 1: 33–55.

———. (1988). Approaches to learning and to essay writing. In *Learning strategies and learning styles*, ed. R. R. Schmeck. New York: Plenum.

Biggs, J. B., and Moore, P. J. (1993). *The process of learning*. Sydney: Prentice-Hall.

Biggs, J. B., and Telfer, R. (1987). *The process of learning*. Sydney: Prentice-Hall.

Bitterman, M. E. (1965). Phyletic differences in learning. *American Psychologist* 20: 396–410.

Bjork, R. A. (1978). The updating of human memory. *Psychology of learning and motivation* 12: 235–59.

Bloom, L. C., and Mudd, S. A. (1991). Depth of processing approach to face-recognition. *Journal of Experimental Psychology: Learning, Memory and Cognition* 17: 556–65.

Bolles, R. C. (1970). Species-specific defense reactions and avoidance learning. *Psychological Review* 77: 32–48.

———. (1988). Nativism, naturalism and niches. In *Evolution and learning*, ed. R. C. Bolles and M. D. Beecher. Hillsdale, NJ: Erlbaum.

Booker, L. B., Goldberg, D. E., and Holland, J.H. (1989). Classifier systems and genetic algorithms. *Artificial Intelligence* 40: 235–82.

Booth, R., and Rachman, S. (1992). The reduction of claustrophobia. *Behavior Research and Therapy* 30: 207–21.

Boring, E. G. (1950). *A history of experimental psychology*. New York: Appleton-Century-Crofts.

Bousfield, W. A. (1953). The occurrence of clustering in the recall of randomly arranged associates. *Journal of General Psychology* 49: 229–40.

Bower, G. H. (1970). Analysis of a mnemonic device. *American Scientist* 58: 496–510.

Bower, G. H., and Clapper, J. P. (1989). Experimental methods in cognitive science. In *Foundations of cognitive science*, ed. M. I. Posner. Cambridge, MA: MIT Press.

Bower, G. H., and Hilgard, E. R. (1981). *Theories of learning*. Englewood Cliffs, NJ: Prentice-Hall.

Bower, G. H., and Mann, T. (1992). Improving recall by recoding interfering material at the time of retrieval. *Journal of Experimental Psychology: Learning, Memory and Cognition* 18: 1310–20.

Boysen, S. T., and Berntson, G. G. (1989). Numerical competence in a chimpanzee. *Journal of Comparative Psychology* 103: 23–31.

Bransford, J. D., and Johnson, M. K. (1973). Consideration of some problems in comprehension. In *Visual information processing*, ed. W. G. Chase. Orlando, FL.: Academic Press.

Breland, K., and Breland, M. (1961). The misbehavior of organisms. *American Psychologist* 16: 681–84.

———. (1966). *Animal behavior.* New York: Macmillan.

Broadbent, D. A. (1958). *Perception and communication.* London: Pergamon.

Brody, N. (1985). The validity of tests of intelligence. In *Handbook of human intelligence,* ed. B. B. Wolman. San Diego: Academic Press.

Brooks, L. W., and Dansereau, D. F. (1983). Effects of structural schema training and text organization on expository prose processing. *Journal of Educational Psychology* 75: 811–20.

Brown, A. S. (1991). A review of the tip-of-the-tongue experience. *Psychological Bulletin* 109: 204–23.

Brown, D. E. (1991). *Human universals.* Philadelphia: Temple University Press.

Brown, N. R. (1990). Organization of public events in long-term memory. *Journal of Experimental Psychology: General* 119: 297–314.

Brown, P., and Jenkins, H. M. (1968). Autoshaping of the pigeon's keypeck. *Journal of the Experimental Analysis of Behavior* 11: 1–8.

Brown, R., and Kulik, J. (1977). Flashbulb memories. *Cognition* 5: 73–99.

Brown, R., and McNeill, D. T. (1966). The 'tip-of-the-tongue' phenomenon. *Journal of Verbal Learning and Verbal Behavior,* 5: 325–37.

Bruch, M., Cavanagh, P., and Ceci, S. J. (1991). Fortysomething: Recognizing faces at one's 25th reunion. *Memory and Cognition* 19: 221–28.

Bruner, J. S., Goodnow, J. J., and Austin, G. A. (1956). *A study of thinking.* New York: Wiley.

Burke, D. M., MacKay, D. G., Worthley, J. A., and Wade, E. (1991). On the tip of the tongue. *Journal of Memory and Language* 30: 542–79.

Burns, D. J. (1993). Item gains and losses during hypernesic recall. *Journal of Experimental Psychology: Learning, Memory and Cognition* 19: 163–73.

Buschke, H. (1976). Learning is organized by chunking. *Journal of Verbal Learning and Verbal Behavior* 15: 313–24.

Buss, D. M. (1989). Sex differences in human mate preferences. *Behavioral and Brain Sciences* 12: 1–49.

Camerer, C. F., and Johnson, E. J. (1991). The process-performance paradox in expert judgment. In *Toward a general theory of expertise,* ed. K. A. Ericsson and J. Smith. New York: Cambridge University Press.

Campbell, C.B.G., and Hodos, W. (1991). The scala naturae revisited. *Journal of Comparative Psychology* 105: 211–21.

Campione, J. C., Brown, A. L., Ferrara, R. A., Jones, R. S., and Steinberg, E. (1985). Breakdown in flexible use of information. *Intelligence* 9: 297–315.

Canfield, R.L., and Ceci, S.J. (1992). Integrating learning into a theory of intellectual development. In *Intellectual development,* ed. R. J. Sternberg and C. A. Berg. New York: Cambridge University Press.

Carbonell, J. (1989). Introduction: Paradigms for machine learning. *Artificial Intelligence* 40: 1–9.

———. (1992). Machine learning: A maturing field. *Machine Learning* 9: 5–7.

Carey, S. (1985). *Conceptual change in childhood.* Cambridge, MA: MIT Press.

Carmichael, L. L., Hogan, H. P., and Walter, A. A. (1932). An experimental study of the effect of language on the reproduction of visually-presented form. *Journal of Experimental Psychology* 15: 73–86.

Caro, T.M., and Hauser, M.D. (1992). Is there teaching in nonhuman animals? *Quarterly Review of Biology* 67: 151–74.

Carrasco, M., and Ridout, J.B. (1993). Olfactory perception and olfactory imagery. *Journal of Experimental Psychology: Human Perception and Performance* 19: 287–301.

Carroll, J. B. (1993). *Human cognitive abilities.* New York: Cambridge University Press.

Castro, C. A., and Larsen, T. (1992). Primacy and recency effects in nonhuman primates. *Journal of Experimental Psychology: Animal Behavior Processes* 18: 335–40.

Cattell, R. B. (1987). *Intelligence: Its structure, growth and action.* Amsterdam: Elsevier.

Caubet, Y., Jaisson, P., and Lenoir, A. (1992). Preimaginal induction of adult behavior in insects. *Quarterly Journal of Experimental Psychology* 44: 165–78.

Ceci, S. J., and Liker, J. (1986). Academic and nonacademic intelligence. In *Practical intelligence,* ed. R. J. Sternberg and W. K. Wagner. Hillsdale, NJ: Erlbaum.

Ceci, S. J., and Ruiz, A. (1992). The role of general ability in cognitive complexity. In *The psychology of expertise,* ed. R. R. Hoffman. New York: Springer-Verlag.

Cerella, J. (1979). Visual classes and natural categories in the pigeon. *Journal of Experimental Psychology: Human Perception and performance* 5: 68–77.

Chambers, M. J., and Alexander, S.D. (1992). Assessment and prediction of outcome for a brief behavior insomnia treatment program. *Journal of Behavior Therapy and Experimental Psychiatry* 23: 289–98.

Charlot, V., Tzourio, N., Zilbovicius, M., Mazoyer, B., and Denis, M. (1992). Different mental imagery abilities result in different regional cerebral blood flow activation patterns during cognitive tasks. *Neuropsychologia* 30: 565–80.

Charness, N. (1983). Age, skill and bridge bidding. *Journal of Verbal Learning and Verbal Behavior* 22: 406–16.

―――. (1991). Expertise in chess. In *Toward a general theory of expertise,* ed. K. A. Ericsson and J. Smith. New York: Cambridge University Press.

Charness, N., and Bieman-Copland, S. (1992). The learning perspective: Adulthood. In *Intellectual development,* ed. R. J. Sternberg and C. A. Berg. New York: Cambridge University Press.

Charniak, E., and McDermott, D. (1985). *Introduction to artificial intelligence.* Reading, MA: Addison-Wesley.

Chase, W. G., and Ericsson, K. A. (1982). Skill and working memory. *Psychology of Learning and Motivation* 16: 1–58.

Chase, W. G., and Simon, H. A. (1973). The mind's eye in chess. In *Visual information processing,* ed. W. G. Chase. Orlando, FL: Academic Press.

Cheng, P. W. (1993). Separating causal laws from casual facts. *Psychology of Learning and Motivation* 30: 215–64.

Chi, M.T.H. (1978). Knowledge structures and memory development. In *Children's thinking: What develops?* ed. R. S Siegler. Hillsdale, NJ: Erlbaum.

―――. (1981). Knowledge development and memory performance. In *Intelligence and learning,* ed. M. L. Friedman, J. P. Das, and N. O'Connor. New York: Plenum.

Chi, M.T.H., and Ceci, S. J. (1987). Content knowledge. *Advances in Child Development and Behavior* 20: 91–142.

Chi, M.T.H., Feltovich, P. J., and Glaser, R. (1981). Categorization and representation of physics problems by experts and novices. *Cognitive Science* 5: 121–52.

Chi, M.T.H., Glaser, R., and Farr, M. J. (1988). *The nature of expertise.* Hillsdale, NJ: Erlbaum.

Chi, M.T.H., and Koeske, R. D. (1983). Network representation of a child's dinosaur knowledge. *Developmental Psychology* 19: 29–39.

Churchland, P. S. (1986). *Neurophilosophy.* Cambridge, MA.: MIT Press.

Churchland, P. S., and Sejnowski, T. J. (1992). *The computational brain.* Cambridge, MA.: MIT Press.

Clark, N. K., and Stephenson, G.M. (1990). Social remembering. *British Journal of Psychology* 81: 73–94.

Claxton, G. (1980). Cognitive psychology: A suitable case for what sort of treatment? In *Cognitive psychology,* ed. G. Claxton. London: Routledge and Kegan Paul.

Clement, C. A., and Gentner, D. (1991). Systematicity as a selection constraint in analogical mapping. *Cognitive Science* 15: 89–132.

Cofer, C. N. (1979). Human learning and memory. In *The first century of experimental psychology,* ed. E. Hearst. Hillsdale, NJ: Erlbaum.

Cohen, B., and Murphy, G. L. (1984). Models of concepts. *Cognitive Science* 8: 27–58.

Cohen, G. (1989). *Memory in the real world.* Hove, U.K.: Erlbaum.

Cole, P. G., and Chan, L.K.S. (1990). *Methods and strategies for special education.* Sydney: Prentice-Hall.

Colley, A. M. (1989). Cognitive motor skills. In *Human skills,* ed. D.H. Holding. Chichester, U.K.: Wiley.

Colley, A.M., and Beach, J. R. (1989). Acquiring and performing cognitive skills. In *Acquisition and performance of cognitive skills,* ed. A. M. Colley and J. R. Beach. Chichester, U.K.: Wiley.

Collins, A. M., and Loftus, E. F. (1975). A spreading activation theory of semantic processing. *Psychological Review* 82: 407–28.

Coltheart, M. (1983). Iconic memory. *Philosophical Transactions of the Royal Society* 302: 283–94.

Conger, R., and Killeen, P. (1974). Use of concurrent operants in small group research. *Pacific Sociological Review* 17: 399–406.

Conners, F. A. (1992). Special abilities of idiots savants, hyperlexic children, and phenomenal memorizers. In *Current topics in human intelligence,* ed. D.K. Detterman. Norwood, NJ: Ablex.

Conway, M. A., Cohen, G., and Stanhope, N. (1991). On the very long-term retention of knowledge acquired through formal education. *Journal of Experimental Psychology: General* 120: 395–409.

Craik, F.I.M., and Lockhart, R. S. (1972). Levels of processing: A framework for memory research. *Journal of Verbal Learning and Verbal Behavior* 11: 671–84.

Craik, F.I.M., and McDowd, J.M. (1987). Age differences in recall and recognition. *Journal of Experimental Psychology: Learning, Memory and Cognition* 13: 474–79.

Craik, K.J.W. (1943). *The nature of explanation*. Cambridge, U.K.: Cambridge University Press.

Crampton, G. H., and Lucot, J. B. (1991). Habituation of motion sickness in the cat. *Aviation, Space, and Environmental Medicine* 62: 212–15.

Crick, F. (1989). The recent excitement about neural networks. *Nature* 337: 129–32.

Crowder, R. G. (1993). Short-term memory: Where do we stand? *Memory and Cognition* 21: 142–45.

Dahlgren, L. O. (1978). Qualitative differences in conceptions of basic principles in economics. Paper presented at Fourth International Conference on Higher Education, Lancaster, U.K.

Dallal, N.L., and Meck, W.H. (1990). Hierarchical structures. *Journal of Experimental Psychology: Animal Behavior Processes* 16: 69–84.

Das, J. P. (1988). Simultaneous-successive processing and planning: Implications for school learning. In *Learning strategies and learning styles*, ed. R. R. Schmeck. New York: Plenum.

Davey, G. (1989). *Ecological learning theory*. London: Routledge.

Davis, H., Memmott, J., and Hurwitz, H.M.B. (1975). Autocontingencies. *Journal of Experimental Psychology: General* 104: 169–88.

Davison, M., and McCarthy, D. (1988). *The matching law*. Hillsdale, NJ: Erlbaum.

Dawkins, M. S. (1977). Do hens suffer in battery cages? Environmental preference and welfare. *Animal Behavior* 25: 1034–46.

Dean, A. L., Duhe, D. A., and Green, D. A. (1983). The development of children's mental tracing strategies on a rotation task. *Journal of Experimental Child Psychology* 36: 226–40.

DeCasper, A. J., and Fifer, W. P. (1980). Of human bonding: Newborns prefer their mothers' voices. *Science* 208: 1174–76.

DeCasper, A. J., and Spence, M.J. (1986). Prenatal maternal speech influences newborn's perception of speech sounds. *Infant Behavior and Development* 9: 133–50.

De Jong, K. A., Spears, W. M., and Gordon, D. F. (1993). Using genetic algorithms for concept learning. *Machine Learning* 13: 161–88.

Dempster, F. N. (1992). The rise and fall of the developmental mechanism. *Developmental Review* 12: 45–75.

Denis, M., and Cocude, M. (1992). Structural properties of visual images constructed from poorly or well-structured verbal descriptions. *Memory and Cognition* 20: 497–506.

Denis, M., and Zimmer, H.D. (1992). Analog properties of cognitive maps constructed from verbal descriptions. *Psychological Research* 54: 286–98.

Dent, H. (1992). The effects of age and intelligence on eyewitnessing ability. In *Children as witnesses*, ed. H. Dent and R. Flin. Chichester, U.K.: Wiley.

Detterman, D. K., and Spry, K. M. (1988). Is it smart to play the horses? *Journal of Experimental Psychology: General* 117: 91–95.

Dinges, D. F., Whitehouse, W. G., Orne, E. C., Powell, J. W., and Orne, M. T. (1992). Evaluating hypnotic memory enhancement (hypernesia and reminiscence) using multitrial forced recall. *Journal of Experimental Psychology: Learning, Memory and Cognition* 18: 1139–47.

Dittrich, W. H., and Lea, S.E.G. (1993). Motion as a natural category for pigeons. *Journal of the Experimental Analysis of Behavior* 59: 115–29.

Domjan, M., and Hollis, K. L. (1988). Reproductive behavior. In *Evolution and learning*, ed. R. C. Bolles and M. D. Beecher. Hillsdale, NJ: Erlbaum.

Dorffner, G. (1993). How connectionism can change AI and the way we think about ourselves. *Applied Artificial Intelligence* 7: 59–85.

Dudai, Y. (1989). *The neurobiology of memory*. Oxford, U.K.: Oxford University Press.

Dunbar, R. M. (1993). Coevolution of neocortical size, group size and language in humans. *Behavioral and Brain Sciences* 16: 681–735.

Dunn, B. R., and Reddix, M.D. (1991). Modal processing style differences in the recall of expository text and poetry. *Learning and Individual Differences* 3: 265–93.

Dunn, R., and Dunn, K. (1978). *Teaching students through their individual learning styles*. Reston, VA: Reston Publishing.

Egan, K. (1984). *Education and psychology*. London: Methuen.

Elias, P. K., Elias, M. F., Robbins, M. A., and Gage, P. (1987). Acquisition of word processing skills by younger, middle-aged and older adults. *Psychology and Aging* 2: 340–48.

Ellis, A. (1977). The basic clinical theory of rational-emotive therapy. In *Handbook of rational-emotive therapy*, ed. A. Ellis and R. Grieger. New York: Springer.

Entwistle, N. (1988). Motivational factors in students' approaches to learning. In *Learning strategies and learning styles*, ed. R. R. Schmeck. New York: Plenum.

Epstein, W. (1993). The representational framework in perceptual theory. *Perception and Psychophysics* 53: 704–9.

Ericsson, K. A., Krampe, R. T., and Tesch-Romer, C. (1993). The role of deliberate practice in the acquisition of expert performance. *Psychological Review* 100: 363–406.

Ericsson, K. A., and Polson, P. G. (1988). A cognitive analysis of exceptional memory for restaurant orders. In *The nature of expertise*, ed. M.T.H. Chi, R. Glaser, and M. J. Farr. Hillsdale, NJ: Erlbaum.

Ericsson, K. A., and Smith, J. (1991). *Toward a general theory of expertise*. New York: Cambridge University Press.

Estes, W. K. (1982). Learning, memory and intelligence. In *Handbook of human intelligence*, ed. R. J. Sternberg. New York: Cambridge University Press.

———. (1988). Human learning and memory. In *Stevens' handbook of experimental psychology*, ed. R. C. Atkinson. New York: Wiley.

———. (1993). Models of categorization and category learning. *Psychology of Learning and Motivation* 29: 15–56.

Evans, J.S.B.T. (1989). *Bias in human reasoning*. Hove, U.K.: Erlbaum.

Eysenck, H. J., and Eysenck, M. W. (1985). *Personality and individual differences*. New York: Plenum.

Eysenck, M. W. (1992). *Anxiety: The cognitive perspective*. Hove, U. K.: Erlbaum.

Eysenck, M. W., and Keane, M. T. (1990). *Cognitive psychology*. Hove, U. K.: Erlbaum.

Fagan, J. F. (1973). Infants' delayed recognition memory and forgetting. *Journal of Experimental Child Psychology* 16: 424–50.

Farah, M. J. (1988). Is visual imagery really visual? *Psychological Review* 95: 307–17.

Farnham-Diggory, S. (1992). *Cognitive processes in education*. New York: HarperCollins.

Ferrara, R. A., Brown, A. L., and Campione, J. C. (1986). Children's learning and transfer of inductive reasoning rules. *Child Development* 57: 1087–99.

Ferretti, R. P., and Butterfield, E. C. (1992). Intelligence-related differences in the learning, maintenance and transfer of problem-solving strategies. *Intelligence* 16: 207–24.

Feuerstein, R., Rand, Y., Hoffman, M. B., and Miller, R. (1980). *Instrumental enrichment*. Baltimore, MD: University Park Press.

Finkbiner, R.G., and Woodruff-Pak, D. S. (1991). Classical eyeblink conditioning in adulthood: Effects of age and interstimulus interval on acquisition in the trace paradigm. *Psychology and Aging* 6: 109–17.

Finke, R. A. (1989). *Principles of mental imagery*. Cambridge, MA: MIT Press.

Firebaugh, M. W. (1989). *Artificial intelligence*. Boston: PWS-Kent.

Fisher, R. P., and Geiselman, R. E. (1988). Enhancing eyewitness testimony with the cognitive interview. In *Practical aspects of memory*, ed. M. M. Gruneberg, P. E. Morris, and R. N. Sykes. Chichester, U. K.: Wiley.

Fitts, P. M., and Posner, M. I. (1967). *Human performance*. Belmont, CA: Brooks/Cole.

Foa, E. B., Ilai, D., McCarthy, P. R., Shoyer, B., and Murdock, T. (1993). Information-processing in obsessive-compulsive disorder. *Cognitive Therapy and Research* 17: 173–89.

Fodor, J. (1983). *The language of thought*. Cambridge, MA: MIT Press.

Fodor, J. A., and Pylyshyn, Z. (1988). Connectionism and cognitive architecture: A critical analysis. In *Connections and symbols*, ed. S. Pinker and J. Mehler. Cambridge, MA: MIT Press.

Forthman, D. L., and Ogden, J. J. (1992). The role of applied behavior analysis in zoo management. *Journal of Applied Behavior Analysis* 25: 647–52.

Fountain, S. B. (1990). Rule abstraction, item memory and chunking in rat serial-pattern tracking. *Journal of Experimental Psychology: Animal Behavior Processes* 16: 96–105.

Friman, P. C., Allen, K. D., Kerwin, M. L., and Larzelere, R. (1993). Changes in modern psychology. *American Psychologist* 48: 658–64.

Frydman, M., and Lynn, R. (1992). The general intelligence and spatial ability of gifted young Belgian chess players. *British Journal of Psychology* 83: 233–35.

Gagné, R. M. (1970). *The conditions of learning*. New York: Holt, Rinehart and Winston.

Gallistel, C. R. (1990). *The organization of learning*. Cambridge, MA: MIT Press.

Garcia, J. (1981). Tilting at the paper-mills of academe. *American Psychologist* 36: 149–58.

Gardiner, M. M., and Christie, B. (1987). Introduction. In *Applying cognitive psychology to user-interface design*, ed. M. M. Gardiner and B. Christie. Chichester, U. K.: Wiley.

Gardner, H. (1983). *Frames of mind*. New York: Basic Books.

Gazzaniga, M.S. (1992). *Nature's mind*. New York: Basic Books.

Gelman, R. (1990). First principles organize attention to and learning about relevant data. *Cognitive Science* 14: 79–106.

_____ . (1993). A rational-constructivist account of early learning about numbers and objects. *Psychology of Learning and Motivation* 30: 215–64.

Gelman, S. A., and Markman, E. M. (1987). Young children's inductions from natural kinds. *Child Development* 58: 1532–41.

Gennari, J. H., Langley, P., and Fisher, D. (1989). Models of incremental concept formation. *Artificial Intelligence* 40: 11–61.

Gentner, D. R. (1988). Expertise in typewriting. In *The nature of expertise*, ed. M.T.H. Chi, R. Glaser, and M. J. Farr. Hillsdale, NJ: Erlbaum.

Gettinger, M. (1984). Individual differences in time needed for learning. *Educational Psychologist* 19: 15–29.

Gettinger, M., and White, M. A. (1980). Evaluating curriculum fit with class ability. *Journal of Educational Psychology* 72: 338–44.

Gibson, E. J. (1991). *An odyssey in learning and perception.* Cambridge, MA: MIT Press.

Gick, M. L., and Holyoak, K. J. (1987). The cognitive basis of knowledge transfer. In *Transfer of training*, ed. S. Cormier and J. D. Hagman. New York: Academic Press.

Gilhooly, K. J., and Green, A.J.K. (1989). Learning problem-solving skills. In *Acquisition and performance of cognitive skills*, ed. A. M. Colley and J. R. Beech. Chichester, U. K.: Wiley.

Glaser, R. (1990). The reemergence of learning theory within instructional research. *American Psychologist* 45: 29–39.

Glenberg, A. M., and McDaniel, M. A. (1992). Mental models, pictures and text. *Memory and Cognition* 20: 458–60.

Globerson, T. (1989). What is the relationship between cognitive style and cognitive development? In *Cognitive style and cognitive development*, ed. T. Globerson and T. Zelniker. Norwood, NJ: Ablex.

Godden, D., and Baddeley, A. (1975). Context-independent memory in two natural environments. *British Journal of Psychology* 66: 325–31.

Golding, J. F. (1992). Cannabis. In *Handbook of human performance*, ed. A. P. Smith and D. M. Jones. San Diego: Academic Press.

Goldman-Rakic, P. S. (1987). Development of cortical circuitry and cognitive function. *Child Development* 58: 601–22.

Goldstein, A. P., and Krasner, L. (1987). *Modern applied psychology.* New York: Pergamon.

Goldstein, F. C., and Harvey, H. S. (1992). Cognitive function after closed head injury. In *Cognitive disorders*, ed. L. J. Thal, W. H. Moos, and E. R. Gamzu. New York: Marcel Dekker.

Goodman, G. S., and Schwartz-Kenney, B. M. (1992). Why knowing a child's age is not enough: Influences of cognitive, social and emotional factors on children's testimony. In *Children as witnesses*, ed. H. Dent and R. Flin. Chichester, U. K.: Wiley.

Gorman, R. P., and Sejnowski, R. J. (1988). Analysis of hidden units in a layered network trained to classify sonar targets. *Neural Networks* 1: 75–89.

Goschke, T., and Kuhl, J. (1993). Representation of intentions. *Journal of Experimental Psychology: Learning, Memory and Cognition* 19: 1211–26.

Gossette, R. L., and O'Brien, R. M. (1993). Efficacy of rational-emotive therapy (RET) with children. *Journal of Behavior Therapy and Experimental Psychiatry* 24: 15–26.

Gould, J. L. (1990). Honey bee cognition. *Cognition* 37: 83–103.

Gould, J. L, and Gould, C. G. (1982). The insect mind. In *Animal mind-human mind*, ed. D. R. Griffin. New York: Springer-Verlag.

Gow, L., and Kember, D. (1990). Does higher education promote independent learning? *Higher Education* 19: 307–22.

Graesser, A. C., Langston, M. C., and Baggett, W. B. (1993). Exploring information about concepts by asking questions. *Psychology of Learning and Motivation* 29: 411–36.

Green, L., Kagel, J. H., and Battalio, R. C. (1987). Consumption-leisure trade-offs in pigeons. *Journal of the Experimental Analysis of Behavior* 47: 17–28.

Green, T.G.R. (1991). User modelling: The information-processing perspective. In *Human-computer interaction*, ed. J. Rasmussen, H. B. Anderson, and N. O. Bernsen. Hove, U. K.: Erlbaum.

Greene, R. L. (1992). *Human memory: Paradigms and prospects.* Hillsdale, NJ: Erlbaum.

Gustavson, C. R., Garcia, J., Hankins, W. G., and Rusiniak, K. W. (1974). Coyote predation control by aversive conditioning. *Science* 184: 581–83.

Haber, R. N. (1983). The impending demise of the icon. *Behavioral and Brain Sciences* 6: 1–11.

Haier, R. J., Siegel, B., Tang, C., Abel, L., and Buchsbaum, M. S. (1992). Intelligence and changes in regional cerebral glucose metabolic rate following learning. *Intelligence* 16: 415–26.

Halford, G. S. (1993). *Children's understanding.* Hillsdale, NJ: Erlbaum.

Hammerton, M. (1989). Tracking. In *Human skills*, ed. D. H. Holding. Chichester, U. K.: Wiley.

Hamond, N. (1987). Principles from the psychology of skill acquisition. In *Applying cognitive psychology to user-interface design*, ed. M. M. Gardiner and B. Christie. Chichester, U. K.: Wiley.

Hamond, N.R., and Fivush, R. (1991). Memories of Mickey Mouse: Young children recount their trip to Disneyworld. *Cognitive Development* 6: 443–48.

Hanley, J. R., Young, A. W., and Pearson, N. A. (1991). Impairment of the visuo-spatial sketchpad. *Quarterly Journal of Experimental Psychology* 43: 101–25.

Harlow, H. F. (1959). Learning set and error factor theory. In *Psychology: A study of a science*, ed. S. Koch. New York: McGraw-Hill.

Harrell, M., Parente, F., Bellingrath, E. G., and Lisicia, K.A. (1992). *Cognitive rehabilitation of memory.* Gaithersburg, MD: Aspen.

Hasher, L., and Zacks, R. T. (1979). Automatic and effortful processes in memory. *Journal of Experimental Psychology: General* 108: 356–88.

Hebb, D. O. (1949). *The organization of behavior.* New York: Wiley.

Hegarty, M., and Just, M. A. (1993). Constructing mental models of machines from text and diagrams. *Journal of Memory and Language* 32: 717–42.

Hepper, P. G. (1992). Introduction: The quest for the developmental origins of behavior. *Quarterly Journal of Experimental Psychology* 44: 161–64.

Hepper, P. G., and Shahidullah, S. (1992). Habituation in normal and Down's syndrome fetuses. *Quarterly Journal of Experimental Psychology* 44: 305–18.

Hepper, P. G., and Waldman, B. (1992). Embryonic olfactory learning in frogs. *Quarterly Journal of Experimental Psychology* 44: 179–98.

Herrnstein, R. J. (1973). *IQ in the meritocracy.* Boston: Little, Brown.

———. (1990). Levels of stimulus control. *Cognition* 37: 133–66.

Herrnstein, R. J., and de Villiers, P.A. (1980). Fish as a natural category for people and pigeons. *Psychology of Learning and Motivation* 14: 59–95.

Herrnstein, R. J., and Loveland, D. A. (1964). Complex visual concept in the pigeon. *Science* 146: 549–51.

Herrnstein, R. J., Loveland, D.A., and Cable, C. (1976). Natural concepts in pigeons. *Journal of Experimental Psychology: Animal Behavior Processes* 2: 285–311.

Herrnstein, R. J., Vaughan, W., Mumford, D. B., and Kosslyn, S. M. (1989). Teaching pigeons an abstract relational rule: Insideness. *Perception and Psychophysics* 46: 56–64.

Hess, T. M. (1982). Visual abstraction processes in young and old adults. *Developmental Psychology* 18: 473–84.

Hick, W. E. (1952). On the rate of gain of information. *Quarterly Journal of Experimental Psychology* 4: 11–26.

Hill, L. B. (1957). A second quarter-century of delayed recall, or relearning at 80. *Journal of Educational Psychology* 48: 65–69.

Hinde, R. A. (1970). *Animal behavior*. New York: McGraw-Hill.

Hinton, G. E. (1989). Connectionist learning procedures. *Artificial Intelligence* 40: 185–234.

Hinton, G. E., Plant, D. C., and Shallice, T. (1993). Simulating brain damage. *Scientific American* 269: 58–65.

Hinton, G. E., and Shallice, T. (1991). Lesioning an attractor network. *Psychological Review* 98: 74–95.

Hintzman, D. L. (1986). "Schema abstraction" in a multiple-trace memory model. *Psychological Review* 93: 411–28.

———. (1990). Human learning and memory. *Annual Review of Psychology* 41: 109–39.

Hirsch, E. D. (1987). *Cultural literacy*. Boston: Houghton-Mifflin.

Hitch, G. J. (1987). Principles from the psychology of memory. In *Applying cognitive psychology to user-interface design*, ed. M. M. Gardiner and B. Christie. Chichester, U. K.: Wiley.

Hodges, J. R., Salmon, D. P., and Balters, N. (1992). Semantic memory impairment in Alzheimer's disease. *Neuropsychologia* 30: 301–14.

Hoffman, R. E., and Dobscha, S. K. (1989). Cortical pruning and the development of schizophrenia: A computer model. *Schizophrenia Bulletin* 15: 477–90.

Holding, D. H. (1965). *Principles of training*. London: Pergamon.

———. (1985). *The psychology of chess skill*. Hillsdale, NJ: Erlbaum.

———. (1987). Concepts of training. In *Handbook of human factors*, ed. G. Salvendy. New York: Wiley.

———. (1989). Skills research. In *Human skills*, ed. D. H. Holding. New York: Wiley.

Holland, J. H. (1975). *Adaptation in natural and artificial systems*. Cambridge, MA: MIT Press.

Holland, J. H., Holyoak, K. J., Nisbett, R. E., and Thagard, P. R. (1986). *Induction*. Cambridge, MA: MIT Press.

Holyoak, K. J. (1991). Symbolic connectionism: Toward third-generation theories of expertise. In *Toward a general theory of expertise*, ed. K. A. Ericsson and J. Smith. New York: Cambridge University Press.

Holyoak, K. J., Junn, E. N., and Billman, D. O. (1984). Development of analogical problem solving skill. *Child Development* 55: 2042–55.

Homa, D. (1984). On the nature of categories. *Psychology of Learning and Motivation* 18: 49–94.

Hopfield, J. J. (1982). Neural networks and physical systems with emergent collective properties. *Proceedings of the National Academy of Sciences* 79: 2554–58.

Horgan, T., and Tienson, J. (1991). *Connectionism and the philosophy of mind.* Norwell, MA: Kluwer.

Horne, P. J., and Lowe, C. F. (1993). Determinants of human performance on concurrent schedules. *Journal of the Experimental Analysis of Behavior* 59: 29–60.

Howard, R. W. (1979). Stimulus generalization along a dimension based on a verbal concept. *Journal of the Experimental Analysis of Behavior* 32: 199–212.

———. (1987). *Concepts and schemata.* London: Cassell.

———. (1991). *All about intelligence: Human, animal and artificial.* Sydney: NSW University Press.

———. (1992). Classifying types of concept and conceptual structure: Some taxonomies. *European Journal of Cognitive Psychology* 4: 81–111.

———. (1993). On what intelligence is. *British Journal of Psychology* 84: 27–37.

Howe, M. (1988). Perspiration beats inspiration. *New Scientist* 24: 58–60.

———. (1989). *Fragments of genius.* London: Routledge.

Howell, W. C. (1993). Engineering psychology in a changing world. *Annual Review of Psychology* 44: 231–63.

Howes, M., Siegel, M., and Brown, F. (1993). Early childhood memories: Accuracy and affect. *Cognition* 47: 95–119.

Hull, C. L. (1952). *A behavior system.* New Haven, CT: Yale University Press.

Hulme, C., and Mackenzie, S. (1992). *Working memory and severe learning difficulties.* Hove, U.K.: Erlbaum.

Hulme, C., Lee, G., and Brown, G.D.A. (1993). Short-term memory impairments in Alzheimer-type dementia. *Neuropsychologia* 31: 161–72.

Humphreys, M. S., Bain, J. D., and Pike, R. (1989). Different ways to cue a coherent memory system. *Psychological Review* 96: 208–31.

Hunt, E. (1976). Varieties of cognitive power. In *The nature of intelligence,* ed. L. B. Resnick. Hillsdale, NJ: Erlbaum.

Hunter, I.M.L. (1982). An exceptional memory. In *Memory observed,* ed. U. Neisser. New York: Freeman.

Hurford, J. R. (1991). The evolution of the critical period for language acquisition. *Cognition* 40: 159–201.

Itakura, S. (1992). A chimpanzee with the ability to learn the use of personal pronouns. *Psychological Record* 42: 157–72.

Itani, J., and Nishimura, A. (1973). The study of infrahuman culture in Japan. In *Precultural primate behavior,* ed. E. Menzel. Basel: Karger.

Jackson, B. (1978). The effects of unilateral and bilateral ECT on verbal and visual spatial ability. *Journal of Clinical Psychology* 34: 4–13.

Jacobs, G. D., Benson, H., and Friedman, R. (1993). Home-based central nervous system assessment of a multifactor behavioral intervention for chronic sleep-onset insomnia. *Behavior Therapy* 24: 159–74.

James, W. (1890). *Principles of psychology*. New York: Holt.

Janikow, C. Z. (1993). A knowledge-intensive genetic algorithm for supervised learning. *Machine Learning* 13: 189–228.

Jenkins, H. (1979). Animal learning and behavior theory. In *The first century of experimental psychology*, ed. E. Hearst. Hillsdale, NJ: Erlbaum.

Jenkins, H. M., and Moore, B. R. (1973). The form of the autoshaped response with food or water reinforcers. *Journal of the Experimental Analysis of Behavior* 20: 163–81.

Jensen, A. R. (1980). *Bias in mental testing*. London: Methuen.

———. (1989). The relationship between learning and intelligence. *Learning and Individual Differences* 1: 37–61.

Johnson, M. K., Hashtroudi, S., and Lindsay, D. S. (1993). Source monitoring. *Psychological Bulletin* 114: 3–28.

Johnson, T. D. (1982). Selective costs and benefits in the evolution of learning. *Advances in the Study of Behavior* 12: 65–106.

Johnson-Laird, P. N. (1983). *Mental models*. Cambridge, U. K.: Cambridge University Press.

———. (1989). Mental models. In *Foundations of cognitive science*, ed. M. I. Posner. Cambridge, MA: MIT Press.

Johnson-Laird, P. N., Hermann, D. J., and Chaffin, R. (1984). Only connections—A critique of semantic networks. *Psychological Bulletin* 96: 292–315.

Just, M. A., and Carpenter, P. A. (1992). A capacity theory of comprehension. *Psychological Review* 99: 122–49.

Kail, R. (1988). Developmental functions of speeds of cognitive processes. *Journal of Experimental Child Psychology* 45: 339–64.

———. (1992). Evidence for global developmental change. *Journal of Experimental Child Psychology* 54: 308–14.

Kail, R., and Bisanz, J. (1992). The information-processing perspective on cognitive development. In *Intellectual development*, ed. R. J. Sternberg and C. A. Berg. New York: Cambridge University Press.

Kamil, A. C., and Maudlin, J. E. (1988). A comparative-ecological approach to the study of learning. In *Evolution and learning*, ed. R. C. Bolles and M. D. Beecher. Hillsdale, NJ: Erlbaum.

Kamps, D. M., Leonard, B. R., Vernon, S., Dugan, E. P., Delquadri, J. C., Gershon, B., Wade, L., and Falk, L. (1992). Teaching social skills to students with autism to increase peer interactions in an integrated first-grade classroom. *Journal of Applied Behavior Analysis* 25: 281–88.

Kaplan, R. M., Sallis, J. F., and Patterson, T. L. (1993). *Health and human behavior*. New York: McGraw-Hill.

Karmiloff-Smith, A. (1992). *Beyond modularity*. Cambridge, MA: MIT Press.

Katz, B. F. (1993). A neural resolution of the incongruity-resolution and incongruity theories of humor. *Connection Science* 5: 59–97.

Kausler, D. H. (1990). *Experimental psychology: Cognition and human aging*. New York: Springer-Verlag.

Keane, M. (1988). *Analogical problem solving*. Chichester, U. K.: Ellis Horwood.

Kehoe, E. J. (1988). A layered network model of associative learning: Learning to learn and configuration. *Psychological Review* 95: 411–33.

Keil, F. C. (1986). The acquisition of natural-kind and artifact terms. In *Language learning and concept acquisition*, ed. W. Demopoulos and A. Marras. Norwood, NJ: Ablex.

——. (1990). Constraints on constraints. *Cognitive Science* 14: 135–68.

Keil, F. C., and Batterman, N. (1984). A characteristic-to-defining shift in the development of word meaning. *Journal of Verbal Learning and Verbal Behavior* 23: 221–36.

Kintsch, W. (1980). Semantic memory: A tutorial. In *Attention and Performance VIII*, ed. R. S. Nickerson. Hillsdale, NJ: Erlbaum.

Kirby, J. R., and Williams, N. H. (1991). *Learning problems: A cognitive approach.* Toronto: Kagan and Woo.

Kirk, S. A., and Gallagher, J. J. (1986). *Educating exceptional children.* Boston: Houghton-Mifflin.

Kisilevsky, B. S., Muir, D. W., and Low, J. A. (1992). Maturation of human fetal responses to vibroacoustic stimulation. *Child Development* 63: 1497–1508.

Koedinger, K. R., and Anderson, J. R. (1990). Abstract planning and perceptual chunks: Aspects of expertise in geometry. *Cognitive Science* 14: 511–50.

Koehler, O. (1950). The ability of birds to "count." *Bulletin of Animal Behavior* 9: 41–50.

Komatsu, L. K. (1992). Recent views of conceptual structure. *Psychological Bulletin* 112: 500–26.

Kopelman, M. D., Christensen, H., Puffett, A., and Stanhope, N. (1994). The great escape: A neuropsychological study of psychogenic amnesia. *Neuropsychologia* 32: 675–91.

Kosslyn, S. M. (1980). *Image and mind.* Cambridge, MA: Harvard University Press.

——. (1983). *Ghosts in the mind's machine.* New York: Norton.

Kow, L., and Kember, D. (1993). Conceptions of teaching and their relation to student learning. *British Journal of Educational Psychology* 63: 20–33.

Kozminsky, E., and Kaufman, G. (1992). Academic achievement and individual differences in the learning processes of Israeli high-school students. *Learning and Individual Differences* 4: 335–45.

Kranzler, J. H., and Jensen, A. R. (1991). Unitary g: Unquestioned postulate or empirical fact? *Intelligence* 15: 437–48.

Krascum, R. M., and Andrews, S. (1993). Feature-based versus exemplar-based strategies in preschoolers' category learning. *Journal of Experimental Child Psychology* 56: 1–48.

Kreutzer, M. A., Leonard, C., and Flavell, J. H. (1975). An interview study of children's knowledge about memory. *Monographs of the Society for Research in Child Development* 40: no. 159.

Kruschke, J. K. (1993). Human category learning: Implications for back-propagation models. *Connection Science* 5: 3–36.

Kuhn, T. S. (1970). *The structure of scientific revolutions.* Chicago: University of Chicago Press.

Kulik, J. A., Kulik, C. C., and Cohen, P. A. (1979). A meta-analysis of outcome studies of Keller's personalized system of instruction. *American Psychologist* 34: 307–18.

Kyllonen, P. C., and Alluisi, E. A. (1987). Learning and forgetting facts and skills. In *Handbook of human factors*, ed. G. Salvendy. New York: Wiley.

Kyllonen, P. C., and Tirre, W. C. (1988). Individual differences in associative learning and forgetting. *Intelligence* 12: 393–421.

Labouvie-Vief, G. (1992). A neo-Piagetian perspective on adult cognitive development. In *Intellectual development*, ed. R. J. Sternberg and C. A. Berg. New York: Cambridge University Press.

Lachman, R., Lachman, J. L., and Butterfield, E. R. (1979). *Cognitive psychology and information processing*. Hillsdale, NJ: Erlbaum.

Lakoff, G. (1987). *Women, fire and dangerous things*. Chicago: University of Chicago Press.

Lakoff, G., and Johnson, M. (1980). *Metaphors we live by*. Chicago: University of Chicago Press.

Lamb, M. R. (1991). Attention in humans and animals. *Journal of Experimental Psychology: Animal Behavior Processes* 17: 45–54.

Landau, B. (1982). Will the real grandmother please stand up. *Journal of Psycholinguistic Research* 11: 47–62.

Landauer, T. K. (1986). How much do people remember: Some estimates of the quantity of learned information in long-term memory. *Cognitive Science* 10: 477–93.

Langley, P., and Zytkow, J. M. (1989). Data-driven approaches to empirical discovery. *Artificial Intelligence* 40: 283–312.

Larson, G. E., and Alderton, D. C. (1992). The structure and capacity of thought: Some comments on the cognitive underpinnings of g. In *Current topics in human intelligence*, ed. D. K. Detterman. Norwood, NJ: Ablex.

Lattal, K. A., McFarland, J. M., and Joyce, J.H. (1990). What is happening in psychology of learning courses? *The Behavior Analyst* 13: 121–30.

Lavelle, J. M., Hovell, M. F., West, M. P., and Dahlgren, D. R. (1992). Promoting law enforcement for child protection. *Journal of Applied Behavior Analysis* 25: 885–92.

Le Cun, Y., Boser, B. L., Denker, J. S., Henderson, D., Howard, R. E., Hubbard, W., and Jackel, L. D. (1992). Handwritten digit recognition with a back-propagation network. In *Neural networks: Current applications*, ed. P.G.J. Lisboa. London: Chapman and Hall.

Lenat, D. B. (1976). AM. Ph.D. thesis, Stanford University.

Lenat, D. B., and Guha, R. V. (1990). *Building large knowledge-based systems*. Reading, MA: Addison-Wesley.

Lenski, G. (1978). Marxist experiments in destratification. *Social Forces* 57: 364–83.

Lesgold, A., Rubinson, H., Feltovich, P., Glaser, R., Klopfer, D., and Wang, Y. (1988). Expertise in a complex skill: Diagnosing X-ray pictures. In *The nature of expertise*, ed. M.T.H. Chi, R. Glaser, and M. J. Farr. Hillsdale, NJ: Erlbaum.

Levelt, W.J.M. (1990). On learnability, empirical foundations, and naturalness. *Behavioral and Brain Sciences* 13: 501.

Levin, J. R., McCormick, C. B., Miller, G. E., and Berry, J .K. (1982). Mnemonic vs. non-mnemonic vocabulary-learning strategies for children. *American Educational Research Journal* 19: 121–36.

Levy-Leboyer, C. (1988). Success and failure in applying psychology. *American Psychologist* 43: 779–85.

Ley, P. (1978). Memory for medical information. In *Practical aspects of memory*, ed. M. M. Gruneberg, P. E. Morris, and R.N.S. Sykes. London: Academic Press.

Lickliter, R., and Stoumbos, J. (1992). Modification of prenatal auditory experience alters postnatal auditory preferences of bobwhite quail chicks. *Quarterly Journal of Experimental Psychology* 44: 199–214.

Light, L. L. (1991). Memory and aging. *Annual Review of Psychology* 42: 333–76.

Ling, C.X., and Marinov, M. (1993). Answering the connectionist challenge: A symbolic model of learning the past tenses of English verbs. *Cognition* 49: 235–90.

Lisboa, P.G.J. (1992). Introduction. In *Neural networks: Current applications*, ed. P.G.J. Lisboa. London: Chapman and Hall.

List, J. A. (1986). Age and schematic differences in the reliability of eyewitness testimony. *Developmental Psychology* 22: 50–57.

Lockhart, R.S., and Craik, F. I. (1990). Levels of processing: A retrospective commentary on a framework for memory research. *Canadian Journal of Psychology* 44: 87–112.

Loftus, E. F. (1984). Expert testimony on the eyewitness. In *Eyewitness testimony*, ed. G. L. Wells and E. F. Loftus. New York: Cambridge University Press.

_____. (1993). Psychologists in the eyewitness world. *American Psychologist* 48: 550–52.

Loftus, E. F., and Burns, T. E. (1982). Mental shock can produce retrograde amnesia. *Memory and Cognition* 10: 318–23.

Loftus, E. F., and Palmer, J. C. (1974). Reconstruction of automobile destruction. *Journal of Verbal Learning and Verbal Behavior* 13: 585–89.

Logue, A. W. (1988). A comparison of taste aversion learning in humans and other vertebrates. In *Evolution and learning*, ed. R. C. Bolles and M. D. Beecher. Hillsdale, NJ: Erlbaum.

Lohman, D. F. (1988). Spatial abilities as traits, processes, and knowledge. In *Advances in the psychology of human intelligence*, ed. R. J. Sternberg. Hillsdale, NJ: Erlbaum.

Longoni, A. M., Richardson, J.T.E., and Aiello, A. (1993). Articulatory rehearsal and phonological storage in working memory. *Memory and Cognition* 21: 11–22.

Lopez, J. C., and Lopez, D. (1985). Killer whales (*Orcinus orca*) of Patagonia, and their behavior of intentional stranding while hunting near shore. *Journal of Mammalogy* 66: 181–83.

Lorenz, K. (1935). Der Kumpan in der Umwelt des vogels. *Journal of Ornithology* 83: 137–213.

Lovelack, E. A., and Marsh, G. R. (1985). Prediction and evaluation of memory performance by young and old adults. *Journal of Gerontology* 40: 192–97.

Lowe, C. F., Horne, P. J., and Higson, P. H. (1987). Operant conditioning. In *Theoretical foundations of behavior therapy*, ed. H. J. Eysenck and I. Martin. New York: Plenum.

Lubow, R. E. (1974). Higher-order concept formation in the pigeon. *Journal of the Experimental Analysis of Behavior* 21: 475–83.

Luria, A. R. (1968). *The mind of a mnemonist*. New York: Basic Books.

Mackintosh, N. J. (1974). *The psychology of animal learning.* New York: Academic Press.

——. (1987). A natural history of intelligence in man and other animals. In *Science and intelligence,* ed. S. Nash. Northwood, U.K.: Science Reviews.

MacPhail, R. M. (1987). The comparative psychology of intelligence. *Behavioral and Brain Sciences* 10: 645–95.

Maddox, H. (1993). *Theory of knowledge.* Castlemaine, Australia: Freshet Press.

Madigan, S., and O'Hara, R. (1992). Initial recall, reminiscence and hypernesia. *Journal of Experimental Psychology: Learning, Memory and Cognition* 18: 421–25.

Mahadevan, S., Mitchell, T. M., Mostow, J., Steinberg, L., and Tadepalli, P. V. (1993). An apprentice-based approach to knowledge acquisition. *Artificial Intelligence* 64: 1–52.

Mandler, J. M. (1984). *Stories, scripts and scenes: Aspects of schema theory.* Hillsdale, NJ: Erlbaum.

——. (1992). How to build a baby II: Conceptual primitives. *Psychological Review* 99: 587–604.

Mane, A. M., Adams, J. A., and Denchin, E. (1989). Adaptive and part-whole training in the acquisition of a complex perceptual-motor skill. *Acta Psychologica* 71: 179–96.

Markman, E. M. (1990). Constraints children place on word meanings. *Cognitive Science* 14: 57–77.

Markowitz, H. (1982). *Behavioral enrichment in the zoo.* New York: Van Nostrand Reinhold.

Marr, D. (1982). *Vision.* New York: Freeman.

Marshall, C., Christie, B., and Gardiner, M. M. (1987). Assessment of trends in the technology and techniques of human-computer interaction. In *Applying cognitive psychology to user-interface design,* ed. M. M. Gardiner and B. Christie. Chichester, U. K.: Wiley.

Martin, A., and Weingartner, H. (1992). Modules, domains and frames. In *Current topics in human intelligence,* ed. D. K. Detterman. Norwood, NJ: Ablex.

Martindale, C. (1991). *Cognitive psychology: A neural-network approach.* Pacific Grove, CA: Brooks/Cole.

Marton, F. (1988). Describing and improving learning. In *Learning strategies and learning styles,* ed. R. R. Schmeck. New York: Plenum.

Massaro, D.W. (1988). Some criticisms of connectionist models of human performance. *Journal of Memory and Language* 27: 213–34.

Massaro, D. W., and Cowan, N. (1993). Information processing models. *Annual Review of Psychology* 44: 383–425.

Mazur, J. E. (1990). *Learning and behavior.* Englewood Cliffs, NJ: Prentice-Hall.

McBride, G. (1987). Ethology and comparative psychology. *Journal of Comparative Psychology* 101: 272–74.

McCartney, J. R. (1987). Mentally retarded and non-mentally retarded subjects' long-term recognition memory. *American Journal of Mental Retardation* 92: 312–17.

McClelland, J.L. (1988). Connectionist models and psychological evidence. *Journal of Memory and Language* 27: 107–23.

McCloskey, M. E., and Glucksberg, S. (1978). Natural categories: Well-defined or fuzzy sets? *Memory and Cognition* 6: 642–72.

McCulloch, W. S., and Pitts, W. (1943). A logical calculus of the ideas immanent in nervous activity. *Bulletin of Mathematical Biophysics* 5: 115–33.

McKee, R. D., and Squire, L. R. (1993). On the development of declarative memory. *Journal of Experimental Psychology: Learning, Memory and Cognition* 19: 397–404.

McNamara, T. P., Halpin, J. A., and Hardy, J. K. (1992). The representation and integration in memory of spatial and nonspatial information. *Memory and Cognition* 20: 519–32.

Medin, D. L., Ahn, W., Bettger, J., Florian, J., Goldstone, R., Lassaline, M., Markman, A., Rubinstein, J., and Wisniewski, E. (1990). Safe takeoffs—soft landings. *Cognitive Science* 14: 169–78.

Mervis, C. B., and Rosch, E. (1981). Categorization of natural objects. *Annual Review of Psychology* 32: 89–115.

Messick, S. (1976). *Individuality in learning*. San Francisco: Jossey-Bass.

Metzler, J., and Shepard, R. N. (1974). Transformational studies of the internal representation of three dimensional objects. In *Theories of cognitive psychology: The Loyola symposium*, ed. R. L. Solso. Hillsdale, NJ: Erlbaum.

Michalsky, R. S. (1987). Learning strategies and automated knowledge acquisition. In *Computational models of learning*, ed. L. Bolc. New York: Springer-Verlag.

Michalsky, R. S., and Chilausky, R. (1980). Knowledge acquisition by encoding expert rules versus computer induction from examples. *International Journal of Man-Machine Studies* 12: 63–87.

Miller, G. A. (1956). The magical number seven, plus or minus two. *Psychological Review* 63: 81–97.

Miller, G. A., Galanter, E., and Pribram, K. A. (1960). *Plans and the structure of behavior*. New York: Holt.

Milner, B. (1966). Amnesia following operations on the temporal lobes. In *Amnesia*, ed. C.W.M. Whitty and O. Zangwill. London: Butterworth.

Minsky, M. A., and Papert, S. (1969). *Perceptrons*. Cambridge, MA: MIT Press.

Minton, S., Carbonell, J. G., Knoblock, C. A., Kuokka, D. R., Etzioni, O., and Gil, Y. (1989). Explanation-based learning: A problem-solving perspective. *Artificial Intelligence* 40: 63–118.

Moely, B. E., Olsen, F. A., Halwes, T. G., and Glavell, J. H. (1969). Production deficiency in young children's clustered recall. *Developmental Psychology* 1: 26–34.

Moran, G. (1987). Applied dimensions of comparative psychology. *Journal of Comparative Psychology* 101: 277–81.

Morgan, M. J., Fitch, M. D., Holman, J. G., and Lea, S.E.G. (1976). Pigeons learn the concept of an A. *Perception* 5: 57–66.

Morris, R. G., and Kopelman, L. D. (1986). The memory deficits in Alzheimer-type dementia: A review. *Quarterly Journal of Experimental Psychology* 38: 575–602.

Morris, R.G.M. (1981). Spatial localization does not require the presence of local cues. *Learning and Motivation* 12: 239–60.

Morse, C. K. (1993). Does variability increase with age? *Psychology and Aging* 8: 156–64.

Moscovitch, M., Winocur, G., and McLachlan, D. (1986). Memory as assessed by recognition and reading time in normal and memory-impaired people with Alzheimer's disease and other neurological disorders. *Journal of Experimental Psychology: General* 115: 331–47.

Mosler, F., Heil, M., and Glowalla, U. (1993). Monitoring retrieval from long-term memory by slow event-related brain potentials. *Psychophysiology* 30: 170–82.

Murphy, G. J., and Medin, D. L. (1985). The role of theories in conceptual coherence. *Psychological Review* 92: 289–316.

Murphy, G. L., and Wright, J. C. (1984). Changes in conceptual structure with expertise. *Journal of Experimental Psychology: Learning, Memory and Cognition* 10: 144–55.

Nagell, K., Olguin, R. S., and Tomasello, M. (1993). Processes of social learning in the tool use of chimpanzees and human children. *Journal of Comparative Psychology* 107: 174–86.

Nebes, R. D. (1989). Semantic memory in Alzheimer's disease. *Psychological Bulletin* 106: 337–94.

Neisser, U. (1967). *Cognitive psychology*. New York: Appleton-Century-Crofts.

———. (1981). John Dean's memory. *Cognition* 9: 1–22.

———. (1982). Memory: What are the important questions? In *Memory observed*, ed. U. Neisser. New York: Freeman.

Nelson, K. (1992). Emergence of autobiographical memory at age four. *Human Development* 35: 172–77.

Nelson, L. J., and Hekmat, H. (1991). Promoting healthy nutritional habits by paradigmatic behavior therapy. *Journal of Behavior Therapy and Experimental Psychiatry* 22: 291–98.

Newell, A. (1990). *Unified theories of cognition*. Cambridge, MA: Harvard University Press.

Newell, K. M. (1991). Motor skill acquisition. *Annual Review of Psychology* 42: 213–37.

Newport, E. L. (1990). Maturational constraints on language learning. *Cognitive Science* 14: 11–28.

Nisbett, R. E., and Wilson, T. D. (1977). Telling more than we can know. *Psychological Review* 84: 231–59.

Nordhausen, B., and Langley, P. (1993). An integrated framework for empirical discovery. *Machine Learning* 12: 17–47.

Norman, D. A. (1988). *The psychology of everyday things*. New York: Basic Books.

Norman, D. A., and Rumelhart, D.E. (1975). *Explorations in cognition*. New York: Freeman.

Norris, D. (1990). How to build a connectionist idiot (savant). *Cognition* 35: 277–91.

Nowak, J. D., and Gowin, D. B. (1984). *Learning how to learn*. New York: Cambridge University Press.

Nussbaum, J. (1979). Children's conceptions of the Earth as a cosmic body. *Science Education* 63: 83–93.

Nussbaum, J., and Novick, S. (1981). Brainstorming in the classroom to invent a model: A case study. *School Science Review* 62: 771–78.

O'Connor, K., and Ison, J. R. (1991). Echoic memory in the rat. *Journal of Experimental Psychology: Animal Behavior Processes* 17: 377–85.

O'Donnell, A., Dansereau, D. F., and Rocklin, T. R. (1991). Individual differences in the cooperative learning of concrete procedures. *Learning and Individual Differences* 3: 149–62.

O'Donohue, W., Plaud, J. J., and Hecker, J. E. (1992). The possible function of positive reinforcement in home-bound agoraphobia. *Journal of Behavior Therapy and Experimental Psychiatry* 23: 303–12.

Olson, D. J., Kamil, A. C., and Balda, R. P. (1993). Effects of response strategy and retention interval on performance of Clark's nutcrackers in a radial maze analog. *Journal of Experimental Psychology: Animal Behavior Processes* 19: 138–48.

Orne, M. T., Soskis, D. A., Dinges, D. F., and Orne, E. C. (1984). Hypnotically induced testimony. In *Eyewitness testimony*, ed. G. L. Wells and E. F. Loftus. New York: Cambridge University Press.

Paivio, A. (1986). *Mental representations*. New York: Oxford University Press.

Palmer, C., and van de Sande, C. (1993). Units of knowledge in music performance. *Journal of Experimental Psychology: Learning, Memory and Cognition* 19: 457–70.

Palmer, S. E. (1978). Fundamental aspects of cognitive representation. In *Cognition and categorization*, ed. E. Rosch and B. B. Lloyd. Hillsdale, NJ: Erlbaum.

Papini, M. R., and Bitterman, M. E. (1990). The role of contingency in classical conditioning. *Psychological Review* 97: 396–403.

Park, D. C., Smith, A. D., and Cavanaugh, J. C. (1990). Metamemories of memory researchers. *Memory and Cognition* 18: 321–27.

Parkes, M. J. (1992). Fetal behavioral states: Sleep and wakefulness? *Quarterly Journal of Experimental Psychology* 44: 231–44.

Parkin, A. J. (1993). *Memory*. Oxford, U. K.: Blackwell.

Pask, G. (1988). Learning strategies, teaching strategies, and conceptual or learning style. In *Learning strategies and learning styles*, ed. R. R. Schmeck. New York: Plenum.

Pask, G., and Scott, B.C.E. (1972). Learning strategies and individual competence. *International Journal of Man-Machine Studies* 5: 17–52.

Patel, V. L., and Groen, G. J. (1991). The general and specific nature of medical expertise. In *Toward a general theory of expertise*, ed. K. A. Ericsson and J. Smith. New York: Cambridge University Press.

Patterson, F. G., and Linden, E. (1981). *The education of Koko*. New York: Holt, Rinehart and Winston.

Pavlov, I. P. (1927). *Conditioned reflexes*. London: Oxford University Press.

Penfield, W., and Perot, P. (1963). The brain's record of auditory and visual experience. *Brain* 86: 595–96.

Pepperberg, I. M. (1987). Evidence for conceptual quantitative abilities in the African Gray parrot. *Ethology* 75: 37–61.

Perner, J. (1991). *Understanding the representational mind*. Cambridge, MA: MIT Press.

———. (1992). Grasping the concept of representation. *Human Development* 35: 146–55.

Peters, D. P. (1988). Eyewitness memory and arousal in a natural setting. In *Practical aspects of memory*, ed. M. M. Gruneberg, P. E. Morris, and R. N. Sykes. Chichester, U. K.: Wiley.

Peterson, L. (1993). Behavior therapy: The long and winding road. *Behavior Therapy* 24: 1–5.

Phillips, W. A. (1988). Brainy minds. *Quarterly Journal of Experimental Psychology* 40: 389–405.

Phillips, W.A., and Baddeley, A. (1989). Learning and memory. In *Research directions in cognitive science: European perspectives*, ed. A. Baddeley and N. O. Bernsen. Hove, U. K.: Erlbaum.

Piattelli-Palmarini, M. (1989). Evolution, selection, and cognition. *Cognition* 31: 1–44.

Pillemer, D. B. (1990). Clarifying the flashbulb memory concept. *Journal of Experimental Psychology: General* 119: 92–96.

Pintrich, P. R., Marx, R. W., and Boyle, R. A. (1993). Beyond cold conceptual change. *Review of Educational Research* 63: 167–99.

Poole, J., and Lander, D. G. (1971). The pigeon's concept of pigeon. *Psychonomic Science* 25: 157–58.

Povinelli, D. J. (1993). Reconstructing the evolution of mind. *American Psychologist* 48: 493–509.

Price, E. O. (1984). Behavioral aspects of animal domestication. *Quarterly Review of Biology* 59: 1–32.

Priest, G. (1991). Protecting primates: The psychology of animal care. *Zoonoos* 64: 7–11.

Puff, C. R. (1979). *Memory organization and structure*. New York: Academic Press.

Quillian, M. R. (1969). The teachable language comprehender. *Communications of the Association for Computing Machinery* 12: 459–76.

Quine, W.V.O. (1960). *Word and object*. Cambridge, MA: MIT Press.

———. (1977). Natural kinds. In *Naming, necessity and natural kinds*, ed. S. P. Schwartz. Ithaca, NY: Cornell University Press.

Quinlan, P. T. (1991). *Connectionism and psychology*. Hertsfordshire, U. K.: Harvester Wheatsheaf.

Quinlan, R. (1986). Induction of decision trees. *Machine Learning* 1: 81–106.

Raaijmakers, J.G.W., and Shiffrin, R. M. (1992). Models for recall and recognition. *Annual Review of Psychology* 43: 205–34.

Rabbitt, P. (1993). Does it all go together when it goes? *Quarterly Journal of Experimental Psychology* 46: 385–434.

Rabbitt, P., Banerji, N., and Szymanski, A. (1989). Space Fortress as an IQ test? *Acta Psychologica* 71: 243–57.

Rajamoney, S. A. (1993). The design of discrimination experiments. *Machine Learning* 12: 185–203.

Ramsden, P. (1983). Institutional variations in British students' approaches to learning and experiences of teaching. *Higher Education* 12: 691–705.

Ratcliff, R. (1978). A theory of memory retrieval. *Psychological Review* 85: 59–108.

Ray, W. S. (1932). A preliminary report on a study of fetal conditioning. *Child Development* 3: 175–77.

Reber, A. S. (1989). Implicit learning and tacit knowledge. *Journal of Experimental Psychology: General* 118: 219–35.

Ree, M. J., and Earles, M. (1991). Predicting training success. *Personnel Psychology* 44: 321–32.

Rescorla, R. A. (1988). Pavlovian conditioning: It's not what you think it is. *American Psychologist* 43: 151–60.

Rescorla, R. A., and Wagner, A. R. (1972). A theory of Pavlovian conditioning. In *Classical conditioning II*, ed. A. H. Black and W. F. Prokasy. New York: Appleton-Century-Crofts.

Reuning, H. (1988). Testing bushmen in the central Kalahari. In *Human abilities in cultural context*, ed. S. H. Irvine and J. W. Berry. New York: Cambridge University Press.

Revusky, S. (1977). Learning as a general process with an emphasis on data from feeding experiments. In *Food aversion learning*, ed. N. W. Milgram, L. Krames, and T. Alloway. New York: Plenum.

Riding, R., and Douglas, G. (1993). The effect of cognitive style and mode of presentation on learning performance. *British Journal of Educational Psychology* 63: 297–307.

Roberts, W. A., and Mazmanian, D. S. (1988). Concept learning at different levels of abstraction by pigeons, monkeys and people. *Journal of Experimental Psychology: Animal Behavior Processes* 14: 247–60.

Robinson, D. A. (1992). Implications of neural networks for how we think about brain function. *Behavioral and Brain Sciences* 15: 644–55.

Rodin, J., and Salovey, P. (1989). Health psychology. *Annual Review of Psychology* 40: 533–79.

Roedinger, H. C. (1990). Implicit memory: A commentary. *Bulletin of the Psychonomic Society* 28: 373–80.

Roitblat, H. L., and von Fersen, L. (1992). Comparative cognition. *Annual Review of Psychology* 43: 671–710.

Rosenblatt, F. (1958). The perceptron. *Psychological Review* 65: 368–408.

———. (1962). *The principles of neurodynamics* New York: Spartan.

Rosler, F., Heil, M., and Glowalla, U. (1993). Monitoring retrieval from long-term memory by slow event-related brain potentials. *Psychophysiology* 30: 170–82.

Ross, A. (1991). Growth without progress. *Contemporary Psychology* 36: 743–44.

Rovee-Collier, C., Borza, M. A., Adler, S. A., and Boller, K. (1993). Infant's eyewitness testimony. *Memory and Cognition* 21: 267–79.

Rubin, D. C., Wallace, W. T., and Houston, B. C. (1993). The beginnings of expertise for ballads. *Cognitive Science* 17: 435–62.

Rumelhart, D. E. (1989). The architecture of mind: A connectionist approach. In *Foundations of cognitive science*, ed. M. I. Posner. Cambridge, MA: MIT Press.

Rumelhart, D. E., and McClelland, J. L. (1986). *Parallel distributed processing*. Cambridge, MA: MIT Press.

Rumelhart, D. E., and Norman, D. A. (1988). Representation in memory. In *Stevens' handbook of experimental psychology*, ed. R. C. Atkinson. New York: Wiley.

Russon, A. E., and Galdikas, B.M.F. (1993). Imitation in free-ranging rehabilitant orangutans. *Journal of Comparative Psychology* 107: 147–61.

Saariluoma. P. (1991). Aspects of skilled imagery in blindfold chess. *Acta Psychologica* 77: 65–89.

Sackheim, H. A. (1992). The cognitive effects of electroconvulsive therapy. In *Cognitive disorders*. ed. L. J. Thal, W. H. Moos, and E. R. Gamzu. New York: Marcel Dekker.

Saljo, R. (1982). *Learning and understanding*. Goteborg, Sweden: Universitatis Gothoburgensis.

Salkovskis, P. M., Clark, D. M., and Hackmann, A. (1991). Treatment of panic attacks using cognitive therapy without exposure or breathing retraining. *Behavior Research and Therapy* 29: 161–69.

Salmoni, A. W. (1989). Motor skill learning. In *Human skills*, ed. D. H. Holding. New York: Wiley.

Salthouse, T. A. (1984). Effects of age and skill in typing. *Journal of Experimental Psychology: General* 113: 345–71.

———. (1985). *A theory of cognitive aging*. Amsterdam: North-Holland.

———. (1986). Perceptual, cognitive and motoric aspects of transcription typing. *Psychological Bulletin* 99: 303–19.

———. (1991). *Theoretical perspectives on cognitive aging*. Hillsdale, NJ: Erlbaum.

Samuel, A. (1959). Some studies of machine learning using the game of checkers. *IBM Journal of Research and Development* 3: 211–29.

Sartori, G., and Job, R. (1988). The oyster with four legs: A neuropsychological study on the interaction of visual and semantic information. *Cognitive Neuropsychology* 5: 105–32.

Scardamalia, M., and Bereiter, C. (1991). Literate expertise. In *Toward a general theory of expertise*, ed. K. A. Ericsson and J. Smith. New York: Cambridge University Press.

Schab, F. R. (1991). Odor memory. *Psychological Bulletin* 109: 242–51.

Schacter, D. L. (1992). Understanding implicit memory. *American Psychologist* 47: 559–69.

Schafer, E.W.P. (1985). Neural adaptability: A biological determinant of g factor intelligence. *Behavioral and Brain Sciences* 8: 240–41.

Schaffer, C. (1993). Bivariate scientific function finding in a sampled, real-data testbed. *Machine Learning* 12: 167–83.

Schaie, K. W., and Strother, C. R. (1968). A cross-sequential study of age changes in cognitive behavior. *Psychological Bulletin* 70: 671–80.

Schaie, K. W., and Willis, S. L. (1993). Age difference patterns of psychometric intelligence in adulthood. *Psychology and Aging* 8: 44–55.

Schank, R. C. (1981). Language and memory. In *Perspectives on cognitive science*, ed. D. A. Norman. Hillsdale, NJ: Erlbaum.

Schmeck, R. R. (1983). Learning styles of college students. In *Individual differences in cognition*, ed. R. F. Dillon and R. R. Schmeck. New York: Academic Press.

———. (1988). An introduction to strategies and styles of learning. In *Learning strategies and learning styles*, ed. R. R. Schmeck. New York: Plenum.

Schmidt, R. A. (1991). *Motor learning and performance*. Champaign, IL.: Human Kinetics Books.

Schneider, S. L., and Laurion, S. K. (1993). Do we know what we've learned from listening to the news? *Memory and Cognition* 21: 198–209.

Schneider, W., Korkel, J., and Weinert, F. E. (1989). Domain-specific knowledge and memory performance. *Journal of Educational Psychology* 81: 306–12.

Schwartz, B., and Reisberg, D. (1991). *Learning and memory*. New York: Norton.

Seidenberg, M.S., and McClelland, J. L. (1991). A distributed, developmental model of word recognition and naming. *Psychological Review* 96: 523–68.

Sejnowsky, T. J., and Rosenberg, C. (1987). Parallel networks that learn to pronounce English text. *Complex Systems* 1: 145–68.

Seligman, M.E.P. (1970). On the generality of the laws of learning. *Psychological Review* 77: 406–18.

Selmes, J. P. (1985). Approaches to learning at secondary school. Ph.D. thesis, University of Edinburgh.

Shallice, T. (1988). *From neuropsychology to mental structure.* New York: Cambridge University Press.

Shepard, R. N. (1987). Toward a universal law of generalization for psychological science. *Science* 237: 1317–24.

Sherry, D. F., and Schacter, D. L. (1987). The evolution of multiple memory systems. *Psychological Review* 94: 439–54.

Shettleworth, S. J. (1993). Varieties of learning and memory in animals. *Journal of Experimental Psychology: Animal Behavior Processes* 19: 5–14.

Shiffrin, R. M. (1993). Short-term memory: A brief commentary. *Memory and Cognition* 21: 193–97.

Shuell, T. J. (1990). Phases of meaningful learning. *Review of Educational Research* 60: 531–47.

Siegal, M. (1991). *Knowing children.* Hove, U. K.: Erlbaum.

Siegler, R. S. (1989). Mechanisms of cognitive development. *Annual Review of Psychology* 40: 353–80.

Simonton, D. K. (1988). *Scientific genius.* New York: Cambridge University Press.

Skemp, R. R. (1979). *Intelligence, learning and action.* Chichester, U. K.: Wiley.

Skinner, B. F. (1938). *The behavior of organisms.* New York: Appleton-Century-Crofts.

———. (1948). Superstition in the pigeon. *Journal of Experimental Psychology* 38: 168–72.

———. (1957). *Verbal behavior.* New York: Appleton-Century-Crofts.

———. (1968). *The technology of teaching.* New York: Appleton-Century-Crofts.

———. (1971). *Beyond freedom and dignity.* New York: Knopf.

———. (1974). *About behaviorism.* New York: Knopf.

Slamecka, N.J., and Katsaiti, L. T. (1987). The generation effect as an artifact of selective displaced rehearsal. *Journal of Memory and Language* 26: 589–607.

Smith, E. E., and Medin, D. L. (1981). *Categories and concepts.* Cambridge, MA: Harvard University Press.

Smith, J .D., Tracy, J. I., and Murray, M. J. (1993). Depression and category learning. *Journal of Experimental Psychology: General* 122: 331–46.

Smolensky, P. (1988). On the proper treatment of connectionism. *Behavioral and Brain Sciences* 11: 1–74.

Sneath, P.H.A., and Sokal, R. R. (1973). *Numerical taxonomy.* New York: Freeman.

Snow, R.E., and Swanson, J. (1992). Instructional psychology. *Annual Review of Psychology* 43: 583–626.

Spear, N. E., Miller, J. S., and Jagielo, J. A. (1990). Animal memory and learning. *Annual Review of Psychology* 41: 169–212.

Spearman, C. (1904). General intelligence objectively determined and measured. *American Journal of Psychology* 15: 201–93.

———. (1927). *The abilities of man.* New York: Macmillan.

Spelke, E. S. (1990). Principles of object perception. *Cognitive Science* 14: 29–56.

Sperling, G. A. (1960). The information available in brief visual presentations. *Psychological Monographs* 74: no. 498.

Squire, L. R. (1987). *Memory and brain.* New York: Oxford University Press.

———. (1989). On the course of forgetting in very long-term memory. *Journal of Experimental Psychology: Learning, Memory, and Cognition* 15: 241–45.

Squire, L. R., Odo, L. R., Knowlton, B., and Musen, G. (1993). The structure and organization of memory. *Annual Review of Psychology* 44: 453–95.

Staddon, J.E.R. (1988). Learning as inference. In *Evolution and learning,* ed. R. C. Bolles and M. D. Beecher. Hillsdale, NJ: Erlbaum.

Standing, L. (1973). Learning 10,000 pictures. *Quarterly Journal of Experimental Psychology* 25: 207–22.

Stephens, D. N., Dahike, F., and Duka, T. (1992). Consequences of drug and ethanol use on cognitive function. In *Cognitive disorders,* ed. L. J. Thal, W. H. Moos, and E. R. Gamzu. New York: Marcel Dekker.

Sternberg, R. J. (1985). *Beyond IQ.* New York: Cambridge University Press.

Sternberg, R. J., and Frensch, P. A. (1992). On being an expert. In *The psychology of expertise,* ed. R. R. Hoffman. New York: Springer-Verlag.

Sternberg, S. (1966). High speed scanning in human memory. *Science* 153: 652–54.

Stewart, D. E. (1991). Hypersensitivity reexamined. *American Journal of Psychiatry* 148: 1416–17.

Stillings, N. A., Feinstein, M. H., Garfield, J. L., Riesland, E. L., Rosenbaum, D. A., Weisler, S. E., and Baker-Ward, L.(1987). *Cognitive science.* Cambridge, MA: MIT Press.

Stones, E. (1984). *Psychology of education.* London: Methuen.

Stuart, E. W., Shimp, T. A., and Engle, R. W. (1987). Classical conditioning of consumer attitudes. *Journal of Consumer Research* 14: 334–49.

Summers, J. J. (1989). Motor programs. In *Human skills,* ed. D. H. Holding. Chichester, U. K.: Wiley.

Swain, I. U., Zelazo, P. R., and Clifton, R. K. (1993). Newborn infants' memory for speech sounds retained over 24 hours. *Developmental Psychology* 29: 312–23.

Swartz, K. B., Chen, S., and Terrace, H. S. (1991). Serial learning by rhesus monkeys. *Journal of Experimental Psychology: Animal Behavior Processes* 17: 396–410.

Sweller, J., Mawer, R. F., and Ward, M. R. (1983). Development of expertise in mathematical problem solving. *Journal of Experimental Psychology: General* 112: 639–61.

Symons, D. (1993). The stuff that dreams aren't made of. *Cognition* 47: 181–217.

Tannenbaum, S. I., and Yukl, G. (1992). Training and development in work organizations. *Annual Review of Psychology* 43: 399–441.

Teasdale, J. D. (1993). Emotion and two kinds of meaning: Cognitive therapy and applied cognitive science. *Behavior Research and Therapy* 31: 339–54.

Terrace, H. S. (1979). *Nim.* New York: Knopf.

Terrace, H. S., and Chen, S. (1991). Chunking during serial learning by a pigeon: II. *Journal of Experimental Psychology: Animal Behavior Processes* 17: 94–106.

Thomas, D. R. (1974). The role of adaptation-level in stimulus generalization. *Psychology of Learning and Motivation* 8: 91–145.

Thompson, R. F., and Spencer, W. A. (1966). Habituation. *Psychological Review* 73: 16–43.

Thorndike, E. L. (1903). *Educational psychology*. New York: Lemcke and Buechner.

Thornton, C. J. (1992). *Techniques in computational learning*. London: Chapman and Hall.

Tierney, A. J. (1986). The evolution of learned and innate behavior. *Animal Learning and Behavior* 14: 339–48.

Treffert, D. A. (1988). *Extraordinary people*. New York: Bantam.

Tryon, W. W. (1993). Neural networks: I. Theoretical unification through connectionism. *Clinical Psychology Review* 13: 341–52.

Tulving, E. (1983). *Elements of episodic memory*. Oxford, U. K.: Oxford University Press.

———. (1985). How many memory systems are there? *American Psychologist* 40: 385–98.

Turner, C. W., and Fischler, I. S. (1993). Speeded tests of implicit knowledge. *Journal of Experimental Psychology: Learning, Memory and Cognition* 19: 1165–77.

Usher, J. A., and Neisser, U. (1993). Childhood amnesia and the beginnings of early memory for early life events. *Journal of Experimental Psychology: General* 122: 155–65.

Uttal, W. R. (1993). Toward a new behaviorism. In *Foundations of perceptual theory*, ed. S. C. Masin. New York: North-Holland.

van der Veer, G. C. (1991). Human-computer interaction from the viewpoint of individual differences and human learning. In *Human-computer interaction*, ed. J. Rasmussen, H. B. Anderson, and N. O. Bernsen. Hove, U. K.: Erlbaum.

van Hamme, L. J., Kao, S., and Wasserman, E. A. (1993). Judging interevent relations. *Memory and Cognition* 21: 802–8.

van Lehn, K. (1989). Problem solving and cognitive skill acquisition. In *Foundations of cognitive science*, ed. M. I. Posner. Cambridge, MA: MIT Press.

Vaughan, W., and Greene, S. L. (1984). Pigeon visual memory capacity. *Journal of Experimental Psychology: Animal Behavior Processes* 10: 256–71.

Vernon, P. A. (1991). Studying intelligence the hard way. *Intelligence* 15: 389–96.

Vicente, K. J., and Brewer, W. F. (1993). Reconstructive remembering of the scientific literature. *Cognition* 46: 101–28.

Vosniadou, S., and Brewer, W. F. (1992). Mental models of the Earth. *Cognitive Psychology* 24: 535–85.

Waber, D. (1989). The biological boundaries of cognitive styles. In *Cognitive style and cognitive development*, ed. T. Globerson and T. Zelniker. Norwood, NJ: Ablex.

Wadden, T. A., and Stunkard, A. J. (1986). A controlled trial of very low-calorie diet, behavior therapy, and their combination in the treatment of obesity. *Journal of Consulting and Clinical Psychology* 54: 482–88.

Waddill, P.J., and McDaniel, M. A. (1992). Pictorial enhancement of text memory. *Memory and Cognition* 20: 472–82.

Wagenaar, W. A. (1986). My memory: A study of autobiographical memory over six years. *Cognitive Psychology* 18: 225–52.

Wallace, B., and Hofelich, B. G. (1992). Process generalization and the prediction of performance on mental imagery tasks. *Memory and Cognition* 20: 695–704.

Warren, P. E., and Walker, I. (1991). Empathy, effectiveness and donations to charity. *British Journal of Social Psychology* 30: 325–37.

Warrington, E. K., and McCarthy, R. A. (1988). The fractionation of retrograde amnesia. *Brain and Cognition* 7: 184–200.

Wasserman, E.A. (1993). Comparative cognition. *Psychological Bulletin* 113: 211–28.

Watson, J. B. (1914). *Behavior*. New York: Holt.

———. (1924). *Behaviorism*. Chicago: University of Chicago Press.

Watson, J. B., and Rayner, R. (1920). Conditioned emotional reactions. *Journal of Experimental Psychology* 3: 1–14.

Weaver, C. A. (1993). Do you need a "flash" to form a flashbulb memory? *Journal of Experimental Psychology: General* 122: 39–46.

Weinstein, C. E. (1988). Assessment and training of student learning strategies. In *Learning strategies and learning styles*, ed. R. R. Schmeck. New York: Plenum.

Weiser, M., and Shertz, J. (1983). Programming problem representation in novice and expert programmers. *International Journal of Man-Machine Studies* 14: 391–96.

Welford, A. T. (1976). *Skilled performance*. Glenview, IL: Scott, Foresman.

Wellman, H. M., and Gelman, S.A. (1992). Cognitive development. *Annual Review of Psychology* 43: 337–76.

Wells, G. L. (1993). What do we know about eyewitness identification? *American Psychologist* 48: 553–71.

White, B. Y. (1993). Thinkertools. *Cognition and Instruction* 10: 1–100.

Whitley, D., Dominic, S., Das, R., and Anderson, C. W. (1993). Genetic reinforcement learning for neurocontrol problems. *Machine Learning* 13: 259–84.

Wilding, J., and Valentine, E. (1994). Memory champions. *British Journal of Psychology* 85: 231–44.

Wilkins, D. C. (1987). Knowledge base refinement using apprenticeship learning techniques. In *Lecture notes in artificial intelligence*, ed. K. Morik. New York: Springer-Verlag.

Williams, J.M.G. (1987). Cognitive treatment of depression. In *Theoretical foundations of behavior therapy*, ed. H. J. Eysenck and I. Martin. New York: Plenum.

Williams, J.M.G., and Broadbent, K. (1986). Autobiographical memory in suicide attempters. *Journal of Abnormal Psychology* 95: 144–49.

Winston, P. (1976). Learning structural descriptions from examples. In *The psychology of computer vision*, ed. P. Winston. New York: McGraw-Hill.

———. (1992). *Artificial intelligence*. Reading, MA: Addison-Wesley.

Wittgenstein, L. (1953). *Philosophical Investigations*. New York: Macmillan.

Wolpe, J. (1958). *Psychotherapy by reciprocal inhibition*. Stanford, CA: Stanford University Press.

Wong, S. E., Floyd, J., Innocent, A. J., and Woolsey, J. E. (1991). Applying a DRO schedule and compliance training to reduce aggressive and self-injurious behavior in an autistic man. *Journal of Behavior Therapy and Experimental Psychiatry* 22: 299–304.

Wood, D. C. (1973). Stimulus-specific habituation in a protozoan. *Physiology and Behavior* 11: 349–73.

Woodley-Zanthos, P. (1993). The effects of level of processing on long-term recognition memory in retarded and nonretarded persons. *Intelligence* 17: 205–21.

Woolfolk, A. E. (1993). *Educational psychology.* Boston: Allyn and Bacon.

Wright, A. A. (1989). Memory processing by pigeons, monkeys, and people. *Psychology of Learning and Motivation* 24: 25–70.

Wright, A. A., and Watkins, M. J. (1987). Animal learning and memory and their relation to human learning and memory. *Learning and Motivation* 18: 131–46.

Zeaman, D., and House, B. J. (1967). The relation of IQ and learning. In *Learning and individual differences,* ed. R. M. Gagne. Columbus, OH: Merrill.

Zelniker, T. (1989). Cognitive style and dimensions of information processing. In *Cognitive style and cognitive development,* ed. T. Globerson and T. Zelniker. Norwood, NJ: Ablex.

Zinbarg, R. E., Barlow, D. H., Brown, T. A., and Hertz, R. M. (1992). Cognitive-behavioral approaches to the nature and treatment of anxiety disorders. *Annual Review of Psychology* 43: 235–67.

Zuriff, G. E. (1985). *Behaviorism.* New York: Freeman.

Index

Accommodation, 70, 92
Age, changes in mental abilities and, 145–46; and learning and memory, 145–48
Aitken, Alexander, 148
AM (automated mathematician), 5, 64
Analogy use, 106–7, 133, 141, 166; and machine design, 210
Analytic machine learning, 166, 168–69, 178
Anderson, James, 171
Animal applications, 188–89
Applications of psychology: areas of, 185; levels of, 183; problems in, 184
Approaches to Study Inventory, 160
Aquino, Benito, 66
Aristotle, 11, 14, 53, 171
Articulatory loop, 60, 62–63
Articulatory process, 63
Artificial grammar learining, 64, 68
Assimilation, 70, 92
Associationism, 14
Autoshaping, 35, 39–40

Back, Aaron, 203
Back-propagation rule, 176–77, 180
Bartlett, Frederick, 17
Basic-level categories, 104–5
Behaviorism, 15–19, 23, 27, 37, 113; assumptions of, 16; and connectionism, 170, 179–80, 183; and education, 184–85, 190–92; and psychotherapy, 198–202
Behavior therapy, 199–202
Binet, Alfred, 149, 183
Bird song learning, 47, 56, 68
Bohr, Niels, 196
British Ability Scales, 150, 198
Burton, Richard, 148

Central executive, 60
Chunking, 22, 30, 48, 49, 61, 62, 73, 96, 98, 106, 142; and aging, 147; and neurological problems, 207; and skill learning, 117, 119, 120
Classical conditioning, 23, 29, 39–43, 45, 46, 64, 68; and aging 146–47; and education, 190; and neural nets, 176, 179; and psychotherapy, 198; and Spearman's g, 153
Cognitive processes, 19, 26; in animals, 48–52; and Spearman's g, 153
Cognitive styles, 157–60, 162
Cognitive therapy, 20, 2–4
Cohort effect, 145
Comparative cognition, 29, 48–53
Competitive learning rule, 176
Computer analogy for learning, 17, 19–20, 29, 56, 106
Computer interface design, 210–11

Computer simulation, 26–27
Concept mapping, 197
Concepts, 23, 98–103; animals and, 50–51; children and, 139–40; computers and, 164–66, 169, 175, 179; domains and, 106–7; education and, 192–97; expertise and, 126, 133; findings about, 99; information contained in, 100–102; knowledge and, 98–103; learning of, 103; machine design and, 210; methods of studying, 25; types of, 102–3; words and, 66–67
Connectionism, 23, 164, 166, 170–81
Constraints on knowledge, 105, 107–9
Contingencies, 7–8, 33, 36, 43, 45, 138, 153, 168; and machine design, 209

Dean, John, 22, 65
Delta rule, 176
Demjanjuk, Ivan, 187
Descartes, René, 15
Development: and behaviorism, 16; causes of 143–44; cognitive metatheory and, 19; connectionism and, 179; learning and, 5; levels of processing and, 59
Discrimination, 3, 41, 45, 50, 52, 70, 121
Domains of knowledge, 105–8; children's learning about, 141; expertise and, 122, 123, 125; skills and, 111
Domestication, 5–6

Ebbinghaus, Hermann, 14–15, 74, 78
Education and learning and memory, 182, 183, 189–98; behavioral applications to, 184–85, 90–92; cognitive applications to, 192–98
Einstein, Albert, 23, 24, 68, 71, 108
Einstellung phenomenon, 121
Electro-convulsive therapy (ECT), 185, 204–5
Embedded Figures Test, 157
Empiricism, 11–14, 137
Encoding specificity principle, 78

Equipotentiality assumption of behaviorism, 16, 18, 108
Ethology, 11, 31
Expertise, 123–24, 163–64; acquisition of, 131–33; definition of, 123–24; development and, 141, 143; education and, 193; novices and, 125–29; processing in domains of 129–31; reasons to study, 123–24; Speraman's g and, 155–56; types of, 124–25
Explanation-based learning, 68, 103, 132, 168–69
Explicit memory, 64, 69, 71, 136
Eysenck Personality Inventory, 38

Features: concepts and, 100–101; prototypes and, 95; as representation device, 90; types of, 90
Feynman, Richard, 196
Field-independence/dependence, 157–59
Fixed-action-pattern (FAP), 33
Flashbulb memory, 74
Flooding, 200
Forgetting, 78–81; age and, 147–48; causes of, 80–81; Ebbinghaus curve and, 15; patterns of, 78–79
Fugue, 81, 206

G. See Intelligence; Spearman's g
Galton, Francis, 92
Generalization, 41, 45–46, 47, 70–71, 121, 179
General processing capacity, 136, 142, 144, 145, 151
Generation effect, 74
Genetic algorithms, 164, 166, 169–70, 178
Genius, 155
Grossberg, Steven, 171
Guthrie, Edwin, 16

Habituation, 37–38, 64, 68, 137–38; domestication and, 5; Spearman's g and, 153
Health promotion, 185, 199, 204
Hebb rule, 171, 175–76

Hemisphericality, 159–60
Hick's law, 116
Hitchcock, Alfred, 81
HM, 1, 2, 26, 63
Holist versus serialist style, 161
Homunculus, 175
Hopfield, John, 171
Hull, Clark, 16–17
Human characteristics: malleability
    of, 13; machine design and, 209–10
Hume, David, 14
Hypnosis, 188

Imagery, 19–20, 65, 71, 90; aging and,
    147; animals and, 49–50; facts
    about, 92–94; Finke's principles
    and, 93–94; infants and, 142; visuo-
    spatial sketchpad and, 60–62
Implicit memory, 64, 69, 71, 136
Imprinting, 5, 47, 56, 68
Inductive learning in computers, 166–
    68, 178
Infantile amnesia, 139, 143
Infant learning, 138–39
Inferences, 85–86, 87, 140
Information-processing metatheory,
    29, 48, 194; assumptions of, 19
Intelligence: fluid and crystallized,
    146; learning and memory and,
    148–56
Inventory of Learning Processes, 160

James, William, 14, 137
Johnson, Marcia, 9

Keller method, 191
Knowledge, 83–109; definition of, 83;
    facts about, 83–87; innate, 32; na-
    ture of 27; organization of, 65–68;
    sources of, 9, 11; types of, 84; units
    of, 83, 97–99; updating, of, 8–9
Knowledge structures, 104–7
Kohonen, Teuvo, 171

Language learning, 3, 6, 47–48, 52, 68,
    142; in animals, 51–52; connection-
    ism and, 170, 179, 181
Law, applications to, 185–87

Learning: age and, 135–48; complex
    learning in animals 50–52; costs
    and benefits of, 34; definitions of,
    2, 163; development and, 5; domes-
    tication and, 5; evolution and, 29–
    36, 52–53, 56–57; examples of, 3;
    history of study of, 11–24; intelli-
    gence and, 148–56; knowledge
    and, 4; methods of studying, 24–
    27; overtaxing of ability, 10; princi-
    ples abstracted by ten-year-olds,
    11; processes, 3, 68–73; questions
    about, 27–28; sets, 50; across spe-
    cies, 52–53; strategies, 71–72;
    things humans need to learn, 6–10;
    types of, 36–48, 53, 68–73; vari-
    ables affecting, 73–74, 135
Learning problems, 197–98
Learning styles, 157, 160–62
Lennon, John, 66
Levels of processing approach, 58–59
Lewin, Kurt, 183
Locke, John, 11, 12, 14
Loftus, Elizabeth, 185
Long-term memory, 30, 57, 58, 60, 63–
    68; age and, 142; capacity of, 84–85;
    multistore model and, 20–22; sche-
    mas and, 91

McCulloch, Warren, 171
McCulloch effect, 43
Machine design, 136, 184, 207–11
Machine learning: connectionist, 170–
    81; parts of system, 165; symbolic,
    163–70; ways systems learn, 165–66
Marcos, Ferdinand, 66
Marr's levels of analysis, 27
Matching law, 44–45
Maturation, 5, 143–44
Memory: animals and, 48–50, 52, 55–
    68; clinical syndromes and, 206–7;
    definitions of, 3, 16, 19; drugs and,
    205; episodic, 64–66; physiological
    basis of, 28; procedural, 64–65;
    questions about, 27–28; relation to
    learning, 3–5; semantic, 65–68
Mental models, 95–96, 101, 209

Methods of studying learning and memory, 24–27
Misconceptions, 102, 109, 132, 160–61; education and, 195–96
Mnemonic devices, 71–72, 133, 148, 207
Multiple intelligences, 152
Multistore memory model, 20–22, 55, 57, 58

Nativism, 11–14
Neisser, Ulric, 22
NETtalk, 175, 177–78
Neural nets, 23, 170–81; engineering and, 177–78; history of, 171–72; learning in, 175–77; neural plausibility of, 172, 178–79, 180–81; parts of, 172–75; problems of, 180–81; psychology and, 23, 178–80; types of, 173
Neurological syndromes, 206–7
Nixon, Richard, 22

Operant conditioning, 43–46, 50, 153, 189; psychotherapy and, 198, 200–201
Orienting response, 37

Partonomy, 104–5
Pavlov, Ivan, 15, 39
Penfield, Wilder, 80
Perceptron, 171
Permastore, 78
PET scan, 25
Phenomenal memorizers, 148–49
Phonological store, 62
Piaget, Jean, 5, 102, 137, 143–44
Pitts, Walter, 171
Plasticity, 3, 35
Plato, 11
Polgar sisters, 155–56
Power law of practice, 113, 118–19
Prenatal learning, 137–38
Preparedness, 36, 69
Priming, 64
Process versus content debate, 192
Production systems, 96, 165
Programmed learning, 90–91

Propositions, 91, 104
Prototypes, 94–95; aging and, 147; concepts and, 100, 105; neural nets and, 179
Psychotherapy, 185, 198–204

Rational-emotive therapy, 202–3
Ravens Progressive Matrices, 150, 157
Reaction potential, 17; net, 16
Recall, 75–78, 79; cues and, 77–78; hypermnesia and, 77; reminiscence and, 77; social, 22
Recognition, 75, 78, 79
Reflective versus impulsive style, 159, 162
Reinforcement: schedules of, 44–45; types of, 44
Representation: cognitive metatheory and, 19, 89; content and format of, 88–89; definition of, 2, 87–88; processes and, 19, 89; types of mental, 90–97
Repression, 80–81
Retrieval: from long-term memory, 75–78; from short-term memory, 74–75
Rosenblatt, Frank, 171

Savings, 15, 25
Scala naturae, 53
Schemas: cognitive therapy and, 202–3; definition of, 91; education and, 193, 196–97; expertise and, 127, 130–31, 132; eyewitness testimony and, 186; field-independence and, 159; forgetting and, 80; machine learning and, 168; skills and, 116; types of, 91
Sensitization, 38–39
Sensory registers, 20–22, 60
Shaping, 43–44, 190
Shereskevski, S. V., 93, 148
Short-term memory, 20–22, 30, 57, 58, 60
Skills, 6, 111–23; age and, 147; definition of, 111–12; education and, 193–94; feedback and, 120; intelligence and, 153–54; learning of, 115–21,

131–33, 210; machine design and, 208; organization of, 116; performance of, 115–16; psychotherapy and, 198; stages of learning, 117–18, 210–11; types and dimensions, of, 113–15

Skinner, B.F., 16, 17, 90–91

Skinner box, 24

Source-monitoring, 9

Spearman's g, 149–57

Species-specific behaviors, 31–33

Spence, Kenneth, 16

Sternberg paradigm, 74–75

Strategies of learning, 136, 141–42, 157, 162, 198; mental retardation and, 206

Superstitions, 7

Surface versus deep processing, 160–61

Systematic desensitization, 200

Taxonomy: of concepts, 102–3; of constraints on knowledge, 107; as a knowledge structure, 104–5; of learning processes, 36–37, 68–73; machine learning of, 166–67; psychiatric, 108, 126, 194

Teachable Language Comprehender, 67

Teaching in animals, 34

Theory of mind, 142–43

ThinkerTools, 196

Thorndike, Robert, 15, 36

Tip-of-the-tongue phenomenon, 76, 148

Token economy, 191–92

Tolaman, Edward, 16

Transfer of skill, 121–23

Universals, 13

Verbal versus imagery style, 158–59

Visuospatial sketchpad, 60–62, 94, 136

Watson, John B., 15, 183

Wearing, Clive, 1–2

Working memory 60–63; age and, 142; learning problems and, 197–98; machine design and, 209; parts of, 60–63

Wundt, Wilhelm, 14

About the Author

ROBERT W. HOWARD teaches at the University of Newcastle, Australia. He is the author of three books—*Coping and Adapting* (1984), *Concepts and Schemata* (1987), and *All About Intelligence: Human, Animal and Artificial* (1991)—and many journal articles.

ISBN 0-275-94641-X

9 780275 946418

HARDCOVER BAR CODE